On the Edge *of Apostasy*

The Evangelical *Romance* with ROME

by Robert M. Zins, Th.M.

A Christian Witness to Roman Catholicism
P.O.Box 325
Herndon, VA 20172 USA
www.cwrc-rz.org

On the Edge of Apostasy: the Evangelical Romance with Rome

Copyright ©1998, 2005 by Robert M. Zins, Th.M. All rights reserved. Printed in the United States of America.

Cover art by Rebekah Sanders

Works by Robert M. Zins, Th.M.:

Romanism
the Relentless Roman Catholic Assault on the Gospel of Jesus Christ!

Formidable Truth
a Vindication of Loraine Boettner

On the Edge of Apostasy
the Evangelical Romance with Rome

For copyright information, write to *A Christian Witness to Roman Catholicism*, P.O.Box 325 Herndon, VA 20172 USA, or visit www.cwrc-rz.org

Unless otherwise noted, all Scripture texts in this work are taken from the *King James Version* (*Authorized Version*, UK) of the Bible

Library of Congress Catalog Card Number: 97-60607
ISBN 0-9637141-6-3

First Edition 0 9 8 7 6 5 4 3 2

Additional copies of *On the Edge of Apostasy* may be obtained by writing to:

A Christian Witness to Roman Catholicism
P.O.Box 325
Herndon, VA 20172 USA

or by visiting www.cwrc-rz.org

This book is dedicated to Mr. Clyde L. Hargrove, whose constant encouragement and support of this ministry has been a gift from God. Clyde has been used of the Lord as a testimony of those called to contend for the faith which was once delivered to the saints.

We are humbled by his example and generosity in upholding this work for the cause of Christ and the truth of His Gospel.

Contents

Foreword

IN OUR FIRST book, *Romanism: The Relentless Roman Catholic Assault on the Gospel of Jesus Christ* we endeavored to answer line upon line, precept upon precept, the Roman Catholic objections to the Gospel of Jesus Christ. We speak in terms of the Roman Catholic objections to the Gospel of Jesus because Roman Catholicism seeks to set forth a different gospel.

Whereas the Bible consistently and authoritatively lifts up the Gospel of the grace of God and salvation by faith alone in Christ alone to the glory of God alone, Rome has a dissimilar gospel. Rome features a gospel dependent upon sacramentalism characterized by baptismal regeneration, incremental justification dependent upon meritorious works done in faith as well as personal satisfaction of sins via penance, indulgences and faithfulness to Rome's other sacraments.

We included in our first book two important appendices. The first is an analysis of *Evangelicals and Catholics Together: ECT*. The second is *Veritas Formidabilis* or *Formidable Truth,* a vindication of Lorraine Boettner's work against the Roman Catholic religion.

In this, our second major work, we have labored over the state of American Evangelicalism and her relationship to Roman Catholicism. We have entitled this work *On the Edge of Apostasy*. We felt at the time of the first printing that there were many confessing Evangelicals who were toiling to reverse the Protestant Reformation and in so doing were undermining the Gospel. After examining their writings we felt that they were on the edge of apostasy. One of the appendices of *On the Edge of Apostasy* examines the follow-up document to the *ECT* manuscript that is entitled *The Gift of Salvation*. We devoted some care in showing that *The Gift of Salvation,* like its predecessor *ECT,* is a departure from biblical Christianity and serves to further emasculate the Gospel of Jesus Christ.

Since our first printing there has been a tidal wave of ecumenism sweeping across America. More position papers have been written by the *ECT* group and a small book entitled *Your Word Is Truth* was released in 2002. Following up on this book has come a third declaration by Charles Colson and Richard John Neuhaus reprinted in the March 2005 issue of *Christianity Today* under the title of *A Distinctive People.*

The English word ecumenical comes from the Latin *oecumenicis* and Greek *oikoumenikos* which refer to the world or inhabited world. The idea is to lay claim to a universal or general Christianity among all in the inhabited world. The theory of ecumenism can be relegated to a better understanding between those of differing faiths. But it can also mean efforts to bring together those of differing faiths under one umbrella. This latter use of the term is most closely associated with what is happening between Evangelicals and Roman Catholics.

Since our first printing of *On the Edge of Apostasy* much has transpired. Some of it is good. There have been several new releases written by men committed to preserving the Gospel of Jesus Christ. There have been conferences dedicated to protecting the biblical principles of *Sola Fide* and *Sola Scriptura.* The warning bell has been sounded and many are responding. Several prominent theologians and church leaders have strengthened their doctrinal positions and reaffirmed justification by faith alone. For this we are thankful.

But there also have been many setbacks. Many Evangelical theologians have ignored our warnings and plunged headlong into a relationship with Rome that has served to inoculate Rome against any meaningful witness of the Gospel. Too many modern confessing Evangelical pastors and churches have openly endorsed or courted Roman Catholicism. In the estimation of one prominent conservative scholar the word "Evangelical" has lost all its meaning. It used to be a good word from the Greek *euangellion* which translates as the good news or the gospel. But, because of Rome's inclusion into many confessing Evangelical quarters, the good news now includes Rome's gospel as well. This is not the *bona fide* "Good News" or the true Gospel. It is also not good news for Evangelicalism. Many Christian men are wondering out loud, "Do we even have a common faith any more?"

When Paul wrote his letter to Titus he encouraged Titus with these words: "To Titus, my true child in a *common faith.*" Due to the ecumenical push that includes Roman Catholicism, it is a good question to ask, "What is a true child in a *common faith*?"

In this short foreword, we wish to draw your attention to two of the latest documents serving the ecumenical crowd. The first is *Your Word Is Truth* and the second is *A Distinctive People.* It would take another brand new work to cover the in-roads Rome has made in the Pro-Life Movement, Prison Ministry Movement, Campus Ministry Movements as well as biblically compromised Seeker Friendly Churches, Purpose Driven Life Movements and the Alpha Movements both here and abroad. Perhaps a sequel to this book is necessary to continue to warn our brothers and sisters in Christ of the dangerous world in which we live. May we with one mind "contend for the faith."

> "Beloved, while I was making every effort to write you about *our common salvation,* I felt the necessity to write to you appealing that you contend earnestly for *the faith which was once for all delivered to the saints.*" (Jude 3)

Your Word Is Truth

The book *Your Word Is Truth* was released in 2002. The general editors are Chuck Colson and Richard John Neuhaus. These are the two men most responsible for *ECT* and *The Gift of Salvation.* This new product is basically a series of articles written by Roman Catholic and Evangelicals centering upon the relationship of tradition and the Scriptures.

As most know, Rome takes tradition to the level of being on a par with the Bible. This presents an insuperable problem for Evangelicals who trust that the Bible alone is the only valid source of God's revelation. Evangelicals, while respecting the teaching ministry of the Body of Christ throughout the years, would not place tradition on the same level of authority as the Bible. Indeed, there is only one book inspired by God and recognized as the only Word of God.

In an attempt to minimize the stark and fatal difference between Rome's insistence that God's revelation is to be understood as both Tradition and the Scripture (rightly interpreted by the Roman See), and the Reformation cry of *Sola Scriptura* (the Bible alone), *Your Word Is Truth* (YWT) begins where *ECT* and *The Gift of Salvation* [GS] leave off.

It is imperative that the reader understand that those who are committed to all four ecumenical statements are absolutely certain that the Roman Catholic belief system is compatible with the Gospel of Jesus Christ. It is further to be noted that every confessing Evangelical involved in the formulation of these proclamations is thoroughly dedicated to the proposition that Roman Catholicism is a valid Christian community in which salvation, justification, redemption and eternal life with God can be attained through faithful adherence to the Roman sacramental system.

> "This statement and this book are part of the ongoing project known as 'Evangelicals and Catholics Together,' commonly called ECT. The project began in 1992 with a conference occasioned by growing concerns, and often violent, conflicts between Catholics and Evangelical Protestants in Latin America. In March 1994 …we explained why it is necessary, as 'brothers and sisters in Christ,' to

> work with one another, and not against one another, in the great task of evangelization, and to support one another in facing up to the ominous moral and cultural threats of our time. The many signers of the statement pledged themselves to that Christian solidarity and, while this initiative has not been without its critics, both Evangelical and Catholic, we are greatly heartened by the thousands who have joined in that pledge." (*YWT*, Introduction)

For this very reason we have argued that those who enlist as soldiers in the army of this ecumenism have forfeited their rights to be called Christian in any meaningful way. Indeed, they have fallen into the pit of apostasy. It is our position that no man who has the mind of Christ and counts himself to be redeemed by faith alone in the finished work of Christ alone for his justification and salvation can countenance another gospel—let alone throw his support behind it.

It remains to be seen what kind of impact this latest attempt to bring Rome and Evangelicals together will have. Thus far *Sola Fide* [justification by faith alone in the finished work of Christ alone] has been the main target. Now, the foundation of *Sola Scriptura* [the Bible alone for faith and practice] is in the sights of those who wish to kill the Gospel by polluting it with what Paul and every other Christian knows as 'another gospel'.

A Distinctive People

On March 3rd 2005 *Christianity Today* published a document with the subtitle: "A new document from Evangelicals and Catholics Together." This document, *A Distinctive People*, [ADP] is a follow-up to all that has already been released by the *ECT* ecumenical group. It is signed by: Charles Colson, Timothy George, J.I. Packer, Harold O.J. Brown, and other prominent Evangelicals. The gist of the document is clear:

> "Over more than ten years, this group of evangelicals and Catholics, speaking as individuals committed to their respective communities but without any official mandate, has explored important areas of agreement and disagreement among us. In our first round of conversations and in the resulting statement of 1994, … we were able to recognize one another as brothers and sisters in Christ and to affirm the positive value of the witness to the gospel rendered by our several communities, notwithstanding differences and disagreements. In 1997, we were able to issue a second statement, "The Gift of Salvation." In that statement we affirmed that the justification of sinners, which is not earned by any good works or merits of our own, leads us toward the fullness of salvation that is promised in the final kingdom.

> "In our third statement, [YWT], we found a notable convergence in our view concerning the transmission of God's saving Word through Holy Scripture and tradition. The following year we took up the interpretation of the phrase "The Communion of Saints" that appears in the Apostles' Creed, and there we affirmed that, by virtue of our communion with Christ, we are in a certain, albeit imperfect, communion with one another in his body, the church."

From this platform the framers of *ADP* seek to address the issue of holiness in the Church of God. As we can see the authors have already concluded beyond a shadow of a doubt that both Evangelicals and Roman Catholics are Christians and share in the same election of God, the New Covenant in Christ and are members of the Body of Christ. It is this very premise that began with the original *ECT* and continues on with such articles as this that we challenge. We do not believe that what is set forth in *ECT*, *GS, YWT* and *ADP* is truth. We believe it to be utterly false and ultimately anti-Christ and hostile to the Gospel of Jesus Christ.

In our first book, *Romanism*, we labored to show that the doctrinal positions taken by the Roman Catholic religion are inimical to the Gospel of Jesus Christ. Of particular interest to us was the immense importance that the Roman Catholic religion places upon her sacrament of baptism. We were very concerned that there are two ecumenical highways leading to Rome. The first is the extrascriptural sources of authority found in non-Roman Catholic religions that claim an Evangelical identity. Relying upon supernatural impressions and alleged Holy Spirit leadings, there have been many who drive to Rome on the charismatic highway. The other road to Rome is not as subtle. It is the insistence by many Evangelicals that Roman Catholic baptism is a *bona fide* biblical baptism that can be interchanged with true Christian baptism.

One of the highlights of *ECT,* and the rest of the ecumenical statements, is the insistence that baptism is integral to the Gospel of Jesus Christ and that regardless of the form it takes or the candidate it is administered upon, it is indispensable to the Gospel. Hence, the ecumenical acceptance of Roman Catholic baptism has become a golden road back to Rome. It does not seem to matter that Rome's baptism entails regeneration, justification and is administered to infants and adults alike. It does not seem to matter that the biblical teaching on baptism is utterly opposite of Rome's. What seems to matter is only that everyone is baptized in one way or another for one reason or another and everyone accepts each other's baptism!

This 'Christianizing' of society through baptism is not dissimilar to the 'Christianizing' of society that led up to the Protestant Reformation. We find strong evidence of this in *ADP*.

> "Our different traditions, notwithstanding their doctrinal differences, agree that faith and baptism, as the sacrament of faith, belong together. Christian faith should always lead to baptism, and baptism, conversely, should always be accompanied by Christian faith. Baptism is mandated, not optional. It is the gateway to the Christian life." (ADP, page 4)

Baptism is not the gateway to the Christian life. This is simply not true. Yet, it is the recurring theme of ecumenists. There is only one entrance into the Christian life: faith alone in the finished work of Christ alone.

In the following pages we have worked hard to enter into the mind-set of the Evangelical ecumenists and expose for all to see the error of their ways. May our Lord have mercy upon His true Church the Body of Jesus Christ and all who are in Christ through faith alone and trust only in His Word as found only in His Scriptures.

— Robert M. Zins, April 2005

Introduction

IN THE FALL of 1997, a controversial new document was released as a follow-up to the now widely known *Evangelicals and Catholics Together: The Christian Mission In The Third Millennium. ECT,* as it has come to be called, compiled under the general supervision of Mr. Charles Colson (a professed Evangelical), and Richard John Neuhaus (a former Lutheran, now a Roman Catholic priest), has had an enormous impact on the Evangelical community. Without doubt, this new document called *The Gift of Salvation,** which *ECT* has spawned, will have a significant impact, as well.

The essence of the new document may be summed up in the following:

> "We give thanks to God that in recent years many Evangelicals and Catholics, ...have been able to express a common faith in Christ and so to acknowledge one another as brothers and sisters in Christ."[1]

Such a bold statement, in light of the theological divide that has separated the Roman Catholic religion from Evangelical Christianity, will be a shock to some. But on the other side, there is a growing sentiment toward an acceptance of Romanism as a "separate but equal" worshipping community.

The *ECT* statement has also spawned a number of books. There are several who have seen *ECT* as a threat to the very fiber of the Gospel of Jesus Christ.[2] But there are those who wish to expand upon the idea of *ECT* and seem committed to validating Roman Catholicism as a *bona fide* Christian

---

* Zins provides an analysis of *The Gift of Salvation* in Appendix I.

1 *The Gift of Salvation*, (November 12) pg. 1

2 Among those authors who have written to expose the danger they perceive in *ECT* are: John Ankerberg, *Protestants and Catholics: Do They Now Agree?*; John Armstrong, *Roman Catholicism: Evangelicals Analyze What Divides and Unites Us*; David Hunt, *A Woman Rides The Beast*; Kevin Reed, *Making Shipwreck Of The Faith*; R. C. Sproul, *Faith Alone*; William Webster, *The Church of Rome at the Bar of History*, and numerous booklets, tracts, articles and flyers warning of the dangers inherent in the broad acceptance and approval of *ECT*.

community. Of course, Rome has always thought of itself not only as *a* Christian community, but *the* Christian community. Also, it is not surprising to find Rome willing to tolerate other worshipping communities which differ from her. Vatican II offers us some insight as to how carefully Rome preserves its high opinion of itself while granting some slack to other professing Christian communities.[1]

Be that as it may, our purpose here is to examine not what Rome thinks of outsiders, but what outsiders think of Rome.

There must always be cause for concern when anyone begins to tinker with the Gospel. It is like listening to fingernails on the chalkboard to hear some of the more popular radio and TV personalities when they are not careful in the preaching of it. However, this may be unavoidable since good theology and popularity are a rare combination of late. But it is of greater distress when high profile, theologically oriented Evangelicals begin to tinker with the Gospel and campaign openly for Roman Catholicism. It is one thing for mistakes and uncareful language to come from popular ministries not noted for their theological depth. It is quite another thing when that deliberate ambiguity comes from well schooled theologians.

It is the task of this book to expose those who have taken themselves to the edge of apostasy in their romancing of the Roman Catholic religion. As we shall see, what is preached and taught by the theologians filters down through the seminaries, into the pulpits and finally to the pews. This is why we are so distressed that the most recent errors are coming from the theologians themselves. This does not bode well for the coming generation of believers. Many Evangelicals are now accepting Roman Catholicism as a valid form of Christian worship. We believe their writings are perhaps the most damaging to have been written since the documents of the Romanist Council of Trent in 1545, in the sense that they compromise and obscure the Gospel of Jesus Christ.

---

[1] While safeguarding the preëminent place of Rome, as the depository of the fullness of grace, Rome nevertheless makes room for what it calls the Separated Churches. There has been a change of thinking over the years as to how Rome should address the "problem" of Evangelical worshipping communities. See the author's book, *Romanism*, for a more intense discussion.

> "It follows that the separated Churches and communities as such, though we believe they suffer from the defects already mentioned, have been by no means deprived of significance and importance in the mystery of salvation. For the Spirit of Christ has not refrained from using them as means of salvation which derive their efficacy from the very fullness of grace and truth entrusted to the Catholic Church." (Vatican II, *Unitatis Redintegratio*, 21 November, 1964)

In the course of our study, we also wish to make comment on a number of popular Evangelicals who, having taken their cue from the theologians, are now openly endorsing the Roman Catholic religion. They have, in one way or another, called Rome a safe harbor for the anchoring of the Gospel of Jesus Christ.

We first wish to examine the writing of two professing Evangelicals: Dr. Norman Geisler and Ralph MacKenzie. They have written a lengthy book (502 pages) which is by far the most comprehensive treatment of Rome in our day. Their book is entitled: *Roman Catholics and Evangelicals: Agreements and Differences*. We next wish to explore Chuck Colson and Richard Neuhaus, and their recent book, *Evangelicals and Catholics Together: Toward A Common Mission*. This book is actually a compendium of six authors who have contributed a total of six chapters (224 pages). Finally, we wish to explore William D. Watkins and Keith A. Fournier in their book entitled *A House United? Evangelicals and Catholics Together: A Winning Alliance For The 21st Century.*[*]

We shall close our analysis with a comment on individuals who have recognized and validated the religion of Rome. There are those who have taken a somewhat neutral position on the matter. But we have been surprised, and in many cases, shocked as to how far American Evangelicalism has drifted away from its moorings of the Protestant Reformation. The following pages will bear this out.

We ask the reader to ponder the fact that Dr. Geisler is the author of over 40 books, many of them extremely helpful to the Gospel. Take note that Ralph MacKenzie holds a degree from Bethel Theological Seminary. William Watkins holds a Master of Theology from Dallas Theological Seminary. Keith Fournier and Richard Neuhaus are avowed Romanists. Mr. Colson is the director of Prison Ministries and is a professed Evangelical. Fournier & Watkins' book represents the historically anomalous combination of a Dallas Seminary graduate laboring with an avowed Roman Catholic to validate Romanism. In the persons of Colson and Neuhaus, we have an extremely popular Evangelical speaker joining with a Roman Catholic priest to forge a pact of mutual admiration. What gives?

This is precisely what many Christians are asking. Has Rome changed? Has the Gospel changed? Have Christians been wrong about the Protestant Reformation? Was it all just one big misunderstanding? What is going on?

---

[*] It will be helpful to the reader to keep in mind the three titles and the six authors mentioned here. In each section, we shall be interacting with their works by referring to them as "the authors," but not always by name or by title.

Having read these authors and pored over material available on some of the more well known professing Evangelicals, we unhappily seem to be coming to the end of the ancient Gospel of Jesus Christ in our nation, unless God has mercy. What is to come? We do not claim to have the gift of prophecy, but we are not pleased with what we have found on the American landscape. We can foresee the possibility of an unprecedented new order of religion that is neither Romanism nor Christianity. Perhaps initially, it will be a hybrid of mutual acceptance and admiration for novel and contradictory ways of presenting Christ and approaching God. Logically paradoxical ideas about God will be paraded throughout the marketplace. Mutually exclusive and bizarre concepts of the Gospel of Jesus will be tolerated, and indeed demanded. The whole concept of an objective Gospel which speaks to all of mankind due to its timeless truth will be thrown down. The net result will be toleration in the name of unity to the point of oblivion. It is at this juncture when Rome may emerge as the strongest religion in America. Ultimately, Rome will do what it has always done: restore order the Roman way. The signs are here and the players are active in their roles. We foresee "the crush" to rush to Rome led by professing Evangelicals who have invented a religion which has *compromise, unity* and *acceptance* as its unholy trinity.

We are not fanatics, doomsday prophets or a cult organization, although we do feel that we might be labeled as such. We are, rather, sober-minded in our appraisal of professing Evangelicalism in America. This disturbing and apostate turn toward Rome is only the beginning of the troubles for all true disciples of Christ. Sadly, there may be many fearful Evangelicals persecuted by the state who will run to Rome much like Israel of old ran to Egypt. The results will be an utter loss of the Gospel. Rome does not have the Gospel of Jesus Christ. Rome has its own religion. It is that simple. All attempts to merge Christianity with Rome will fail in the end. The window-dressing may change in Rome but it is the same religion inside. Evangelicals who say they are of Christ, and yet push an acceptance of Rome, will try in vain to find the middle ground. It does not exist. One is either of Christ and His Gospel or of Rome and her religion.

We have endeavored to prove this beyond a shadow of a doubt in the upcoming pages. We realize that we are pushing a boulder uphill in our efforts. It seems the whole world resists the notion that Rome is fatal to Christianity. We pray that we have argued well on behalf of the Master Himself, His great Apostles, His saints and martyrs throughout the centuries, and for all true believers of this age. We are beyond all concern for offense at this stage, and reputations mean nothing, for the Gospel itself is at stake.

At this juncture, we lead the reader into a sharper focus of the foray. The most compelling questions facing Christianity since the Protestant

Reformation is this: "Is Romanism a Christian religion?" and, "Has Rome accepted the Gospel of Jesus Christ?" Let the battle be put into perspective for us by the following two writers separated by 450 earthly years and perhaps an eternity:

> "Nevertheless, when all is said and done, evangelical Protestants and traditionalist, believing Roman Catholics have so many convictions and commitments in common that it would be foolish as well as wrong in the sight of the One whom we all claim as our Lord Jesus Christ to *wrangle* with each other in the face of the common enemy. ...while evangelical Protestants and Roman Catholics have and will continue to have *differences* that cannot be swept under the table, in the words or Cardinal Suenens, 'the walls of separation do not reach up to heaven.'"[1]

We contrast these words with one who "wrangled" with the "differences" between Christianity and the Romanist religion:

> "In a corruption of sound doctrine so extreme, in a pollution of the sacraments so nefarious, in a condition of the church so deplorable, those who maintain that we ought not to have felt so strongly, would have been satisfied with nothing less than a perfidious tolerance, by which we should have betrayed the worship of God, the glory of Christ, the salvation of men, the entire administration of the sacraments, and the government of the church. There is something specious in the name of moderation, and tolerance is a quality which has a fair appearance, and seems worthy of praise; but the rule which we must observe at all hazards is, never to endure patiently that the sacred name of God should be assailed with impious blasphemy; that his eternal truth should be suppressed by the devil's lies; that Christ should be insulted, his holy mysteries polluted, unhappy souls cruelly murdered, and the church left to writhe in extremity under the effect of a deadly wound. This would be not meekness, but indifference about things to which all others ought to be postponed."[2]

---

[1] Geisler, Norman L. & MacKenzie, Ralph E., *Roman Catholics and Evangelicals: Agreements and Differences,* (Grand Rapids: Baker Books, ©1995) pp. 12,13, emphasis added. Taken from the foreword, written by Harold O. J. Brown, a professing evangelical.

[2] Calvin, John, *The Necessity of Reforming the Church*, (Dallas, TX: Protestant Heritage Press, ©1995) pp. 7,8

At the Outset

IN THE INTRODUCTION to their work, *Roman Catholics and Evangelicals: Agreements and Differences*, Norman Geisler and Ralph MacKenzie set the tone for the entire book:

> "Before Vatican II, Roman Catholics and Protestants had little contact with each other. On the Protestant side, many thought that the Pope was the anti-Christ, that Catholics worshiped Mary, and that even Unitarians were to be preferred to Roman Catholics."[1]

After the above citation, an illustration is given of a "well known Catholic 'basher' of a generation ago"[2] who is dismissed as having been a secular humanist. The point intended is that it would be foolishness to say, "The Pope *today* is the anti-Christ." Or, to say, "Roman Catholics *today* worship Mary." It is insinuated that such statements *today* are to be considered either archaic or outlandish Catholic bashing. Even worse, to make such

---

[1] Geisler & MacKenzie, pg. 15. The clear implication is that anyone who would think that the Pope is the anti-Christ or that Catholics worship Mary is to be linked with those saying that Unitarians are to be preferred to Roman Catholics. However, there were many Reformed and many modern era Christians who still believe that the Pope is part of the anti-Christ system and that the final 'anti-Christ' may just be a pope! Also, it is not far off at all to say that Catholics worship Mary. Geisler and MacKenzie surprisingly arrive at this very conclusion:

> "And, despite technical distinctions to the contrary, evangelicals argue that there are no practical differences between the veneration of Mary and the worship of God in the minds of devout Marian Catholics. Of course, only God knows the heart, but judging by the fervor of Catholics' devotion and the actual words used of Mary and God there is little visible difference between their devotion to Mary and their devotion to God. And many of the folk Catholics involved in this are not even aware of the official theoretical distinction between the kind of devotion due to God alone and that due to Mary." (chapter on Mariology, pp. 329-330, 330n)

[2] Geisler & MacKenzie, pg. 15. In this case the "Catholic basher" mentioned is Paul Blanshard, author of *American Freedom and Catholic Power*. There is also intimation here that Vatican II represents a new ball game with Romanism. We shall see.

observations could land one into league with a "secular humanist" or some other enemy of orthodoxy.

Likewise on the Catholic side, illustration is given of those Catholics who, in the past tense, regarded Protestants as little better than pagans.[1] This too is considered to be a part of dark history. The impression is clearly given that both sides have erred and there needs to be a new understanding. We shall be investigating thoroughly the definitions and implications of any new understanding recommended between Evangelicals and Roman Catholicism put forth by the authors.

Preliminary Remarks

To start with, Geisler & MacKenzie admit that ultimately there will be no "ecclesiastic union"[2] with Roman Catholicism as long as Rome holds as dogma some of the things mentioned in Section II of their book. But this admission falls far short of any actual *declaration on the status* of the Roman Catholic religion. We are not sure what the terms "ecclesiastic union" define. Also, the authors are convinced that the impossibility of an "ecclesiastic union" *does not* exclude a whole-hearted endorsement of cooperation on moral, social and educational efforts. We shall investigate whether this latter endorsement of social cooperation contains, inherently, an admission that Rome is a suitable place for one to hear and experience the life-changing Gospel of our Lord Jesus Christ.

We ask plainly, "Can one be saved believing what Rome affirms about Jesus Christ, while also believing what Rome denies about the *Gospel* of Jesus Christ?"

---

[1] While some disclaimer may be found in the documents of Vatican II, which suggests that Protestants are now to be considered "separated brethren," this is a meaningless concession if coming from a non-Christian religion. What solace, comfort or joy is to be found in having the Gospel of Christ declared to be "a brother" with any outside religion? Unless Romanism is proven to be "of Christ," it hardly qualifies to make a determination on anything pertaining to the Gospel! If Rome, in fact, dismisses the Christian gospel then it is disqualified from classifying anyone as to their spiritual relationship with God. Despite Vatican II and the declaration that evangelicals are "separated brethren," we find it implausible to use the past tense when describing a negative Roman Catholic opinion toward evangelicals. There are dozens of Catholic apologetic ministries, in full operation today, out to protect Romanism from the likes of these "separated brethren," and they increase in their boldness daily!

[2] The terminology "ecclesiastic union" is not defined. The real question is left open to conjecture. Can we not have "ecclesiastic union" with Rome because it embraces and disseminates a false gospel? Or, can we not have "ecclesiastic union" with Rome because it embraces such odd communal worship practices? Ultimately, this is the question that we all need to have answered.

It is this question which demands our utmost attention. We suspect the authors would have us conclude that our differences with Rome as far as the Gospel is concerned are far outweighed by our alleged need of Rome in order to survive the cultural wars. Also, we are led to believe by Geisler & MacKenzie that our agreements with Rome on *some* creedal statements, concerning *some* important beliefs shared by Christians and Romanists, are far more important than any differences we may have over the Gospel itself. This underlying assumption needs to be examined.

Dangerous Liaisons

The portent of danger summons us early in the introduction of Geisler & MacKenzie's book. Immediately following the authors' contention that Evangelicals should work with Catholics on a common social agenda we read these sobering words:

> "Rather, in view of the devastating effects of both *Western secularism* and *Eastern mysticism* on our culture, the time is overdue for Catholics and Protestants to hang together before we hang separately."[1]

By identifying the enemies as Western secularism and Eastern mysticism, the authors tip their hand. They propose to forge a common moral, social and educational union with Rome in order to combat the above named enemies. There are two immediate problems here. The first is that Eastern mysticism references a group of religions that do not believe the Gospel of Jesus Christ. We question the assumption that Christians should unite with Rome to fight against the false hope of Eastern religions. The cost is too great. It means a surrender of the Gospel. The authors summarize, "...the time is overdue for Catholics and Protestants to hang together before we hang separately."[2] How odd! Why not go the other way? Why not join with the Eastern religions to fight the never ending invasion of the Romanist religion? Why not say, "We might as well join with the Muslims. We will either hang together or hang separately?" The answer is found in the lingering underlying supposition of the entire book.

This assumption is that *Romanism is a suitable Christian partner* for the purposes of resisting the advancement of Eastern mysticism, and regaining ground lost to Western secularism.

---

[1] Geisler & MacKenzie, pg. 16, emphasis added

[2] Geisler & MacKenzie, pg. 16. We notice also that the nomenclature of this book identifies the religious parties as "Protestant" and "Catholic." We suspect this is a presuppositional *fait accompli*, the idea being that there are at least two major kinds of Christianity, i.e., "protestant brand" and "catholic brand." But is this presupposition a "given" in light of the gospel?

We shall be keeping this assumption before us in our examination. In the first place, we wish to point out that historically, it was not Eastern mysticism which butchered and destroyed Christians in the counter-Reformation. It was not Eastern mysticism which formed the Inquisition. It is not now Eastern mysticism which lays a dubious claim to the Christian Gospel. Everyone knows Eastern mysticism is not Christianity! Can the same be said about Roman Catholicism? The hard fact of the matter is that neither Romanism nor Eastern mysticism were considered to be compatible with the Gospel by those who gave their lives in the Protestant Reformation. We might ask, "What has changed?" and "Why join with either?" Furthermore, it seems to us that to join with Rome against Eastern mysticism is akin to hiring the fox to guard the hen house. Rome has already sanctioned Eastern mysticism as a suitable alternative avenue to God.[1] If this is true according to Rome, then how can Rome help Christians resist what Rome herself has sanctioned?

In the second place, we are called upon by Geisler & MacKenzie to fight against the forces of Western secularism. Secularism is the "worldly spirit" which has no room for the religious, especially in the affairs of public domain. Secularism can be good when it protects us against religious zealotry which threatens our right to worship. It can be bad when it pushes out our right to be heard in the marketplace of ideas, and punishes religious thought. We find it equally odd that the authors wish to join with Rome against secularism. This only makes sense if the religion of Rome is to be preferred to the Western secularism of our day. This is not stated explicitly but their conclusion can hardly be missed that Rome will help Christians combat secularism. But we point out: so will the Mormons. So will the Muslims for that matter. Why the rush to Rome?

Having laid the groundwork for an appeal to the Christian community to jump on the bandwagon with Rome in areas of cultural need, the authors set about to present why this is a good idea. Actually, there would be no need to be overly concerned about their work if they had simply left it with the political. The marshalling of conservative forces for the sake of establishing a particular political and social agenda is hardly new. If Geisler & MacKenzie had merely stated that Rome had recently thrown its weight behind such things as home schooling, the rights of the unborn, private education, protection from laws designed to demand radical gay rights in the private arena, a strong defense, strong families, strong penalties for criminals and a few other things that many Christians believe in as well, it would have been a helpful reminder. But then we might ask, "Why limit it to the Romanists?" Why not include the Mormons and Muslims as well? We

---

[1] See chapter 18 on "The Changing Face of Rome" in *Romanism: The Relentless Roman Catholic Assault on the Gospel of Jesus Christ,* (Huntsville, AL: White Horse Publications, ©1995)

should think any politically conservative national organization would help stem the tide of arrogant Western decadence. But, as we shall see, Geisler & MacKenzie have a different agenda. Theirs is a theology book long before it is a political book. Their agenda goes much deeper than mere co-belligerency on social, moral and political matters. The authors wish to go far beyond these boundaries and actually, in our opinion, work toward an acceptance of Rome both as a political ally and a legitimate Christian community. Because of this we need a careful critique of their book, as it appears to be yet another attempt to minimize our differences with Rome on the Gospel, while maximizing agreements with Rome on some aspects of perceived orthodoxy. We ask, "Is this done to legitimize the Romish religion?" We ask further, "Have the authors hamstrung the Gospel from fear of a secular or Eastern mystical world?" Or even, "Have Geisler & MacKenzie simply used the occasion of social disintegration to promote the gospel of Rome, which has already been received into their hearts?" We shall see.

Analysis

We ask the reader to keep in mind that in competing systems of thought, there often exist similar phrases and ideas; but the meaning of the phrases and ideas is determined by the system itself. We begin here because it is alleged by many Evangelicals that there exists a healthy body of doctrinal agreement with Roman Catholicism. The general assumption is that the agreements far outweigh the disagreements. But is this true? Are there really such doctrinal agreements? If so, do they make the differences trivial by comparison? Geisler & MacKenzie have broken up their book into three main sections: I) Areas of Doctrinal Agreement; II) Areas of Doctrinal Differences; and III) Areas of Practical Cooperation. For the sake of cohesiveness, we shall analyze them in the same order but will concentrate mostly on their section on "Areas of Doctrinal Agreement." This is critical since the authors are unwilling to allow the evidence of our differences with Rome to prevail. It is essential that we put their alleged *agreements* to the severest test. Even though the authors have amassed weighty—absolutely insurmountable, in our opinion—differences with Rome, the conclusion persists with them that the alleged *agreements* with Rome win the day. But if the alleged agreements themselves are not valid, then the entire issue is utterly settled. We believe the differences do outweigh the agreements and, when considered alone, prevent Rome from being confused with Christianity. But as we shall see, an obliteration of the alleged agreements will end all doubt that Roman Catholicism is a religion all its own, and not Christianity.

Our comments will be made using Geisler & MacKenzie as a backdrop. However, we will quote extensively from other sources that speak to the issues as well. But we do not wish to make this an "us versus them" episode. Rather we hope to expand the debate throughout all of Christendom for the sake of the Gospel of Jesus Christ and the cause of God and truth. It is our hope to improve upon the motto exhibited on the first page of Part 1 of Geisler & MacKenzie's book. They quote Vincent of Lerins to the effect that:

> "One should believe only what has been held 'always, everywhere and by all.'"[1]

We doubt the Apostle Paul would have found much use for this citation of Vincent. After all, Paul was guilty of joining Jesus in not putting new wine in old wine skins. Vincent's slogan would have fit the Pharisees. They rejected the New Covenant of Christ's blood on Vincent's grounds. Vincent definitely fits well with Rome which champions Traditions and other tales of old.

We prefer a more balanced quotation attributed to Martin Luther at the Council of Worms:

> "Unless I am convinced by the testimony of the Scriptures or by clear reason (for I do not trust either in the pope or in councils alone, since it is well known that they have often erred and contradicted themselves), I am bound by the Scriptures I have quoted, and my conscience is captive to the Word of God. I cannot and will not retract anything, since it is neither safe nor right to go against conscience. I cannot do otherwise, here I stand, may God help me, Amen."[2]

---

[1] Geisler & MacKenzie, pg. 17

[2] *The New International Dictionary of the Christian Church*, J. D. Douglas editor, (Grand Rapids, MI: Zondervan, ©1978) pg. 1062

Part I
Things Held in Common?

The Question of Revelation

IT MAY BE A common perception that Christians and Roman Catholics share a rich historical background and that there is a "body of doctrine shared by Roman Catholics and evangelicals."[1] For instance, it is proposed that three ancient creeds are held in common. They are the *Apostles' Creed,* the *Nicene Creed* and the *Athanasian Creed.* We produce for you the *Apostles' Creed*:

> "I believe in God, the Father almighty; and in Christ Jesus, His only-begotten Son, our Lord, who was born of the Holy Spirit and the Virgin Mary, was crucified by Pontius Pilate, and was buried; the third day He arose again from the dead; He ascended into heaven, sits at the right hand of the Father, whence He is coming to judge the living and the dead; and in the Holy Spirit, the holy [Church] *the forgiveness of sins*, the resurrection of the body. Amen."[2]

We take the space to reproduce this Creed because it discloses to us what will become a disturbing trend among Evangelicals. It is true that the Roman Catholic religion and Evangelicals can both affirm this creed. But what is to be gained from it? This creed attests to a distinctive Trinitarianism but little else. Nothing is said about the Gospel of Jesus Christ. Nothing is said about salvation or justification or the *way* sins are forgiven. What is disturbing is that the mention of a common creed without clarification of *how* the creed is interpreted gives the wrong impression. The *meaning* of the creed in Roman Catholicism and the *meaning* of the creed in Evangelicalism is radically different. In this case the *way* sins are forgiven is absolutely contrary between Evangelicals and Roman Catholics. As we shall see later in this book, even the word "Almighty" means something different for Roman Catholicism than it does for Christianity. The *words* of

---

[1] Geisler & MacKenzie, pg. 19

[2] *Sources of Catholic Dogma,* Translated by Roy J. Deferrari from 13th. Edition of Henry Denzinger's *Enchiridion Symbolorum*, (St. Louis, MO: Herder Book Co., ©1957) pp. 4,5, emphasis added

the creed—and the different meanings assigned to them—only set the stage for radically opposing religions.[1]

We next move to the so-called *Athanasian Creed*.[2] A striking teaching of this creed is the threefold repetition that there is no salvation without belief in the words of this creed:

- "Whoever wishes to be saved, needs above all to hold to the Catholic faith; unless each one preserves this whole and inviolate, he will without a doubt perish in eternity…
- "Therefore let him who wishes to be saved, think thus concerning the Trinity…
- "This is the Catholic faith; unless every one believes this faithfully and firmly, he cannot be saved."[3]

By the term "catholic" the writers did not have in mind Roman Catholicism. Catholic means universal. So it is the universal Church which is warned, in this creed, that disbelief in the contents of the creed leads to condemnation. Yet we notice that the *Athanasian Creed* contains the *Filioque* clause (Latin for "and the Son") with reference to the procession of the Holy Spirit. The Eastern Church rejected this part of the creed preferring to leave out the *Filioque* clause. Does this mean that they cannot be saved? The answer according to the creed is yes; but not according to modern Roman Catholicism which considers the Eastern Church as part of the Body of Christ. Also, the Muslim world rejects the Trinity and it too has been more or less sanctioned by the Vatican.[4]

---

[1] We should point out that Denzinger lists for our perusal three forms of the Apostolic Creed. The Eastern form is much more elaborate and has the additional sentence "…and in one baptism of repentance in the dismissal of sins…" (Denzinger, *Sources of Catholic Dogma*, pg. 9). What this "one baptism" means is crucial. It is left to the interpreter. Many different religions could come from this one little sentence!

[2] Of the origin of this creed, we read the following: "Two creeds need to be distinguished: (1) the Nicene Creed; (2) the Athanasian Creed or the *Quicunque Vult,* known as the *Fides Catholica.* How the latter became known as the Athanasian Creed (beyond the fact that it expresses Nicene sentiments) is unknown, but it was apparently written in Latin, then translated into Greek, and is later than Athanasius." (*The New International Dictionary of the Christian Church*) pg. 81

[3] Denzinger, *Sources of Catholic Dogma*, pp. 15,16

[4] We find this accommodation to the Eastern churches:

> "These Churches, although separated from us, yet possess true sacraments, above all—by apostolic succession—the priesthood and the Eucharist, whereby they are still joined to us in closest intimacy." (Decree on Ecumenism, *Unitatis Redintegratio*, Vatican II)

continued on following page

We see that Rome does not, in virtue of Vatican II, embrace the *Athanasian Creed,* since Rome sanctions non-Trinitarian religions. Also Evangelicals well might ask whether they want to embrace this creed wholeheartedly. On the one hand, Christians will affirm a strong Trinitarian stance. But are we ready to anathematize those not holding to the "procession" of the Holy Spirit from both the Father and the Son (*filioque* clause)? In either case, Rome does not have this creed in common with Evangelicals as long as non-Christian religions are given approbation by the Vatican. Rome is a far cry from the *Athanasian Creed*!

Any contention that Roman Catholics and Evangelicals have the *Apostles' Creed* and the *Athanasian Creed* in common is misleading and in the case of the *Athanasian Creed*, dishonest. With respect to the Nicene Creed, it is easy to see to what extent Evangelicals can harmonize with Rome. The Nicene Creed is very short and to the point with a clear emphasis on '*homousion*' i.e., the Father and Son being of one substance. There is nothing in the creed concerning the Gospel of Christ.

We can say of these creeds that they hammer out some bedrock foundational statements on the concepts of Monotheism, the Trinity and the substance of Christ. But they also leave open the door for disagreements and they say nothing about the *message* of the messenger. It is our observation that Roman Catholics are inconsistent with the *Athanasian Creed.* As we shall see, they are inaccurate in applying a part of the *Apostles Creed* in their sacramental system. They are also far from consistent in their understanding of the *Nicene Creed.* We must point out that Rome may have some thread of continuity with orthodoxy on the Person of Christ, but this will be to no credit should the *message of Christ* be misunderstood.

The Question Of Councils

Should Christians believe that Evangelicals have in common with Roman Catholicism four major early Church Councils? These Councils are: First

---

We find these somewhat startling words concerning the Muslim religion:

> "The Church has also a high regard for the Muslims. They worship God, who is one, living and subsistent, merciful and almighty, the Creator of heaven and earth, who also has spoken to men. They strive to submit themselves without reserve to the hidden decrees of God, just as Abraham submitted himself to God's plan, to whose faith Muslims eagerly link their own. Although not acknowledging him as God, they venerate Jesus as a prophet, his virgin Mother they also honor, and even at times devoutly invoke. Further, they await the day of judgment and the reward of God following the resurrection of the dead. For this reason they highly esteem an upright life and worship God, especially by way of prayer, alms-deeds and fasting." (*Nostra Aetate*, Vatican II)

Nicea (AD 325), First Constantinople (AD 431), Ephesus (AD 431) and Chalcedon (AD 451).

As in the case of the creeds, in order for Evangelicals to embrace a Council the Council must be in accord with the Scriptures. Also, the truths expressed by a Council must be abided by all who agree. It will not do to say that something is "held in common" unless "held in common" means what it says.*

Some think that because the First Council of Nicea dealt primarily with Arianism[1] that we have the entire Council in common with Rome. This is misleading and highly gratuitous. What Geisler & MacKenzie omit speaks volumes. The Council of Nicea taught in unambiguous terms that no one Bishop should seek to expand his authority beyond his local territory:

> "Let the ancient customs in Egypt, Libya and Pentapolis prevail, that the Bishop of Alexandria have jurisdiction in all these, since the like is customary for the Bishop of Rome also. Likewise Antioch and the other provinces, let the Churches retain their privileges." (Canon VI, Council of Nicea, AD 325)

> "But in every province the ratification of what is done should be left to the Metropolitan." (Canon IV, Council of Nicea, AD 325)

With respect to the Council of Constantinople, we observe the same idea:

> "The bishops are not to go beyond their dioceses to churches lying outside of their bounds, nor bring confusion on the churches; but let the Bishop of Alexandria, according to the canons, alone administer the affairs of Egypt; and let the bishops of the East manage the East alone, the privileges of the Church in Antioch, which are mentioned in the canons of Nice, being preserved; and let the bishops of the Asian Diocese administer the Asian affairs only; and the Pontic bishops only Pontic matters; and the Thracian bishops only Thracian affairs." (Canon II, Constantinople, AD 381)

We cite these canons from these Councils in order to prove beyond a shadow of a doubt that Rome does not honor these Councils. As in the

---

* We have had conversations with some Roman apologists who would not, for example, concede that "unanimous consent of the Fathers" meant that all of the Church Fathers agreed! For obvious reasons, it would be difficult to continue such a discussion and have it be productive in any way. The same applies here.

[1] This is the Christological controversy which ultimately branded as heresy the teaching of Arius. Arianism espoused that Christ was created by God and not eternal. Hence it was said of Arius that he believed there was a time when Christ was not!

Athanasian Creed, Rome disqualifies itself from any meaningful common bond with Evangelicals. When it came to the question of Papal primacy, the Councils taught local Bishop authority. Rome teaches a universal Romish Bishop authority.[1] The best any Christian could hope for is that the Vatican holds in common with Evangelicals *some of the teachings of some of the early Church Councils*. It is certainly misleading to say that the Roman Catholic religion has in common with Evangelicals these Creeds and these Councils.

Additionally, we find it most disturbing that some say Evangelicals and Rome have in common not only three Creeds and four councils but five centuries of history! This is incredible in light of Romanist doctrinal expansion and elastic dogma.[2] What may have been held by the Councils and Creeds during the first five centuries has been undone by modern

---

[1] We read these telling words from Vatican II:

> "The Lord made Peter alone the rock-foundation and the holder of the keys of the Church. He gave him keys of his Church and instituted him as Shepherd of the whole flock. The office of binding and loosing which was given to Peter was also assigned to the college of apostles united to its head. This pastoral office of Peter and the other apostles belongs to the Church's very foundation and is continued by the bishops under the primacy of the Pope. For the Roman Pontiff, by reason of his office as Vicar of Christ, and as pastor of the entire Church has full, supreme, and universal power over the whole Church, a power which he can always exercise unhindered." (*Lumen Gentium*, Dogmatic Constitution of the Church, Vatican II. paragraph 22)

Clearly Rome has rewritten the Councils of Nicea and Constantinople in favor of Roman authoritarianism!

[2] Karl Keating, a modern day Romanist apologist, in his book, *Catholicism and Fundamentalism: the Attack on "Romanism" By "Bible Christians,"* borrows from Vincent of Lerins to describe what we would call the elasticity of Roman doctrine:

> "In answering these questions, the Church develops—we perhaps can say 'matures'—doctrines, but does not alter their essence. It is not a matter of inventing new beliefs, but of clearing up obscurities regarding old ones. Vincent of Lerins, in about 450, explained it this way: 'But perhaps someone is saying, Will there then be no progress of religion in the Church of Christ? Certainly there is, and the greatest... But it is truly progress and not a change of faith. What is meant by progress is that something is brought to an advancement within itself; by change, that something is transformed from one thing into another.'"

Quoting from *Die verbum* (Vatican II), Keating offers more explanation:

> "For as the centuries succeed one another, the Church constantly moves forward toward the fullness of divine truth until the words of God reach their complete fulfillment in her." Keating, *Catholicism and Fundamentalism*, (San Francisco: Ignatius Press, ©1988) pp. 143,144

Roman Catholic Councils. We have illustrated this in the case of the *Athanasian Creed* and the Councils of Nicea and Constantinople.

Does the early period of Church history support the Romanist religion as well as Evangelicalism? In the first place, there was not a Roman Catholic religion in the first five centuries as we know of Rome today. Secondly, the commonality is a forced one. Not one person signing any of the aforementioned Creeds or Council canons would recognize what has come to be known today as the Roman Catholic Church. Rome must be reckoned with on what is believed today in its Councils and Canons. There is precious little Evangelicals have in common with modern Rome and there is precious little Rome has in common with early Church history despite *some* orthodoxy on *some things* pertaining to Christianity. We are reminded from Scripture that even the demons are seemingly orthodox in their appraisal of Monotheism, Trinitarianism, Christology and the reality of the incarnation.[1] What the demons could not suffer was the *message* of the messenger. By way of historical reminder, the following citation from Philip Schaff helps to put things into perspective:

> "There is a vast difference between Catholicism and Romanism. The former embraces all Christians, whether Roman, Greek, or Protestant; the latter is in its very name, sectarian, and exclusive. The holy Catholic Church is an article of faith; the Roman Church is not even named in the ancient creeds. Catholicism extends through all Christian centuries; Romanism proper dates from the Council of Trent. Medieval Catholicism looked towards the Reformation; Romanism excludes and condemns the Reformation. So ancient Judaism, as represented by Abraham, Moses, and the prophets, down to John the Baptist, prepared the way for Christianity, as its end and fulfillment; while Judaism, after the crucifixion of the Messiah, and the destruction of Jerusalem, has become hostile to Christianity, 'Catholicism is the strength of Romanism; Romanism is the weakness of Catholicism.'"[2]

We remind the reader that there is a vast chasm which exists between "Catholicism," i.e., the early Church Universal, and "Roman Catholicism" i.e., the provincial and sectarian religion which emerged out of the great Council of Trent.

---

[1] "Thou believest that there is one God; thou doest well: the devils also believe, and tremble" (James 2:19). "And there was in their synagogue a man with an unclean spirit; and he cried out, Saying, Let us alone; what have we to do with thee, thou Jesus of Nazareth? art thou come to destroy us? I know thee who thou art, the Holy One of God" (Mark 1:23-24).

[2] Schaff, Philip, *The Creeds of Christendom*, (Grand Rapids: Baker Books, ©1993) Vol. I, pp. 83,84

The Question Of Biblical Data

We move our discussion now to the biblical data. But before leaving this section, let us remember that the desire of some Evangelicals to show forth areas of *doctrinal agreement* with *Roman Catholicism* is very high. However, one can play fast and loose with the Creeds and Councils. One can make an impression that a connection exists between the Roman Catholic religion and Evangelicals by using the early Church Councils and Canons incorrectly. Such impressions are unreliable, and such efforts must be carefully investigated before commonality is considered proven.[1]

Suppose for illustration that we wanted to show commonality between an elephant and a rat. We would begin by saying that rats and elephants both have two eyes, two ears, a mouth and a stomach. To this we might add that both have four legs and a tail. They have a circulatory system along with bones, muscles and nerve endings. We might go on and on in an effort to prove that the rat and the elephant are *essentially* the same. But at some point, we would have to concede that a rat and an elephant are really very different and cannot be classified together. An alligator has all of these characteristics as well, but is neither a rat nor an elephant. We use this illustration because it serves the point. Citation of superficial commonalities is pervasive throughout the Evangelical community. In many cases the similarities are strained beyond reason and balance. In fact, to our dismay, sometimes things which are asserted as a commonality are absolutely contradicted in later writings. For instance, see how a hope for doctrinal agreement between Christians and Romanists, served up in one section, is utterly crushed by the same authors in another section of their book. With respect to Romish Tradition being allegedly on a par with Scripture, we read from Geisler & MacKenzie's book:

> Scripture Alone
>
> "Although many Catholic theologians see tradition as a second source of revelation, Roman Catholic scholar Louis Bouyer notes that 'according to both the Council of Trent and *Vaticanum* Scripture *alone* can be said to have God as its author.' In this we can see a

[1] We must reiterate that this is the section of Geisler & MacKenzie's book which defines the commonalities with Roman Catholicism. If this section fails, then there is nothing of substance that would attract us to the supposition that Roman Catholicism is a Christian religion. We shall see that the authors amass a mountain of material (204 pages) divulging our differences with Rome, which should settle the question. However, the weight of differences is not overthrown by the alleged weight of commonality in the minds of these authors. So, it behooves us to examine these so-called areas of doctrinal agreement and see if they are plausible and then see if they neutralize the weight of what we consider insurmountable divergences.

basic accord concerning the central place that revelation has in Christian theological formation."[1]

Scripture Not Alone

> "Whether or not extra-biblical apostolic tradition is considered a second source of revelation, *there is no question that both sides agree that the Roman Catholic Church believes apostolic tradition is both authoritative and infallible*. The Council of Trent was *emphatic* in proclaiming that the Bible alone is not sufficient for faith and morals; God has ordained tradition in addition to the Bible to faithfully guide the church."[2]

On the one hand, the authors quote a Roman Catholic who is *sure* that Trent says Scripture alone has God as its author. Yet, on the other hand, the authors are *certain* that Trent was *emphatic* that the Bible alone is *not* sufficient for faith and morals.

In reality, the Council of Trent teaches that both the Scriptures *and* unwritten traditions of the Romanist religion come from the mouth of Christ:

> "It also clearly perceives that these truths and rules are contained in the written books and in the unwritten traditions, which, received by the Apostles from the mouth of Christ Himself, or from the Apostles themselves, the Holy Ghost dictating, have come down to us, transmitted as it were from hand to hand."[3]

So why would the authors, knowing this, present this information in such a way early on in their writing? Our guess is that all attempts are made to give a lasting and favorable impression of the Roman Catholic religion so as to confirm it as Christian. This is done even though the authors explode the very thing they try to establish. So sparse is the commonality between the religion of Rome and the Christian faith that the beginning of their book would be an embarrassment if they did not at the outset attempt to prove similarities in this clever manner.

Here is another typical sentence from the authors with regard to their vain attempt to put Evangelicals and Romanists on the same page when it comes to the value of Scripture:

---

[1] Geisler & MacKenzie, pg. 21, emphases in original

[2] Geisler & MacKenzie, pg. 181, emphases added

[3] Schroeder, H. J., *The Canons and Decrees of the Council of Trent*, (Rockford, IL: TAN Books and Publishers Inc., ©1978) pg. 17

> "That the Scriptures are *central* to an understanding of God's revelation is a truth stated throughout the documents of the Roman Catholic Church."[1]

This is true. But what does the word *central* mean? It certainly does not mean *sola scriptura* (Bible alone). And if it does not mean *sola scriptura*, then something else is *equally* as central as the Bible in the Roman Catholic religion. This, the authors readily admit!

> "Roman Catholics, by contrast, believe that the Bible, apart from any outside information or authority *is not sufficient* to explain all essential points of doctrine. That is why they believe an infallible teaching magisterium is necessary."[2]

Of course, the above citation as to the insufficiency of Scripture in Romanism ruins the previous superficial claim that the Bible is *central* in the Roman Catholic religion. We are troubled that the authors are not willing to conclude that their own research in the "areas of doctrinal difference" adequately and finally undoes all their efforts to prove a commonality with Rome. One might view this as theological schizophrenia.

In another attempt to link the Christian with the Romanist, we are given this loaded sentence by the authors:

> "For both Catholics and Protestants it is in the New Testament that God's plan of salvation enters its final phase."[3]

What exactly the "plan of salvation" consists of is not mentioned in this segment. Also, there is not a separate section devoted to the Gospel in all of the book. The closest we come to a discussion on the plan of salvation is found in the difference section under the topic of justification. It is in this section that we find a remarkable job of clarifying the Romanist position compared to the Christian position on the principle of forensic justification. Ironically, Geisler & MacKenzie conclude that Romanism[4] does carry a different concept of obtaining eternal life:

---

[1] Geisler & MacKenzie, pg. 21, emphasis added

[2] Geisler & MacKenzie, pg. 190n, emphasis added

[3] Geisler & MacKenzie, pg. 22

[4] Incidentally, "Romanism" is our term. It is a term which defines the Roman Catholic religion which we believe to have gone apostate with the official teachings of the Council of Trent in the middle 16th century. Romanism is a term that evidently the authors deem inappropriate. We prefer it to Catholicism and obviously, we do not apply the name Christian to the Romanists.

> "Catholicism teaches that even justification (in adults) is preconditioned on faith plus the resolution to do good works. Hence, the promise to do good works is a condition of initial justification. Thereby sanctification is frontloaded into justification. That is, the promise to live a godly life is a condition for receiving the gift of eternal life. But if this is so then it is *not of grace but works*. And for Roman Catholics, salvation in the ultimate sense, not just in the initial justification, *always requires faith plus works to obtain eternal life."*[1]

Does not this excellent summary of Romanism's gospel underscore the superficiality which is presented in earlier sentences on a presumed commonality? There is no real point of commonality in assuring us that both Romanists and Christians believe that the "plan of salvation" enters its final phase in the New Testament, when the two have radically opposite plans!

The Question Of Theological Development

We shall make only a few comments on this section. We would agree that Romanists believe in the general revelation of God. General revelation describes the effects of God's decree to create. All the visible universe which is open to the scrutiny of man is classified as general revelation. However, neither Romanists nor Christians have cornered the market on the *concept* of general revelation. Not all religions make assertions based on general revelation, but many that do make varying and contradictory conclusions based on the data available. Rome and Christianity, for example, do not agree on the *interpretation* of general revelation. The fact that man exists and that there exists apart from man a world too wonderful for him to comprehend sometimes leads to the notion of a supreme being, but sometimes it does not. We know of at least one astronomer who, when contemplating the vastness of the universe, concludes that the universe itself is supreme and should itself be worshipped. Yet he deduces this from his observations of the natural world which, incidentally, he cannot bring himself to call "creation," since he does not believe it to be created. The deduction from the evidences of nature of an un-caused cause, or the deduction from the evidences of creation of a creator, is found in any number of man-made religions. Yet their deductions all lead to the wrong god whom they freely worship, compounding their offense. The fact that Romanists hold to general revelation does not represent a point of common interest in the Gospel of Jesus Christ. Many religions recognize a supreme being from the evidence surrounding them in nature. But these "supreme beings" that they worship are examples of men suppressing the truth, not agreeing with it! Christians can in no way claim commonality with Rome—

---

[1] Geisler & MacKenzie, pp. 238-239, emphasis added

or with pagan religions, for that matter—based simply on the evidence that Rome calls her "supreme being" by the same name that we do! Theirs is a different gospel, based on a strange fire offered on the wrong altar before a false god whose arm is too short to save.

The Question Of The Natural Law

There are certain assumptions concerning what is called the "Natural Law." Common ground is sought with the Romanist religion on the assumption that Christians and Romanists both believe in a "Natural Law" which is resident in all of mankind. The assumption of a universal "Natural Law" is sometimes presented as a proof that we have some deep truth in common with the Romanist appraisal of mankind. Yet, is this so? Obedience to a so-called "Natural Law" is certainly not the *cause* of salvation. Nor is disobedience to a so-called "Natural Law" the *cause* of condemnation. Christians do not believe that adherence to a "Natural Law" is sufficient to experience God, as Rome teaches. To bend Christianity toward the Roman point of view, it is alleged that Romans 2:14,15 is proof of a "Natural Law" written by God in the hearts of unbelievers. *Romans 2 does not teach a universal "Natural Law,"* which, if obeyed, leads one to eternal life.[1] Paul writes:

---

[1] We are very concerned with any careless exegesis which forces us into a corner on the ability of natural man. Romans 2:14,15 is normally translated in this manner, as evidenced by the KJV version among others:

> "For when the Gentiles, which have not the law, *do by nature* the things contained in the law, these, having not the law, are a *law unto themselves:* which show the work of law *written in their hearts, their conscience also bearing witness,* and their thoughts the mean while accusing or else excusing one another." (Romans 2:14,15, emphases added)

The interpretation which comes from this translation tends to lead one into sticky and often contradictory conclusions. The fact that these verses fall directly after Paul's warning that, "the doers of the law shall be justified" (Romans 2:13), could give us the impression that natural man can be justified if he obeys the law of God written on his heart. It also leaves open the door that the native in the jungle will be justified if he obeys the "natural law" written on his heart, and likewise for non-Christian religions to have a satisfactory relationship with God if only they obey the "natural law" or some sort of "natural light."

We believe the better translation puts the "naturally" with "not having the law" with the understanding that the law which is vacant (among Gentiles) is the Mosaic Law: "Gentiles which have not the law *naturally*." Gentiles are naturally bereft of the Mosaic Law, yet they will judge those who have the Law because of a greater Law of Christ put in their hearts as those among the Gentiles called and regenerated of God. These are not, as Paul says, Jews outwardly, but Jews inwardly, circumcised of the heart (Romans 2:29).

> "For when Gentiles who do not have the Law (Mosaic) by nature, do the things of the Law (Mosaic), these not having the Law (Mosaic) are a law to themselves, in that they show the work of the Law (Mosaic) written in their hearts, their conscience bearing witness, and their thoughts alternately accusing them or else defending them" (Romans 2:14-15).

Notice our translation of Paul seeks to correct the common assumption that the Gentiles spoken of here are unbelievers. The ordinary assumption is that the Gentiles here are unbelievers and that they obey some sort of "Natural Law" instinctively, which obedience is sufficient for heaven. But the translation which leads to this interpretation has been adequately exposed for its deficiencies.[1] The Bible nowhere asserts that natural man gains from nature some degree of reconciliation to God through obedience to a "Natural Law." Scripture testifies that God condemns all men in their unbelief while simultaneously holding them "without excuse": "For God hath concluded them all in unbelief, that he might have mercy upon all" (Romans 11:32). It also testifies, that God has made man in such a way that he *cannot* understand what God has done from the beginning to the end:

> "He hath made every thing beautiful in his time: also he hath set the world in their heart, so that no man can find out the work that God maketh from the beginning to the end" (Ecclesiastes 3:11).

Compare this with Rome's take on Romans 2:14,15;

> "The beginning and end of all things can be known with certitude by the natural light of human reason from created things."[2]

Rome's conclusion is due to the faulty assumption that the "Gentiles" in Romans 2:14,15 are unbelievers, *contra* Jeremiah 31:33, which teaches that God writes His Law on the hearts of believers as a sign of the New Covenant in Christ. It is better exegesis to see in Romans 2:14,15 Gentiles who have been circumcised in the heart (Romans 2:26,27), who are obeying the law of the Holy Spirit written by God on their hearts (Hebrews 8). It is not that Gentiles *do* the law naturally. It is rather that Gentiles do not *have* the law naturally, i.e., by descendency from Abraham, yet do His Law because of the work of God in regeneration by the Spirit: "And I will

---

[1] We ask the readers to consider the fine work of C. E. Cranfield in his commentary on the book of Romans (ICC series, Edinburgh, Scotland: T & T Clark, ©1975). This two volume set is perhaps the finest and most complete commentary in print on the subject. Cranfield takes the position that the Gentiles here are believers who do not have the Law naturally (by descendency from Abraham) but nevertheless have the law of God written on their hearts by virtue of regeneration.

[2] Denzinger, *Sources of Catholic Dogma*, pg. 443

put my spirit within you, and cause you to walk in my statutes, and ye shall keep my judgments, and do them" (Ezekiel 36:27). It is interesting to us that C. E. Cranfield quotes Augustine and Ambroisaster as interpreting Romans 2:14 in this manner.[1] The doctrine of "Natural Law" which Rome longs to find in Romans 2 is not to be found. We take the time to run through all this because it is important to see how "Natural Law"—the ability of man to be just before God by his own natural reasoning—is used by Romanists to champion their "Natural Theology." Many, Romanists among them, have too high a regard for the natural light of mankind, as evidenced by this citation:

> "It is 'the natural light of reason, by which we discern what is right and wrong.' In it is 'naught else but the impression on us of divine light.' All rational creatures, not just believers, share in natural law. It is the law that is written on human hearts of which Paul speaks in Romans 2:12-15."[2]

We do not believe that Romans 2 teaches the "Natural Law" written on the heart of unbelieving mankind. Nor do we agree with the conclusion of this exegesis:

> "For Catholics, as well as many Protestants, natural law is the moral basis from which social issues are addressed."[3]

The Christian position on the state of natural man is that he is a law unto himself and that the common thread between all mankind is found in their depravity—*not* in their enlightened obedience. Natural law, if there is such a common aspect of mankind, is so corrupted and self-seducing that there is

---

[1] Cranfield, *The International Critical Commentary: Epistle to Romans, Volume I,* pg. 156n

[2] Geisler & MacKenzie, pg. 25

[3] Geisler & MacKenzie, pg. 25. We would also remind the reader that this "Natural Law" of which the authors speak so highly is that same "Natural Law" which, according to Rome, morally binds us to obey our consciences even when our consciences instruct us to do wrong: "The position of St. Thomas is, in fact, well known: He is so consistent in his respect for conscience that he maintains that it is wrong for one to make an act of faith in Christ if in one's own conscience one is convinced, however absurdly, that it is wrong to carry out such an act. (cf. Summa Theologica 1-2.19.5) If man is admonished by his conscience—even if an erroneous conscience, but one whose voice appears to him as unquestionably true—he must always listen to it. What is not permissible is that he culpably indulge in error without trying to reach the truth." (John Paul II, *Crossing the Threshold of Hope*, (New York: Alfred A. Knopf, Inc., ©1994) pg. 191) It is baffling to us that Rome can simultaneously hold to this belief that the Gentiles who "do by nature the things contained in the law" (Romans 2:14) are those self-same Gentiles who are bound by their consciences to disobey it! This is where Rome's "natural light of human reason" has taken us, and Geisler & MacKenzie have let her take us there!

no hope of a moral consensus or moral basis. Observation and Scripture soundly refute the moral capabilities of natural man. One need only look from culture to culture to see the common depravity of mankind which formulates laws in accordance with his demented nature. Thus we have a general law of *disorder* and *disunity* in the field of law and ethics. To rely on *this* as the bridge of unity between Roman Catholicism and Protestant Christianity is evidence of a willingness to reach for the very lowest common denominator in order to create the appearance of union. In short, a "Natural Law" theology is dangerous if it leads one to believe that obedience to "Natural Law" puts one right with God, and we see that Rome arrives at this very conclusion. Christians cannot. We also believe, unlike Rome, that man's capacity for self-governing and self-improvement based upon a "Natural Law" is suffocated and annihilated by mankind's depravity. Because of this, Rome's attempt to build a "Natural Theology" on the foundations of the "Natural Law" in all men is precisely where her theology begins to break down because she thinks too highly of man in his fallen state.

The Question Of Natural Theology

It is only a small step to move from "Natural Law" to "Natural Theology," which is precisely what the Romanist religion does. We have already shown that a "Natural Law" is the most unlikely teaching from Romans 2. We have also pointed out that a "Natural Law" salvation is dangerous, as it leads to an obedience-based system of salvation. Romanism is evidence of this, as seen by the following statement from a Roman Catholic apologist:

> "Now we come to the personal issue—the individual issue—how the individual relates to God. Now we get into a different area. And that's where Vatican II is coming closer. Vatican II is now saying the individual, though he does not hold the same doctrine as the Catholic Church in a general sense—a general theological dogmatic sense—he has a certain degree of truth. And the Catholic Church is well noted for that. Everything is not black and white in the Catholic Church. There are degrees of truth. Even the Hottentot in Africa can have salvation even though he doesn't know Jesus Christ, because he has a certain degree of truth with the capacity that God has given him *so that he can obey and still be saved.* And there are varying degrees of truth coming up from that. And so you get up to the pope. And that is what Vatican II is trying to look at, these different degrees of truth, and saying with this degree of truth, yes, you can know God, too, and you can be saved as well."[1]

---

[1] Sungenis, Robert, "Evangelicals and Catholics Together in Cult Ministry Panel Discussion," Evangelical Ministries to New Religions annual conference, Atlanta, GA, *continued on following page*

Some assume that Christians are in agreement with Rome in all this. "Natural Theology" speaks of the ability of man to know God apart from special revelation. It is said to be man's natural understanding of God apart from God's personal revelation. The "Natural Theology" of man consists in his understanding of God based only on general revelation. Rome views "Natural Theology" as something good and something to build upon. They see in mankind some sort of divine light or spark, a natural goodness, as it were.

However, Christians believe that "Natural Theology" is nothing more than man's vain attempts to construct deities for his use and disposal. There is nothing to be gained from an admission that all men in some way set out to make their own gods. Because Romanists believe in a "Natural Theology" does not at all make their religion closer to Christianity in the least, because *all* false religions have some sort of "Natural Theology." This is well illustrated by the number of religions on the face of the earth. Also, the fact that Romanists approach "Natural Theology" in a manner radically different from the Christian actually illustrates our differences rather than showing forth any commonality. This is why we are surprised to see any attempt to build a bridge on this point. Christians have seen "Natural Theology" as part of the overall problem of mankind—not part of the solution.

Thus, it is not true that the Christian shares with the Romanist religion (*contra* all other religions) the same understanding of a "Natural Law" leading to a "Natural Theology." There is no commonality to be found here at all. The Christian believes that the heart, mind and conscience of the natural man is so infected with sin that any remnant of law and theology is entirely warped and actually is an impediment to the Gospel. Whereas the Romanist believes that God has imprinted His law on mankind (a faulty interpretation of Romans 2:14,15) and mankind is capable of understanding God with a "Natural Theology" while obeying the "Natural Law." Ultimately Rome concludes that obedience to "Natural Law," and worship which is consistent with "Natural Theology," will be sufficient to have a satisfactory relationship with God, as evidenced by the Roman apologist's statements, above.

Special Revelation

This brings us to the point of special revelation. It is assumed that Christians and Rome can at least agree on the necessity of special revelation. But even this alleged agreement is highly suspect. Putting aside the fact that Christians and Rome radically disagree on the *content* and *purpose* of special revelation, we need to ask first if Rome sees special revelation as

USA, October, 1995. Tape 1 Side 1. (©1995, Evangelical Ministries to New Religions, PO Box 20352, Philadelphia, PA, 19137), emphasis added

necessary to the salvation of those outside of Rome. We see Rome speaking out of both sides of the mouth on this issue.

Before leaving this section it would be wise to investigate a misleading comment from Geisler & MacKenzie. Keep in mind that the trend is to scrape the bottom of the barrel to find something in common with Rome. Some think they have found it in this segment under "Natural Theology":

> "Both traditional Roman Catholics and conservative Protestants agree that general revelation is insufficient to lead one to a saving knowledge of the gospel."[1]

This is only partially true and therefore not a trustworthy claim. In the first place, even though Rome holds that general revelation is not sufficient to lead one to a saving knowledge of the Gospel, Rome *does* hold that general revelation *is sufficient to lead one to a saving knowledge!* According to Rome, one does not need to hear, understand and believe the Gospel to be saved, making the above citation disingenuous. In the second place, we do not have the same gospel as Rome. What is left out of the above statement speaks volumes as to our differences with Romanism. Does Rome even have a "saving knowledge of the Gospel" at her disposal? We answer, "No!" How then is it that Rome "agrees" with Protestants that general revelation is insufficient to lead one to *a saving knowledge of the Gospel?* Is it not more honest to say that Rome believes general revelation is not sufficient to get people to heaven within the constructs of their religion? Of course, any number of religions can make this claim, and Christianity can hardly be charged with having something worthwhile in common with those who do.

In the third place, Rome's understanding of just how far natural reason—in light of "Natural Theology" and "Natural Law"—can take someone, is quite disturbing:

> "Our holy mother, the Church, holds and teaches that God, the first principle and last end of all things, can be known with certainty from the created world by the natural light of human reason."[2]

Notice that the citation here says that God *can* be known. It does not say merely, "the *fact* that God exists can be known." We point this out because Vatican II has determined that the light of general revelation to peoples who lie outside the special revelation of God now affords access to God. Apparently, by faithfulness to their particular light as found in "Natural

---

[1] Geisler & MacKenzie, pg. 26

[2] *1994 Catechism of the Catholic Church*, pg. 16, paragraph 36

Theology" or obedience to "Natural Law," Buddhists, Hindus and Moslems are on the right path and lack only a *fullness* of revelation—but do not lack salvation. This position of Vatican II cannot be left out of this discussion, and is of critical importance. Christians know that the Bible forbids even the thought of "natural light obeyed properly" as being sufficient to lead one to heaven. But this appears to be exactly the modern position of Romanism. So the claim of ecumenists that natural revelation, according to Rome, is insufficient to lead one to a saving knowledge of the Gospel, is an idle boast when Rome actually teaches a natural revelation which leads people to a saving knowledge *apart* from the Gospel. Listen to Vatican II:

> "The Catholic Church rejects nothing of what is true and holy in these religions. She has a high regard for the manner of life and conduct, the precepts and doctrines which, although differing in many ways from her own teaching, nevertheless often reflect a ray of that truth which enlightens all men."[1]

Some Closing Comments On Revelation

The Catholic Church (universal Church), prior to the Roman Catholic Religion, was in many respects orthodox and we have roots of heritage with many of the pre-Tridentine theologians and writers. But it is wrong to lump together anyone of note from the first 1500 years of Christianity into what we now recognize as the *Roman Catholic* religion. So, while it is true that *Catholics* held to the Bible as *the* source of authority prior to the Protestant Reformation, these *Catholics* were not *Roman* Catholics. They were members of the *Catholic* (universal) Body of Christ that actually had it right with respect to *sola scriptura*! Some have no problem lumping together *Catholics* as one and the same with *Roman Catholics*. This is unfortunate. We have already noted that most of the early members of the Body of Christ would reject *Roman* Catholicism as an apostate aberration.

We also find it highly disturbing that many ecumenists today wish to push for a Romanist credibility by quoting authors who are not representative of Roman Catholicism as we know it today:

> "On this subject, Donald G. Bloesch notes that 'For the most part both the patristic fathers and the medieval theologians before the fourteenth century taught that the Bible is the unique and sole source of revelation.' Bloesch continues: 'The priority of Scripture over tradition was clearly enunciated by Thomas Aquinas: 'Arguments from Scripture are used properly and carry necessity in matters of faith; arguments from other doctors of the Church are proper, but

---

[1] Vatican II, *Nostra Aetate,* pg. 739, paragraph 2

> carry only probability; for our faith is based on the revelation given to the apostles and prophets who wrote the canonical books of the Scriptures and not on revelation that could have been made to other doctors.'"[1]

Yet we believe that even Thomas Aquinas would find current Rome to be out of line and not in concert with his appraisal of *sola scriptura*. So what is to be gained from this quotation? It shows us that Aquinas would have a hard time getting a post in Roman Catholicism today. His view of tradition flies in the face of Trent and the Vatican Councils. Our point here is to say that Aquinas cannot be mustered up to support the Roman Catholic religion against *sola scriptura*. On the contrary, he speaks with us against Rome!

We must not play a shell game with history. In essence, we cannot say, "Let us look at Aquinas; he was a Roman Catholic and he believed in *sola scriptura*." The conclusion hoped for is that Rome has *sola scriptura* as part of its foundation. But Rome openly repudiates *sola scriptura* and does so in irreformable Canons and Councils which came after Aquinas. So, we might ask, "Was Aquinas a Roman Catholic?" Certainly not on *sola scriptura*. Therefore, references to Aquinas are worthless except to show that Rome has no room for Aquinas today on this issue. We cannot have both Aquinas and Roman Catholicism when it comes to *sola scriptura*.

Geisler & MacKenzie have done a masterful job of minimizing the differences between Christianity and Romanism. In so doing, they actually hide from some pretty obvious conclusions. What gives here? Any clear thinker can see that modern Rome's insistence on Scripture *plus* Tradition, and Faith *plus* Works nullifies any testimony mustered from antiquity to somehow make Roman Catholicism digestible.

Finally, we are appalled at the cavalier way in which the writers "wave off" the fatal differences with Rome as though they were mere trivia in essence. Here is one such fantastic statement.

> "Concerning *sola Scriptura*, at least in the material sense, there is more unanimity than one would expect. Of course, Roman Catholics deny the formal sufficiency of Scripture, insisting on the need for the infallible teaching magisterium of the Church."[2]

What shall we say to these kinds of sentences? A denial of the formal sufficiency of Scripture amounts to a denial of the material sense of Scripture. Since Rome will forever claim that it alone has the authority to

---

[1] Geisler & MacKenzie, pp. 32-33

[2] Geisler & MacKenzie pg. 33

properly interpret the Scripture, the material agreement that Scripture is the Word of God is destroyed by a magisterium which claims sole authority to tell us what it means!

Evidently, this is not a fatal difference between Christianity and Romanism in the minds of Geisler & MacKenzie. We could not possibly disagree more.

The Question of Human Beings

THE ROMAN CATHOLIC religion shares with Christianity many of the basic concepts of the human being as to nature and origin. It is noted that humans are material but also, "by virtue of their minds, possess a transcendence that marks them as different from the nature that surrounds them and orients them toward God."[1]

It is noted that Romanists believe that the human race stems from one human pair.* Also, there is a duality of the human being in the form of body and soul. Geisler & MacKenzie seem to favor the creationist theory of the origin of the soul of man. They at least quote Roman theologians approvingly with respect to its origins: "Concerning the creation of the soul, Roman Catholicism teaches that this occurs at the moment of its unification with the body."[2]

Here the Biblical data is present in a nonconflicting account of the creation of man; Genesis 1 and 2 are blended appropriately, and they include a short review of the New Testament revelation on the origin, creation and nature of mankind. Most of the material presented in this section of *Agreements and Differences* is presented from a distinctly Evangelical point of view, with the mention of a few Roman Catholic writers who have endorsed a similar framework for the creation of mankind and the nature of man.

We do not have a problem with the admission that Rome teaches that man was created by God and that man is at least dichotomous (body and soul). We also can appreciate that Rome uses the book of Genesis as a starting point for the fact of God's creation. However, there is some question as to Rome's toleration of evolution and we shall close this section with some

---

[1] Geisler & MacKenzie, pg. 53

* Although, even this has been questioned by Rome as of late. See John Paul II's comments on evolution to the academy of sciences.

[2] Geisler & MacKenzie, pg. 55

comments relating to that. But before we get to evolution, we must take great care in analyzing the alleged doctrinal agreements between Romanists and Christians concerning the fall of man. The authors state simply that, "Catholics and evangelicals also agree that human beings are fallen."[1] They go on to say, "The official Roman Catholic position on original sin is evangelical at the core."[2] They then quote the fifth session of the Council of Trent which states, in essence, that Adam's offense cost him his holiness, his justice, incurred the wrath of God and that Adam was changed in body and soul for the worse. The authors quote from Ludwig Ott, a well respected Roman Catholic writer, who rightly concludes that Adam's sin was disobedience. So far so good. We would not quibble about the original sin of Adam as one of disobedience which changed him for the worse. But we begin to feel a bit uneasy with the descriptive terms used to describe exactly *what* Adam lost. We wish to pause here to comment on what will lead to trouble down the road. The authors continue with a sentence which needs to be challenged. They say:

> "The transgression of Adam and Eve resulted in the loss of sanctifying grace (i.e., the spiritual life of the soul)."[3]

There is no definition of grace given after this sentence. It behooves us to understand here that Romanists see grace as a substance infused by God which transforms from within. Christians see grace just the opposite. Grace is the disposition of God wherein He is propitious toward His own. Grace, like love, is viewed by Christians as the kindness of God. It is His kindness toward us on account of Christ (Ephesians 2:7). It is not a *substance* which is transmitted. We concur with Chemnitz who wrote the most comprehensive refutation of Trent on justification of both his time and ours:

> "The word 'grace' in Scripture often means favor, good will, or mercy; sometimes, indeed, it also means the gifts which are conferred from good will. However, the question is what in particular the term 'grace' means in those passages in which Paul argues that we are justified freely through the grace of God. Likewise: 'You are saved by the grace of God.' The testimonies are not obscure or ambiguous but clear, certain, and firm that the word 'grace' is to be understood in this argument of the gratuitous mercy, goodness, good will, or favor, of God who embraces in His grace and receives into grace the unworthy for the sake of His Son, the Mediator."[4]

---

[1] Geisler & MacKenzie, pg. 57

[2] Geisler & MacKenzie, pg. 58

[3] Geisler & MacKenzie, pg. 59

[4] Chemnitz, Martin, *Examination of the Council of Trent,* translated by: Fred Kramer, (St. Louis, MO: Concordia Publishing House, ©1971) pg. 494

It is critical here to understand that Biblical "grace" is God's disposition toward His children, because the authors at this point go on to ask an important question given the presupposition that grace is a *substance* which is infused. It is this "substance" which Adam is said to have lost. They frame the debate between Roman Catholics and Protestants on the issue of grace as whether grace *perfects* nature (Roman Catholic) or whether grace *changes* nature (Protestant). We are more comfortable saying that grace is the nature of God's attitude toward His own in Christ. God changes and perfects those for whom He sent His son. Grace is not to be construed apart from the reality of God's affection. The disposition of God as gracious is part of describing His loving character in the Bible. God is gracious and we stand in the grace of God.

Incidentally, the question they pose under the misguided assumption of the nature of grace is never answered. To set the record straight, it is the Roman Catholic position that grace is infused through the sacramental system. To the Roman Catholic, grace *perfects* from the inside out, and to get this grace requires only that you participate in their Sacraments. This is why Rome can assert so easily that Adam lost sanctifying grace. In so doing, Rome sets the stage for recapturing sanctifying grace through the Romanist system. Instead of offering a solution to the real problem of fallen man, Rome rewrites the fall to make it fit their solution! There is not one place in Scripture that states either directly or indirectly that Adam lost something called "sanctifying grace"; neither is it a necessary deduction from other Scriptural data. Adam was cursed for his disobedience and forfeited all hope of spiritual life apart from the forgiveness and mercy of God. Adam died both spiritually and physically due to his sin. It was the grace of God—unmerited favor stemming from His loving disposition—which provided a type of covering for forgiveness until the shed blood of Christ was applied to Adam.

Typical Romanist language, seemingly sanctioned by many Evangelicals, is illustrated in Geisler & MacKenzie's use of this citation from Ludwig Ott, a Roman Catholic theologian:

> "In the New Testament, Ott notes that 'The passage which contains the classical proof is Rom. 5:12-21, in which the Apostle draws a parallel between the first Adam, from whom sin and death are *transmitted* to all humanity, and Christ, the second Adam, from whom justice and life are *transmitted* to all men."[1]

We are astounded that this assessment by Ott of Romans 5 is implied to be doctrinally sound. It is not the Christian position that Adam merely transmitted sin and death to the human race. It is the Christian position that

---

[1] Geisler & Mackenzie, pg. 59, emphasis added

Adam's sin and guilt were imputed to the human race so that all are guilty of Adam's sin *and not just of their own sinning* (Romans 5:12). Also, Christ did not become the second Adam simply to transmit justice and life to His elect so they could attain a righteousness of their own. He came to impute His righteousness to them. This *alien righteousness* is at the heart of the Gospel message, and is utterly at odds with the Roman gospel.

Further, Romans 5 speaks of all being in Adam for the ground of our guilt and damnation, and the elect being in Christ for the ground of their righteousness. The analogy cannot be broken. Our death in Adam is replaced by our life in Christ. And equally important, the *way* we died in Adam is the same *way* we live in Christ. Sin is imputed by virtue of Adam, and righteousness is imputed by virtue of Christ. Again, this is utterly at odds with the Roman gospel.

In short summary, Christians do not understand the original sin of Adam in the same sense as the Romanist. We are not inclined to talk in terms of a loss of sanctifying grace. We are not inclined to view grace as an infused substance which is in need of replacing. We do not accept the Roman assertion that God's undertaking to remedy the fall of Adam consists in the dispensing of grace. Grace neither changes the nature nor perfects the nature. Grace is the disposition of God. As love which never fails describes the activity of God, so grace also describes God's disposition and activity in the realization of this love.

A Word About The Remedy

We switch gears somewhat to examine Geisler & MacKenzie's alleged Evangelical and Roman Catholic similarities concerning the *remedy* of Adam's calamity:

> "Likewise, the *final remedy* for this woeful situation is the same as the common evangelical view."[1]

To substantiate this claim the authors quote again from the 5th Session of the Council of Trent. We produce their citation:

> "If anyone asserts that this sin of Adam, which in its origin is one, and by propagation, not by imitation, transfused into all, which is in each one something that is his own, is taken away either by the forces of human nature or by a remedy other than the merit of the one mediator, our Lord Jesus Christ …let him be anathema."[2]

---

[1] Geisler & MacKenzie, pg. 58, emphasis added

[2] Geisler & MacKenzie, pg. 58

Here perhaps is one of the most blatant examples that we have ever encountered of misusing a historical document to assert a dubious allegation. The authors would have us believe that Rome and Christians share the same "final remedy" of Adam's sin. We produce for you the rest of the paragraph from Trent left out by the authors. After "...our Lord Jesus Christ," the article from Trent continues:

> "...who has reconciled us to God in his own blood, made unto us justice, sanctification and redemption; or if he denies that merit of Jesus Christ *is applied both to adults and to infants by the sacrament of baptism rightly administered in the form of the Church,* let him be anathema."[1]

There are two problems here. First, there is a deliberate attempt to mislead the reader into thinking that Rome and the Christian can agree on the *way* the final remedy for sin is applied. This is done by leaving off the sacramental method of the Romanist remedy. For these two theologians to deliberately omit this information is unconscionable. Secondly, Rome *does* say the final solution for sin is to be found in the person and work of Jesus Christ, but this is nothing but cosmetic fluff. Mormons can say the same, as can the Jehovah's Witnesses and myriad other religions which have Christ as a "touchstone" to their peculiar forms of religious rituals. But this has nothing in common with the Gospel of Jesus Christ! This is perhaps the most difficult concept to get across to the reader. We must reiterate that *superficial commonality does not equate to a proper assessment of the Gospel of Jesus Christ.* We shall be coming back to this time and time again. We have to wonder why the authors would lead their readers down such a path.

We are further confused by the admission of Geisler & MacKenzie that the Romanist religion *does not* admit to the same remedy for original sin as Evangelicals. Once again, as is so often the case, Evangelicals have confounded themselves in the space of one page! The following two contradictory assessments are made just paragraphs apart:

Same Remedy

> "Likewise, the *final remedy* for this woeful situation is *the same* as the common evangelical view."[2]

---

[1] Schroeder, *The Canons and Decrees and of the Council of Trent,* pg. 22, emphasis added

[2] Geisler & MacKenzie, pg. 58

Different Remedy

> "While Catholics and evangelicals share belief in the *fact* of original sin *there are differences concerning the remedy* for Adam and Eve's transgression."[1]

We think we understand what is going on here, and we cannot appreciate it. The authors know fully well that the only thing we have in common with the Romanist on the *remedy* for sin is the fact that Jesus Christ is the Son of God and has come down to earth with a message of salvation. But the Romanist understanding of the message of Christ is absolutely irreconcilable with the Christian faith. Anxious to get out of this section, the authors place no value or primacy on the vast chasm that separates us from Rome. Perhaps they cannot, for, oddly enough, they are laboring in this section to prove areas of doctrinal agreement. Their task is proving to be formidable, even given their penchant for compromise. This most unsatisfactory conclusion of theirs is becoming more and more the main stream in Evangelicalism:

> "Although based in Christ's atoning death, the Catholic understanding of original sin is that it is remedied by the sacrament of baptism and what remains is *concupiscence*, which is not sin proper but a tendency toward sin. 'Thus, although concupiscence is not itself, strictly speaking, sinful, it is as it were, a weight dragging even the regenerate downwards into sin.' Although the Catholic view on the extent of depravity is not significantly different from that of most Arminian Protestants, it does differ from a strongly Reformed position. The latter, in contrast to Catholicism, places a stronger emphasis on people's total inability to even cooperate with God's grace by their free will in the process of their salvation."[2]

Here again, we notice what is wrong with *Agreements and Differences*. No attempt is made to discriminate between good or bad theology. We are left to assume that it is acceptable to believe in concupiscence* as a non-sinful lump of weight which drags down the regenerate man after being regenerated in the waters of Romanist baptism. We are left to assume that it is acceptable to address the Romanist understanding of man's will as nothing but a minor "difference" with some Protestants. We are left to

---

[1] Geisler & MacKenzie, pg. 59

[2] Geisler & MacKenzie, pg. 59

* Concupiscence, as defined by Rome, is "Any tendency of the sensitive appetite. The term is most frequently used in reference to desires and tendencies for sinful sense pleasure" (*1994 Catholic Almanac*, Our Sunday Visitor Publishing, Huntington, Indiana, ©1993, pg. 303)

assume that there is nothing wrong with the "cooperation with God's grace in the *process* of salvation." And yet, these very theological questions and issues are at the center of the chasm which separates us from Rome.

We are therefore struck by the number of times the authors have to resort to the word "*difference*" in a section devoted to describing "*agreement*" with Rome. We further point out that nothing of essence has been determined as an agreement, and we begin to grow weary of the word "difference" when it is used without any conclusions or punch. We already consider some of the differences pointed out to be *fatal* to the Gospel, and they have not yet even gotten to the "Differences" section! We would ask the reader to consider the danger of calling something merely "different" from the Gospel and at the same time failing to recognize that it is in fact *fatal* to the Gospel.

Post-Adamic Man

We are at a loss to explain why some Evangelicals think there is an essential agreement with Rome on the doctrine of *imago Dei* (image of God), when there is a radical and violent disagreement on the capacity of man's freedom and the ability to make use of justice and law. We are left hanging with the following:

> "Although there are some differences between Catholics and many evangelicals to the doctrine of the *imago Dei*, or 'image of God,' nevertheless, there are *essential similarities*."[1]

After saying the above, the authors fail to give any of the purported "essential similarities" which are held in agreement. Instead, we are treated to yet another difference. The authors are quick to point out that the Reformers' view of post-Adamic man was radically opposed to the prevailing Romanist position. But it cannot go unnoticed that even while the authors are supposed to be pointing out areas of doctrinal agreement, they instead find themselves having to admit even more radical differences. We also notice that in so doing, they seem to want to play down the real *fatality* of these differences. They likewise distance themselves from all logical deductions which conclude Rome as a non Christian religion.

Sin's Cure

Romanists and Evangelicals realize the far-reaching effects of sin. The authors conclude rightly that, "human beings are totally unredeemable apart

---

[1] Geisler & MacKenzie, pg. 60, emphasis added

from the grace of God."[1] Then, incomprehensible as it may seem, the authors quote the Romanist Ott:

> "As Ott notes, 'Internal supernatural grace is absolutely necessary for *the beginning* of faith and of salvation.'"[2]

The authors continue without a break in the paragraph by quoting the Council of Trent:

> "In fact it is a matter of Catholic dogma that 'in adults *the beginning* of that justification must be derived from the predisposed grace of God through Jesus Christ ...whereby without any existing merits on their part they are called.'"[3]

But this is the same old Roman misrepresentation of grace! Can it be said that Christians have something in common with Rome when it comes to the grace of God in salvation? We are at a loss! Romanism indeed believes in supernatural grace which enlightens a man to a choice as to whether he will believe in the Romanist gospel. Thus, in Romanism, all of salvation is said to hang by the thread of man's willingness to be saved. This is why Romanists also believe that grace is resistible. Men can, according to Rome, say "No" to the God Who desires to save them according to the Romanist system. There is no such thing as irresistible grace to the Romanist, for if God saved men completely apart from man's willing or running—and He does (Romans 9:16)—it would introduce into Rome a concept of grace—*grace that is truly unmerited*—which is deadly to their system of works. Therefore Rome must—and does—teach that supernatural grace, if accepted, leads to the sacramental dispensary of attaining more graces through more sacramental works. Roman justification, therefore, is a process; hence the words the *beginning* of faith and salvation are highlighted by us. Rome teaches a *beginning* of justification which eliminates true Christian justification which is an *act* of God rather than a *work* or a *process*. The end of justification, in Rome, is predicated on good works done in faith, and not the imputed righteousness of Christ alone through faith alone. Thus, Roman justification begins in the flesh (man's accepting or cooperating), and ends in the flesh (man's persevering). This is not the Gospel of Christ.

When Christians say, "We cannot be saved without the grace of God," we have in mind God's unmerited favor to us. This results in a mighty work wrought deep in our nature freeing us to have faith in Jesus Christ and His righteousness alone for our justification. The Romanist system is absolutely

---

[1] Geisler & MacKenzie, pg. 60
[2] Geisler & MacKenzie, pg. 60, emphasis added
[3] Geisler & MacKenzie, pp. 60-61, emphasis added

the opposite. Rome teaches that grace is a supernatural influence upon the soul which, if accepted, will lead one to Roman sacramental works. How honest is it to imply that Rome believes *the same as the Christian* just because Rome says, "grace is absolutely necessary"? In the same breath, which Geisler & MacKenzie muffle with their ecumenical flag-waving, Rome mutters that grace *is not sufficient.*

There is by now a familiar hint of scandal in the way Trent is quoted by these two men. The above citation of Trent on the necessity of grace is taken from Denzinger, a recognized authority among Roman Catholic resource books. Denzinger is quoting Trent on justification. The authors give us the first part of the paragraph in hopes of showing some sort of commonality with Rome on this critical issue of grace and justification. But we produce for you the entire paragraph. We have highlighted below the portion that Geisler & MacKenzie quoted. Judge for yourselves, by what they left out, if the authors have once again played fast and loose with the evidence in order to deliberately mislead the reader:

> "It [the Synod] furthermore declares *that in adults the beginning of that justification must be derived from the predisposing grace [can. 3] of God through Jesus Christ,* that is, from his vocation, *whereby without any existing merits on their part they are called*, so that they who by sin were turned away from God, through His stimulating and assisting grace are disposed *to convert themselves* to their own justification, by freely assenting to and cooperating with the same grace [can. 4 and 5], in such wise that, while God touches the heart of man through the illumination of the Holy Spirit, man himself receiving that inspiration does nothing at all inasmuch as he can indeed reject it, nor on the other hand can he [can. 3] of his own free will without the grace of God move himself to justice before Him."[1]

Notwithstanding the altogether misleading use of the Council of Trent, we notice that in light of the rest of the story—the part which Geisler & MacKenzie opted not to provide—Rome does not have a Christian understanding of justification.[2]

---

[1] Denzinger, *Sources of Catholic Dogma*, no. 797, pg. 250, emphasis added

[2] We notice the authors point out that "there are other disagreements between Roman Catholics and many evangelicals (viz. Calvinists), such as the traditional Catholic distinction between venial and mortal sin. Mortal sin is defined as that which 'kills' grace in the soul. For Catholics, this grace may be renewed by the sacrament of penance. Venial sin is less serious and does not destroy grace" (Geisler & MacKenzie, pg. 61n). This note of interest is relegated to a footnote in Geisler & MacKenzie. We mention it here because we want to point out the pattern. The authors should know that the Romanist imagination in fabricating a distinction between Mortal and Venial sins is fatal to the Gospel. It is fatal because forgiveness of so-called Mortal sins is dependent upon

continued on following page

The Question Of Evolution

We close this section with some comments on the treatment afforded Rome concerning evolution. We are baffled by this short two-page section. The authors have no difficulty admitting the following:

> "Catholics are permitted to believe in evolution (in both the micro and macro senses)."[1]

This admission is technically a difference with mainstream Evangelicalism. It is basically non-Christian in its approach to the Bible. It certainly does not represent any normal and literal rendering of the book of Genesis. The authors are willing to admit more:

> "According to some modern Catholic sources, 'the inspired writers of Genesis did not intend to produce a scientific cosmology, nor did they intend to indicate *how* God accomplished His creation. That God is the author, creator, and governor of the universe is the religious truth imported; it remains for science to discover, if possible, the times, the places, and the modes of origins.'"[2]

The above citation is taken from the *New Catholic Encyclopedia* and is given as a fact with no comment by the authors. The fact that some Romanists are on the slippery slope of scientific modernism is mentioned here because it bears the identical marks of some modern professing Evangelical denominations. Evidently, the commonality we have with Rome is illustrated in the fact that Rome has conservatives who hold to a literal six day creation and liberals who do not. But we soon see that this is a set-up. In the following paragraphs the authors mention certain *avant garde* Catholic

---

Penance dispensed within the sacrament of reconciliation administered by man. The sacrament of Penance, says Rome, gets rid of Mortal sins. Christians know that the blood of Christ cleanses us from all unrighteousness. Christians know that the Bible contains nothing of a sacrament of Penance for the forgiveness of sins. Christians believe Penance stands in the way of the free and full forgiveness of Christ and blocks the Gospel. Yet the authors wish to treat the *manner* of forgiveness as only a "difference" in this section. What a remarkable understatement! We continue to ask, "When is another gospel, another gospel?" Evidently, the word "difference" has replaced "fatal" in the eyes of these two authors. We shall continue to remind the reader of what is really taking place here. There appears to be a wholesale compromising of the Gospel in order to produce an alliance to fight off disintegrating forces within Western society. Apparently, to the authors, Rome is some sort of gift horse to the Evangelical Church. We cannot help but conclude there is, by the effort of these two authors, a Roman Horse looming whose very bowels bear the destruction of the ones receiving such a gift!

[1] Geisler & MacKenzie, pg. 63

[2] Geisler & MacKenzie, pg. 63, emphasis in original

thinkers who have gone well beyond the limit of Roman acceptability in their philosophies and existentialism. Riding to the rescue of orthodoxy, say the authors, is Pope Pius XII. His encyclical, *Humani Generis*, is said to have quieted the stormy waters and set things right. The authors find some comfort that Pius XII restated traditional Catholic teachings:

> "Concerning the Scripture he wrote: 'the encyclical condemned as specific errors the exegesis of Scripture that ignores or is opposed to the analogy of faith... and that which is marked by either ignorance or contempt for the literal meaning of the text in favor of a purely spiritual interpretation.' Finally, concerning historical speculations, 'the encyclical condemns those who empty the Genesis accounts in the Old Testament of any historical sense.' *The above quoted statements sound as if they could have been taken from a number of contemporary evangelical treatments concerning the inerrancy of Scripture*."[1]

It seems to us that such quotations as these are deliberately selective from Papal Encyclicals and highly gratuitous in their linking such extracts to Christianity. We wonder if Christians can be comfortable with the rest of Pope Pius XII's encyclical, quoted below. This is a portion of what was left out:

> "The teaching of the Church does not forbid that the doctrine of evolutionism, in so far as it inquires into the origin of the human body from already existing living matter, be, according to the present state of human disciplines and sacred theology, treated in research and discussion by experts on both sides."[2]

So much for Pius XII riding to the rescue and rebuilding this breach in the protective wall God has built around His Word.

Summary

We have waded through short discussions on revelation, the Councils, the Creeds, biblical data, "Natural Theology" and "Natural Law," the nature of man, original sin, tradition, the image of God, post-Adamic man and evolution. We have labored to show that the Roman Catholic religion has, at best, only superficial similarities with Christianity. Theirs is a parallel world. They use similar language but with radically different meanings. We have noted that the Romish religion does not adhere to the ancient Councils;

---

[1] Geisler & MacKenzie, pg. 64, emphasis added

[2] *The Christian Faith*, Neuner, J. and Dupuis, J., (New York: Alba House, ©1981) pg. 125, Encyclical Letter *Humani Generis* (1950)

rather they change them. Also, the ancient Creeds are so vague on the *manner* of salvation that they could be summoned to support any number of religious ideologies. We pointed out that Rome does, indeed, believe that the Bible is the Word of God but not above the Magisterium and the opinion of the Pope or their Traditions. Rome believes in grace and faith, but it is a grace infused and a faith in their sacramental system. Rome has a radically different *remedy* for the involvement of mankind in the sin of Adam. In fact, Rome describes Adam's sin and our subsequent involvement in terms that have little correspondence to Christianity. We have seen that Rome does not object to the teaching of evolution within its religion. We have questioned Rome's use of the Bible to substantiate its religious paraphernalia which undermines the Gospel.

What has been proven thus far? What does Rome have in common with Christianity? The answer, at best, is a triune God Who has created the heavens and the earth and all that is within them. Christians also have in common with Rome the belief that God sent His Son Jesus Christ, as the second member of the Trinity, to die for the sins of the world. But after this, the similarities are only superficial. *What* God has done in Christ is radically different. *How* God saves man is radically different. The *nature* of man is radically different. The *manner* in which God forgives sin is radically different. The *content* of the Bible is radically different. The *source* of authority is radically different. The *object of allegiance* is radically different. The *consequences* of sin are different for Rome, and because of that, the Roman gospel is different as well. Rome offers the wrong cure due to a fatal misdiagnosis of the problem of man. Therefore, we cannot agree with the summation that,

> "Despite some differences on the extent of sin and the possible use of evolutionary processes by God in producing the human body, there are essential similarities in the Roman Catholic and evangelical understanding of human beings."[1]

How many religions on the earth would deny that they were created in some sense by a god? How many religions on earth would deny the existence of evil or sin in some sense? How many religions on earth would deny that after this life there is an encounter with some type of supreme being? These tenets of belief are shared, to some degree, by the human experience. It is not surprising that Rome and Christianity share some similar outlooks on man. It may be helpful for the readers to understand that we have only essential agreement in the fact of Adam. We have no agreement in the *extent* of the fall and the *result* of Adam's sin onto mankind. It is silly to keep pressing the point that we have in common with Rome that man is a sinner

---

[1] Geisler & MacKenzie, pg. 64

and in need of God's grace. We, along with Rome and Mormons and Jehovah's Witnesses and Orthodox Jews with many others affirm the very same. The conversation begins and ends only with the fact of Adam and the fact of sin and fact of God. After this there is no essential agreement whatsoever on *the* issue where there *must* be agreement for Biblical unity: the Gospel of Christ.

We would remind Geisler & MacKenzie that the mark of apostate religions and a false gospels is not that they *look* on the outside like apostate religions and false gospels! On the contrary, the best counterfeits often pass through the first and second inspection before the trained eye detects the imperfection which exposes the pretender. But we have been shown that some are willing only to take Rome through a first and second inspection, but no further. Thus far, the claim for "areas of doctrinal agreement" alleged by the writers is a curious and, in each designation, a spurious claim when time is taken to sort out the language, its meaning, and the context which these authors are so inclined to ignore.

It appears to us that a sort of dreadful death march is on. Will Rome arrive at more suitable ways of finding common areas of agreement with Muslims, Hindus and Buddhists faster than professing Evangelical Christians can find common ground with Rome? Not if these authors and others like them have their way!

The Question of Salvation

OUR ATTENTION NOW is naturally riveted to any Evangelical attempt to show forth common ground with Romanism in so far as salvation is concerned. We are met with this startling sentence:

> "Catholics and evangelicals share a common core of beliefs about salvation."[1]

And again:

> "As a current catechism puts it, 'Believing in Jesus Christ and in the One who sent him for our salvation is necessary for obtaining that salvation (cf. Mk. 16:16; Jn. 3:36; 6:40 et al.).'"[2]

This citation is taken from the *1994 Catechism of the Catholic Church,* which was recently released in English and serves as a modern standard for the Romanist religion. We need to examine the above use of the Catechism and the initial claim that Evangelicals and Roman Catholics share a *common core* of beliefs about salvation. All will depend upon what we define as *common core* beliefs.

Using an analogy of a dramatic play entitled, "The Salvation of the Lord," let us examine if the Roman Catholic rendition and the Christian rendition share the same *common core* of beliefs. Now, if we wish to say that the *common core* beliefs of salvation concern only the cast of characters and the major theme of eternal salvation, then Rome may have a legitimate claim. We can all agree that the triune God had compassion on mankind and sent His Son, Jesus Christ, to seek and to save the lost. Rome and Christianity have the same cast of characters. God, Jesus Christ, the Holy Spirit, Satan, Demons, unfallen angels and mankind compose the players. No one disputes this! However, assignment of role, meaning of dialogue, method of achieving the goal of salvation and the content of the play are so radically

---

[1] Geisler & MacKenzie, pg. 81

[2] Geisler & MacKenzie, pg. 81

contradictory between Rome and Christianity that we end up with two separate dramas. The same cast of players are arranged in the Roman rendition so as to make its drama completely unique to itself. Which play depicts reality? Is it the Christian or the Roman Catholic? We ask the readers to contemplate, "Is it a *common core* of beliefs just because the players are the same, or is it a *common core* of beliefs only when the *meaning of the dialogue within the play* is the same?" In Romanism, the meaning of the dialogue is completely foreign to the Gospel of Jesus Christ.

We take note, for example, that the word "obtain" is used by the *Catholic Catechism* to describe salvation. This is consistent with the *core* of Romanism which believes that salvation needs to be *obtained*; but Christians believe that salvation cannot be *obtained*, at least not in the sense that Rome does. Christians believe that salvation is the state in which the sinner finds himself when he realizes that God forgives his transgressions for Christ's sake alone. The *Catechism*, however, is misleading, as it presents a hope of salvation being "obtained" through obedience to a new set of rules. We give you only one small example from the rest of the *Catholic Catechism* which explodes the myth that Evangelicals have a *common core* of beliefs with Rome concerning salvation:

> "The Church affirms that for believers the sacraments of the New Covenant are *necessary for salvation*. 'Sacramental grace' is the grace of the Holy Spirit, given by Christ and proper to each sacrament. The Spirit heals and transforms those who receive him by conforming them to the Son of God. The fruit of the sacramental life is that the Spirit of adoption makes the faithful partakers in the divine nature by uniting them in a living union with the only Son, the Savior."[1]

Trudging through a grace-dispensing sacramental system administered by human priests is a different drama altogether. It certainly is not the Christian rendition of the "Salvation of the Lord." Evangelicals lose all integrity when they present superficial commonalities and label them as *common core* beliefs. Not only are the things set forth not *core* beliefs, but terms which are used to show the alleged commonality have vastly different definitions. Incredibly, more and more ecumenists are concluding that, although Rome cannot agree with Evangelicals on justification by faith alone, they yet share a *common core* of beliefs on salvation. This is pure nonsense—not only is justification by faith alone *the core* belief of the true Church; it is the doctrine on which the Church stands or falls! When Protestant ecumenists leave justification by faith alone outside of the "core beliefs of the Church" in order to be one with Rome, they have truly arrived at the edge of apostasy, and have forsaken the truth of God!

---

[1] 1994 *Catechism of the Catholic Church*, pg. 292, paragraph 1129, italics in original

The Question Of Grace

In a very positive and well stated introduction of Augustine (AD 354-430), Geisler & MacKenzie wish to press home a point which they think is a significant element of "doctrinal agreement" with Rome. The gist of the proposition is that Rome and Christians believe in the *necessity* of God's grace *prior* to justification. Herein lies another bit of theological intrigue that needs to be unraveled. We ask, "Is it fair to say that Rome is Christian because it asserts the necessity of grace prior to justification?" We say, No. We answer thus because Rome defines the *nature* of grace, the *delivery* of grace, the *recipients* of grace and the *value* of grace in terms which lead to a system which is antithetical to the Christian Gospel.

In hopes of showing how bafflingly confused Evangelicals have become as they attempt to capitalize on the fact that Romanists believe grace is involved in salvation, we produce for you this citation from Geisler & MacKenzie:

> "Despite the later Protestant emphasis on forensic justification, there is a *common core* of teaching on salvation that unites Catholics and Protestants; namely, that *salvation is by God's grace*. That is, no good works precede justification (regeneration). Recently, some have claimed that the *common core* is 'salvation by grace through faith,' but this is misleading since Roman Catholics believe that justification occurs at baptism when the infant is too young to express any conscious or explicit faith in Christ. Further, they believe works are necessary for salvation, whereas Protestants believe salvation is by faith alone."[1]

---

[1] Geisler & MacKenzie, pp. 85-86, emphasis added. We would note here the theological error that underlies Geisler & MacKenzie's natural affinity for Romanism, i.e., defining justification as regeneration. The Reformers held these two to be separate acts performed by God: God regenerates the unbeliever (rebirth) and then gives faith to the regenerated person, and by that faith imputes the righteousness of Christ (justification). This is the meaning of John's words, "Whosoever believeth that Jesus is the Christ is born of God..." (1 John 5:1). To make rebirth and justification the same thing, is to assert that God grants rebirth in exchange for believing the gospel, making faith the work which God requires of man prior to rebirth. But Christ taught that those who were not born from above could not see the Kingdom of God (John 3:3), that those who were not "of God" could not understand his words (John 8:47), and Paul declared that those who are not reborn cannot comprehend the things of the Spirit (1 Corinthians 2:14). Rebirth (regeneration) is necessary prior to faith, faith then being the means by which Christ's righteousness is imputed to those born from above (justification). We emphasize this here because to believe that we are saved or reborn by the "work" of faith or because of our faith, is not far from Rome's assertion that we are saved by the "works" God produces in us. Geisler & MacKenzie have stumbled into the heart of Romanism here without even realizing it.

Notice that in spite of the admission that Romanists believe works are necessary for salvation, these men are desperately trying to bring the two antithetical thoughts together:

> "Nonetheless, both Catholics and Protestants believe in the *necessity of grace*. That is, without God's grace there would be no salvation."[1]

In response to this we must ask the question, "What difference does this 'agreement' make since Romanists redefine grace and salvation according to their system of works?" Would we be so eager to defend the Mormon religion because we have in common a belief in God? Shall we relegate the Mormon denial of the Trinity as only a divergence? Shall we relegate the Mormon concept of God first being a man as only a discrepancy? Should we keep pounding away at the fact that Mormons believe in God despite their hope of one day being as their god is now? After all, Mormons see salvation as a *grace* from their heavenly father. Geisler & MacKenzie ignore the fact that the Roman Catholic system sees grace operative everywhere—in the works, sufferings and efforts of man—and thus obliterates the biblical lines drawn by God between grace and works. Romanists think the entire concept of suffering to obtain the grace necessary for salvation is a grace in itself!

> "It [the council] teaches furthermore that the liberality of the divine munificence (generosity) is so great that *we are able through Jesus Christ to make satisfaction to God the Father not only by punishments voluntarily undertaken by ourselves to atone for sins*, or by those imposed by the judgment of the priest according to the measure of our offense, but also, and this is the greatest proof of love, *by the temporal afflictions imposed by God and borne patiently by us*."[2]

When Is Grace Not Grace?

In the New Testament the apostle Paul was ever ready to make clear the absolute contrast between grace and works of the law. We believe the burden of the apostle was to leave no doubt that grace was grace and works were works, and they could not both be the ground of justification:

> "And if by grace, then is it no more of works: otherwise grace is no more grace. But if it be of works, then is it no more grace: otherwise work is no more work" (Romans 11:6).

---

[1] Geisler & MacKenzie, pg. 86, emphasis in original

[2] Schroeder, *The Canons and Decrees and of the Council of Trent,* pp. 98,99, emphases added

"Therefore we conclude that a man is justified by faith without the deeds of the law" (Romans 3:28).

"Now to him that worketh is the reward not reckoned of grace, but of debt" (Romans 4:4).

"Which shew the work of the law written in their hearts, their conscience also bearing witness, and their thoughts the mean while accusing or else excusing one another;) In the day when God shall judge the secrets of men by Jesus Christ according to my gospel" (Romans 2:15-16).

One can see here that to be "of grace" excludes being "of works" when it comes to justification. But the question remains to be answered, "What does it mean to be *of grace*?" The battle lines over this very question are alluded to in *Agreements and Differences*:

"For normative Catholicism, *sola gratia* means only the primacy and necessity of grace, but not the exclusivity of grace."[1]

To be 'of grace' in Rome means to be in a state of grace. Grace, according to Rome, is a substance which is infused for moral renewal; it can be increased and lost; it is dispensed through the sacramental system, and is offered to the faithful in return for their obedience to the system. So far as salvation is concerned, Rome begins salvation with grace. The infant is passive when grace is dispensed in the ritual of Roman infant baptism. Thus, Rome can say that it all *starts* with the grace of God. All men need the grace of God! Indeed, the old *Catholic Encyclopedia* devotes over 25 pages of double column fine print to the meaning of grace in the Roman Catholic system!

R. C. Sproul, commenting on the Pelagian controversy of the fifth century, gives us this appropriate insight:

"The Pelagian controversy settled the issue of the necessity of grace for salvation. What was not settled was the question of the degree to which grace is necessary and the full efficacy of grace."[2]

Simply put, the Roman Catholic religion believes that grace is the impetus of meritorious works which are then rewarded with eternal life. To Rome, all "human originated" works of mankind are worthless for the reward of

---

[1] Geisler & MacKenzie, pg. 86, italics in original

[2] Sproul, R. C., *Faith Alone: The Evangelical Doctrine of Justification,* (Grand Rapids, MI: Baker Books, ©1995) pg. 137

eternal life. But all "grace-produced works"—that is, those good works produced by God's grace in man—are meritorious and worthy of eternal life since they trace their origin to the grace of God. All of this makes the following quotation from Geisler & MacKenzie rather meaningless:

> "Whatever can be said of others, the two greatest theologians of the Catholic church, Augustine and Aquinas, clearly believed that *salvation is completely dependent on God's grace.*"[1]

Upon closer inspection, we notice that neither Augustine nor Aquinas lived to see the Council of Trent which clarified that, according to Rome, God's 'grace' makes the 'work' acceptable, and therefore meritorious. Neither Aquinas nor Augustine were a part of the Roman Catholic religion as outlined in Trent. And, most importantly, the above boast is neutralized by the fact that Rome sees *everything* beginning by God's grace, but nothing ending *solely* on God's grace. Thus Rome states that justification has its *beginning* in grace, but the full efficacy and sufficiency of grace is foreign to the Romanist religion. As we have already stated, we must wonder which gospel Geisler & MacKenzie have in mind when they assert that Evangelicals share certain *common core* beliefs with Roman Catholicism on salvation. They have yet to produce any credible evidence to support the assertion.

The Issue Of Aquinas

We cannot let go of this subject until we reproduce the footnote given by the authors in the midst of their efforts to show areas of doctrinal agreement with Rome on the issue of salvation. After extolling the virtues of Aquinas, the authors give us the following caveat:

> "Of course, Aquinas did believe in the doctrine of merit and the necessity of good works. So in this sense he would fall short of the Protestant understanding of salvation by faith alone. But since these good works come in the overall context of God's operative grace, some evangelicals have embraced Aquinas as 'Protestant.'"[2]

It cannot be proven that Aquinas and Augustine would have endorsed the Council of Trent. It is beyond our grasp. The simple truth is that Trent denied the Christian doctrine of justification by faith alone in the finished work of Christ alone for our salvation. Rome is Trent, and Trent is Rome, and that is where our argument must be directed. To admit that Aquinas endorses merit and falls short of the Protestant understanding of salvation

---

[1] Geisler & MacKenzie, pg. 93, emphasis in original

[2] Geisler & MacKenzie, pg. 93n

by grace through faith alone *is to admit to a fatal error in Aquinas—it does nothing to acquit Rome!* Can the reader see the huge leaps that are being taken here? Geisler & MacKenzie take some people's inference that Aquinas was *Roman* in his Catholicism, join it with some people's perception that he was somehow *Protestant* in his understanding of operative grace, and then attempt to stretch this caricature of Aquinas to the breaking point and wrap it all the way around the enormity of Trent, and *Presto!*, Rome and Evangelicals agree! But their attempt is made without regard for a proper definition of grace, and without any resolution on the matter of justification. Yet this is the whole point of the battle with Rome. That Augustine and Aquinas were not accustomed to separating the declarative act of God's justifying the ungodly from the resultant moral transformation of the justified sinner does not excuse Rome. It remains for historians and theologians to argue whether, given the clearer light of the Reformation, Augustine and Aquinas would have joined Calvin, Knox, Luther and Beza to uphold the distinction between justification and sanctification. But again, this does not excuse Roman Catholicism. Whatever anyone might say of Augustine and Aquinas on the issue of forensic justification, (God's act of declaration whereby the ungodly are proclaimed acquitted solely on the ground of Christ's righteousness received by faith alone), the Council of Trent, and the entire Roman Catholic religion with it, became apostate in the eyes of God by condemning to hell justification as it is presented in the Gospel of Christ.

We ask the reader to ponder the serious and most significant points of our discussion so far. Christians believe in salvation by grace alone and view the grace of God as His loving disposition toward undeserving sinners. Christians believe in the total sufficiency and efficacy of God's grace alone. *Christians do not believe the ground of their justification is in anything which grace produces.* Roman Catholics, on the other hand, believe in a different grace of God. They believe that it is dispensed from heaven upon sinners to awaken them to their need to be filled with grace. They believe grace starts the ball rolling. They believe grace softens the will toward God and produces works which are pleasing to God. These grace-produced works are then said to be part of the ground of justification.

The Christian understanding of justification is that God acquits the sinner on the basis of Christ's righteousness alone, resulting in a moral transformation in the believer by the indwelling of the Spirit in the one justified. Rome's understanding has God's grace and man's cooperation producing the moral transformation. Then God acquits the sinner based on the good behavior produced by man's cooperation and God's grace. *These two views absolutely cannot be reconciled.* It should be obvious by this that any theologian vending a *common core* of beliefs between Rome and Christianity—as pertaining to grace and salvation—is marketing swampland to the unsuspecting and naïve.

Conclusions

Geisler & MacKenzie wrap up their discussion on salvation with a summing up of what they label as "Our Common Soteriological Roots."[1] We produce the four points of commonality as proposed by the authors, with our comments following each:

- "First, both believe salvation is historical. The Old Testament view of salvation as effected through historic, divine intervention is affirmed in the New Testament. Against Gnosticism, we jointly affirm that man is not saved by wisdom; as against Judaism, *man is not saved by moral and religious merit apart from the grace of God*."[2]

We believe this to be a serious distortion of the truth. The authors can only say this due to Rome's insistence that grace is the necessary first step in the meriting of salvation. Rome's true position is that man is saved by moral and religious merit produced by the grace of God if that grace is accepted. This is another gospel. The assertion of the authors notwithstanding, Rome's gospel has nothing in common with the soteriological roots of Christianity. The authors do err and mislead.

- "Second, both evangelicals and Catholics believe salvation is moral and spiritual. *Salvation is related* to a deliverance from sin and its consequences and hence from guilt (Rom. 5:1; Heb. 10:22), from the curse of the law (Gal. 3:13; Col. 2:14), from death (1 Pet. 1:3-5), from judgment (Rom. 5:9), from fear (Heb. 2:15); and, finally, from bondage (Gal. 5:1f.; Titus 2:11-3:6)."[3]

The distortions continue. We are not certain if the use of the term *related* is deliberate here. What does *related* mean? We suspect it is an ambiguous term used specifically here to cover all the bases. But we notice what is missing, and it speaks volumes. The certain knowledge that one has peace with God is missing from the authors' description of salvation. The method of becoming saved is missing. The Gospel of salvation is missing, and most importantly, *freedom from paying the penalty of sins* is missing.

Christian salvation entails deliverance from both guilt *and penalty* due to sin, but we notice that the authors have left out the second half of this. They do so because Rome believes that man must pay the penalty of sin even though he is "forgiven" the guilt of his sin. This, too, is another gospel.

---

[1] Geisler & MacKenzie, pg. 103

[2] Geisler & MacKenzie, pg. 103, emphasis added

[3] Geisler & MacKenzie, pg. 103, emphasis added

- "Third, salvation is eschatological for both Catholics and evangelicals. ...All that is now known about salvation is preliminary and a foretaste of the fullness which awaits the completing of the kingdom at the *parousia* of the Lord."[1]

We see no reason to have this commonality listed under the heading of 'Common Soteriological Roots.' The authors are truly grasping at straws here! There are a number of religions which believe in a future eternal (eschatological) state which is a salvation from the decrepit conditions of our mortality. What is to be gained by saying that the Roman Catholic religion believes in an eschatological salvation? The real point is Rome does not believe in a *present* salvation! The entirety of the Roman system is a denial of any true knowledge of having enough peace with God to ensure the woeful soul a place in heaven. Roman Catholics do not have the *same* eschatological hope as the Christian. Christians deny the need for and existence of Purgatory, believing rather that salvation is a reality both *now* and then with certainty, "for he is faithful that promised" (Hebrews 10:23b).

- "Fourth, initial justification is unmerited. As the new *Catechism of the Catholic Church* puts it, 'Our justification comes from the grace of God' (1996) and even 'the merits of our good works are gifts of the divine goodness' (2009). Although the forensic aspect of justification stressed by Reformed theology is scarcely found prior to the Reformation, there is continuity concerning salvation between medieval Catholicism and the Reformers. Thus, Colin Brown can speak of 'the Augustinian orthodoxy of Geneva and Rome.' For both groups salvation is by grace and is not prompted by human works."[2]

Let us take a deep breath and count to ten! The authors fail miserably here in an attempt to show common soteriological roots with Roman Catholicism. The folly is evident in the assertion that "initial justification is unmerited." Let us be reminded that for Rome, justification is ongoing, hence the need for the artificial bifurcation of the term *justification* into subcategories called *initial justification* and *final justification*. The authors must know that in Rome, although *initial justification* is by "grace," *final justification* is merited by work. This is antithetical to the Christian Gospel which knows nothing of 'stages' of justification. The reason for our distress on this point is that once again, Geisler & MacKenzie cannot see the logical implications of their own research. To assert that "initial justification" is not merited is to confess that Rome believes that "final justification" *is* merited. This ruins the Gospel of Christ, a Gospel which Geisler & MacKenzie cannot bring

---

[1] Geisler & MacKenzie, pg. 103

[2] Geisler & MacKenzie, pp. 103-104

themselves to defend. In Roman Catholicism, justification begins through the waters of infant baptism, but the Christian Gospel knows nothing of baptismal justification. The ground of Roman justification is meritorious works which are said to be produced by grace after the initial passive entrance of grace through the waters of baptism, but the Christian Gospel knows Christ alone as the ground of our justification. The Romanist position is that justification can be improved on or lost depending on the faithfulness of the man, but the Christian Gospel knows nothing of *earning* or *losing* justification, and speaks only of Christ as the sole ground of justification; hence there can be no increase or decrease, for justification depends on the faithfulness of God.

Thus, to insinuate that 'salvation is by grace' in Romanism is to assassinate grace and ridicule it by giving it a new and morbid definition. In the Roman Catholic scheme of things, God is said to give the spark from which all manner of merit, penalty, sufferings and work are called 'grace.' In the Christian scheme of things, God is said to give the spark that starts a never ending relationship of love and acceptance for the sake of Christ alone Who died for the ungodly that they may live for God. These two positions cannot be reconciled to each other, let Geisler & MacKenzie try as they may.

Finally, what little correspondence may be made between the forensic justification of the Reformers and pre-Trent theologians of the Catholic (universal) church era is dwarfed by the Council of Trent. Trent defines Roman Catholicism, and denies the sufficiency of the righteousness of Christ as the ground of justification. It will do no good to try an end run of this by saying 'The merits of our good works are gifts of the divine goodness.' As we have seen, Rome teaches that it is mandatory to suffer for the penalty of sins committed and to atone for our own sins either by our present sufferings or by the future tortures of purgatory. They boast that to do so is actually a gift of God. We trust the readers can see by now that it is no *gift* to require one to work or to suffer for what he is given:

> "Now to him that worketh is the reward not reckoned of grace, but of debt" (Romans 4:4).
>
> "Even as David also describeth the blessedness of the man, unto whom God imputeth righteousness without works" (Romans 4:6).

Throughout the first 158 pages of their book, the authors have labored to build a house on a foundation of sand. The more weight considered, the more the sand gives way and ultimately when the rains of biblical exposition test the house, it washes away to destruction. We have argued that if the areas of alleged *doctrinal agreements* can be shown to be erroneous, then the Roman Catholic religion cannot be reclassified as a Christian religion, as much as the authors would have it so. We have also argued that the areas of doctrinal disagreement are so severe and fatal that they should carry the day against Rome. But before moving on to consider the differences given to us by the authors of *Agreements and Differences*, we should review:

- Roman Catholicism is defined by the dogma and doctrine of the Council of Trent. Any appraisal of Rome begins and ends with Trent. Vatican 1 and Vatican 2 both affirm Trent. The *1994 Catechism* of the Roman Catholic religion does nothing to steer a course away from Trent, but rather cites the Council of Trent more than 80 times.

- Theologians writing in the pre-Trent era cannot be taken as *Roman* Catholics. Any number of theologians have written on numerous topics, some closer to scriptural fidelity than others. It is absolutely incorrect to call either Augustine or Aquinas a *Roman* Catholic. They both died before Trent and we have no way of knowing if they might have been the champions of the Reformation.

- Roman Catholicism uses the same language as Christianity but with an entirely different meaning. Grace in the Roman system is radically and fatally opposite to grace in the Christian Gospel.

- It is misleading and disingenuous to zip in and out of history, hop-scotching over Trent and appealing to historical testimonies which pre-date Trent, in order to validate a modern Catholicism.

- When it comes to the presentation of the Gospel of Jesus Christ and the *way of salvation*, nothing could be more untrue than to say that there is a *common core* of understanding between Rome and Christianity.

- The early Church Councils were not *Roman* Catholic Councils. Any Roman profession of loyalty to the Church Councils is circumvented by Rome's use of the "elastic theology clause" of the teaching magisterium.

- Roman Catholicism presents the dramatic play, "The Salvation of the Lord," in such a way as to make it a *Roman* play replete with *Roman* meaning and a *Roman* ending. Though the cast of characters is in name Christian, the meaning of the dialogue and method of eternal salvation, as well as the representation of the person of God and Christ, are unique to Rome. Rome's play is not Christian.

By any fair assessment, modern Rome has nothing in common with historic Christianity other than naked terminology. However, when the terms are dressed in Roman garb and fashioned in Roman definitions, it is the end of the Gospel and the faith once delivered to the saints. With that in mind, let us move on to Part II and see how Geisler & MacKenzie will deal with the differences between Rome and Christianity.

Part II
Irreconcilable Differences

Sorting It Out

IN PART I of our analysis, we labored to show that allegations of "doctrinal agreements" could not withstand close scrutiny. We cautioned the reader to be discerning in the definition of terms and cited numerous occasions where terms meant one thing to the Christian and quite another to the Roman Catholic. We also pointed out that superficial commonalities do not constitute a basis for the recognition of Romanism as a Christian community.

We come now to the "differences" between Roman Catholicism and Evangelicalism, as expressed by Geisler & MacKenzie. We feel the authors are at times brilliant in pointing out these differences. But we are in utter disbelief that no conclusions of substance are drawn from the research. We ask the readers to conclude for themselves whether or not these differences are fatal to biblical Christianity. It is obvious to us that if the serious lack of doctrinal agreement alone sounds the death knell for Rome, how much more should the avalanche of doctrinal disagreement bury all claims that she is true Christianity. Strangely enough, the authors are unwilling to conclude from their own presentation that Rome is not Christian. The evidence amassed against Rome in this section is overwhelming, but the obvious conclusion is withheld. There is no doubt in our minds that the authors wish to be honest with the data while keeping strangely silent as to the only conclusion that the data can provide. They have defined a duck and concluded that it is, in essence, a swan.

The authors begin Part II of their treatise, "Areas of Doctrinal Agreement," under the same rubric with which they closed their first section. We reproduce their introductory paragraph:

> "In the first part of this volume we have stressed what evangelicals have in common with Roman Catholics. In short, this includes the great fundamentals of the Christian faith, including a belief in the Trinity, the virgin birth, the deity of Christ, the creation and subsequent fall of humanity, Christ's unique atonement for our sins, the physical resurrection of Christ, the necessity of God's grace for

> salvation, the existence of heaven and hell, the second coming of Christ, and the verbal inspiration and infallibility of Scripture."[1]

Here again we have a repetition of the "cast of characters" of our hypothetical play. We have already alerted the reader to the danger of assuming that the same characters, props and themes equals the same drama. Romanists and Christians do believe in the Trinity, the virgin birth, and the deity of Christ. But believing these things does not make one a Christian. Christians do not believe anything like the Roman Catholic when the bald terms of "creation," "fall," "atonement," and "the necessity of God's grace" are fleshed out with theological understanding. For example, to defend the verbal inspiration and infallibility of the Bible apart from the word *alone* is nonsense. We notice again the conspicuous absence of any reference to the Gospel of Jesus Christ. Having extolled what, in their opinion, amounts to be the fundamental agreements with Rome, above, the authors begin to mark the differences:

> "Catholics affirm and evangelicals reject the immaculate conception of Mary, her bodily assumption, her role as coredemptrix, the veneration of Mary and other saints, prayers to Mary and the saints, the infallibility of the pope, the existence of purgatory, the inspiration and canonicity of the Apocrypha, the doctrine of transubstantiation, the worship of the transformed Host, the special sacerdotal powers of the Roman Catholic priesthood, and the necessity of works to obtain eternal life. Since all these have been proclaimed as infallible dogma by the Roman Catholic Church, and since many are contrary to central teachings of evangelicalism, there appears to be no hope of ecumenical or ecclesiastical unity."[2]

For most, this shocking admission of heresy would be an end to it. To admit that the Roman Catholic Church claims as infallible dogma the 'necessity of works for salvation' along with purgatory, papal infallibility, Marian veneration, transubstantiation, canonicity of the apocrypha and worship of the transformed host would be enough to convince all but the authors that we are dealing with another religion. But perhaps the clue to the authors' indifference to the Gospel of Jesus Christ is found in the fact that the above citation pits Romanism against *Evangelicalism* rather than the Bible. There would be no need for this book were it not for the fear of the authors to say that the above Romish heresies are contrary to the *central teachings of the Bible*. Instead, they opt for a safer haven by casting the differences as those between Roman Catholics and Evangelicals. Notice that the picture is painted in such a way that the central question is "ecclesiastical

---

[1] Geisler & MacKenzie, pg. 155
[2] Geisler & MacKenzie, pg. 155

unity." The real question should be, "Is Roman Catholicism of Christ?" Despite the mountain of evidence which they themselves have produced, Geisler & MacKenzie cannot bring themselves to answer in the negative.

What is obviously missing is any discussion on whether one community is right and the other wrong in their assessment of the Christian Gospel. The authors seem content not to ask the question. We, however, do not hesitate to ask this very question loudly and clearly. For if we can be convinced that Rome is nothing other than a "different" Christian worshiping community, then we have lost all sense of an objective Gospel. How can two radically opposite portrayals of God, His Son and His Gospel both be acceptable in heaven?

The authors devote 200 pages to "Areas of Doctrinal Differences." We will be content to give you the highlights of their reasoning followed by their inconsistent conclusions and our comments. The areas to be explored are the Apocrypha, Scripture, Justification, Sacramentalism, and Purgatory. We present these "differences" in the hopes that you will keep before you at all times the question of whether or not the Roman views on these are fatal to the Christian Gospel and the revelation of God in Christ. We shall begin each section by giving you the weighty evidence set forth against the teaching of the Roman Catholic religion *in the authors' own words.* We shall then give you their rebuttal followed by their illogical conclusion and our assessment of it.

The Apocrypha

WE WOULD ASK the reader to consider the weighty evidence that the authors of *Agreements and Differences* compile against the Roman apocrypha. We have only included a few short excerpts of their argument. Keep their excellent arguments in mind as you see Geisler & MacKenzie ultimately arrive at a conclusion which is timidity itself in comparison to their statements here.

The Roman Catholic Position

"As we have already seen in chapter 1, both Catholics and Protestants affirm the inspiration and divine authority of the sixty-six books of the Protestant canon (thirty-nine in the Old Testament and twenty-seven in the New Testament). A crucial difference emerges, however, over eleven pieces of literature (seven books and four parts of books) that the Roman Catholic Church infallibly pronounced part of the canon in A.D. 1546 at the Council of Trent."[1]

"In spite of some current speculative usage by Catholic scholars to the contrary, the Council of Trent affords these books full canonical status and pronounces an anathema (excommunication) on any who reject them. After enumerating the books, including the eleven apocryphal books, the Council stated: 'If anyone, however, should not accept the said books as sacred and canonical, entire with all their parts ...and if both knowingly and deliberately he should condemn the aforesaid tradition let him be anathema.' The same language affirming the Apocrypha is repeated by Vatican II."[2]

Geisler & MacKenzie's Rebuttal

"Actually, all that the arguments used in favor of the canonicity of the apocryphal books prove is that various apocryphal books were

---

[1] Geisler & MacKenzie, pg. 157

[2] Geisler & MacKenzie, pp. 157-158

given varied degrees of esteem by different persons within the Christian church, usually falling short of canonicity. Only after Augustine and the local councils he dominated mistakenly pronounced them inspired did they gain wider usage and eventual acceptance by the Roman Catholic Church at Trent. This falls far short of the kind of initial, continual, and complete recognition of the canonical books of the Protestant Old Testament and Jewish Torah (which exclude the Apocrypha) by the Christian church. It exemplifies how the teaching Magisterium of the Catholic church proclaims infallible one tradition to the neglect of strong evidence in favor of an opposing tradition because it supports a doctrine that lacks any real support in the canonical books."[1]

"There is strong evidence that the apocryphal books are not prophetic. But since propheticity is the test for canonicity, this would eliminate the Apocrypha from the canon. First, no apocryphal books claim to be written by a prophet. Indeed, as already noted, one apocryphal book even disclaims being prophetic (1 Macc. 9:27). Second, there is no divine confirmation of any of the writers of the apocryphal books, as there is for prophets who wrote canonical books (e.g., Exod. 4:1-2). Third, there is no predictive prophecy in the Apocrypha, such as we have in the canonical books (e.g., Isa. 54; Dan. 9; Mic. 5:2) and which is a clear indication of their propheticity. Fourth, there is no new messianic truth in the Apocrypha. Thus, it adds nothing to the messianic truths of the Old Testament. Fifth, even the Jewish community, whose books they were, acknowledged that the prophetic gifts had ceased in Israel before the Apocrypha was written. Sixth, the apocryphal books were never listed in the Jewish Bible along with the 'Prophets,' or any other section for that matter. Seventh, never once is any apocryphal book cited authoritatively by a prophetic book written after it. Taken together, this provides overwhelming evidence that the Apocrypha was not prophetic and, therefore, should not be part of the canon of Scripture."[2]

"Philo, an Alexandrian Jewish teacher (20 B.C.—A.D. 40), quoted the Old Testament prolifically from virtually every canonical book. Never once, however, did he quote the Apocrypha as inspired text. Josephus (A.D. 30—100), a Jewish historian, explicitly excluded the Apocrypha, numbering the Old Testament as twenty-two books (= thirty-nine books in the Protestant Old Testament)."[3]

---

[1] Geisler & MacKenzie, pg. 165

[2] Geisler & MacKenzie, pg. 167

[3] Geisler & MacKenzie, pg. 168

"Jesus and the New Testament writers never once quoted the Apocrypha as Scripture, even though they were aware of these books and possibly even alluded to them at times."[1]

"The Jewish scholars at Jamnia (c. A.D. 90) did not accept the Apocrypha as part of the divinely inspired Jewish canon."[2]

"No canonical list or general council accepted the Apocrypha as inspired for nearly the first four centuries of the Christian church. This is especially significant since all the lists available and most of the Fathers from this period rejected the Apocrypha. The first councils to accept the Apocrypha were only local ones without ecumenical force. Many of the early Fathers of the Christian church spoke out against the Apocrypha, including Origen, Cyril of Jerusalem, Athanasius, and the great Roman Catholic Bible translator, Jerome. Jerome (A.D. 340-420), the greatest biblical scholar of the early medieval period and translator of the Latin Vulgate, explicitly rejected the Apocrypha as part of the canon."[3]

"The infallible pronouncement by the Council of Trent that the Apocrypha is part of the inspired Word of God is unjustified for many reasons… The occasion of Trent's infallible pronouncement on the Apocrypha was part of a polemical action against Luther, supporting teaching that he had attacked, such as prayers for the dead (cf. 2 Macc. 12:45-46). Not all the Apocrypha was accepted at Trent. In fact, they arbitrarily accepted a book favoring their belief in prayers for the dead (2 Maccabees) and rejected one opposing such prayers (2 [4] Esdras; cf. 7:105)."[4]

"In exercising its magisterial role, the Roman Catholic Church chose the wrong course in rendering its decision about the Apocrypha."[5]

Our Comments

As one can see, the authors present a vast array of solid arguments as to why Rome is in error when it places the Apocryphal books on the same level as the Scriptures, not the least of which arguments is that the *Jews* did not consider the Apocrypha to be canonical; this is extremely important, because, as Paul asserts, "unto them were committed the oracles of God"

---

[1] Geisler & MacKenzie, pp. 168-169
[2] Geisler & MacKenzie, pg. 169
[3] Geisler & MacKenzie, pg. 169
[4] Geisler & MacKenzie, pp. 171-172
[5] Geisler & MacKenzie, pg. 174

(Romans 3:2). That is, God entrusted the Old Testament to the care of the Jews until the time of the Apostles, and the Jews exercised their custodial role meticulously, but did not include the Apocrypha in that task. We applaud such sound reasoning on behalf of Geisler & MacKenzie.

But we observe that they are willing to call the insertion of the Apocryphal books a 'serious error' but not a fatal error. Neither do they wish to make comment on the anathemas cast upon their heads by the infallible Magisterium for not accepting the Apocryphal books as part of the canon. Presumably, the authors are not willing to let the anathema—the *curse*—of the Roman Catholic religion affect their conclusion that the Romish religion only seriously errs here. Corresponding to that, we wonder how reasonable it is for them to hold the following views in light of sitting under the curse of Rome:

> "Unlike some evangelicals, we believe that there is no need to exaggerate our differences or to condemn Catholics for holding beliefs they do not hold. Nor should our doctrinal differences keep us from personal fellowship with other believing Catholics and social cooperation with them on common moral, social, and educational causes."[1]

We certainly agree with the authors that it is not right to condemn Catholics by attributing beliefs to them that they do not hold. This we do not do. But we wonder why these authors are so careful not to reject Rome based on beliefs Rome *does* hold.

And what of the Roman Catholic penchant for cursing to hell those who do not believe what they do? We ask, "Is the Roman assertion of the canonicity of the Apocrypha and that those resisting it are to be accursed, grounds for a denial of Rome as a Christian community?" We answer "Yes," if it can be shown that the addition of books into the canon affects the central message of the canon. The insertion of I Maccabees and II Maccabees, and the subsequent appeal to them to promote the anti-Gospel of Purgatory, links the use of the Apocryphal to a proclamation of a false gospel. This the writers freely admit:

> "Trent has all the markings of a dogmatic and polemical pronouncement, geared by Roman Catholicism to bolster support for doctrines for which they cannot find clear support in any of the sixty-six canonical books."[2]

---

[1] Geisler & MacKenzie, pg. 156

[2] Geisler & MacKenzie, pg. 175

We cannot help but notice that Rome has introduced non-revelational material into the Word of God. This material reigns in Rome as the Word of God, fully authoritative. To the Christian, it is nothing more than an extra authority existing along side the Scriptures, not unlike the Book of Mormon and the writings of Ellen G. White so championed by the Seventh Day Adventists. This aspect of Romanism gives it the markings of a cult, not a Christian denomination. Such a conclusion is not in the least bit unwarranted. It is, however, a conclusion conspicuously absent from *Agreements and Differences*. How ironic that right from the start, in the "Areas of Doctrinal Disagreement" section, the authors, by virtue of their denial of the Apocryphal books as canon, place themselves under the curse of Rome. Is this not more than mere serious error on the part of Rome? Is Rome serious? If not, then Rome is openly contradictory. If the authors accept Rome's word on this, they must somehow reconcile their zeal to proclaim themselves 'friends of Rome,' with Rome's zeal in condemning them to hell!

Scripture

WHEN FACED WITH the Roman Catholic assertion that the Bible alone is not both materially and formally sufficient, Geisler & MacKenzie are brilliant in their defense of Christian orthodoxy *contra* Rome. In a carefully laid out and cogently argued 15-page rebuttal to the Romanist position, the authors champion the Reformation cry of *sola scriptura*. We produce only a small portion of their arguments to provide a taste of their excellent work. Our comments will follow.

The Roman Catholic Position

> "One of the basic differences between Catholics and Protestants is over whether the Bible alone or the Bible plus extra-biblical apostolic tradition is the sufficient and final authority for faith and practice. Roman Catholics affirm the latter and Protestants the former. For, while Catholics allow the Protestant teaching on the material sufficiency* of Scripture, they deny its formal sufficiency. Catholics insist that there is a need for a teaching Magisterium to rule on just what is and is not authentic apostolic tradition."[1]

> "Whether or not extra-biblical apostolic tradition is considered a second source of revelation, there is no question that both sides agree that the Roman Catholic Church believes apostolic tradition is both authoritative and infallible. The council of Trent was emphatic in proclaiming that the Bible alone is not sufficient for faith and

---

* By "material sufficiency" is meant the actual words of the Bible or the Bible itself. The Bible is said to contain in itself all that is necessary for salvation. This is the evangelical and Christian position. Some in Rome agree with this. The difference lies in the formal sufficiency of the Bible. Christians believe the Bible is sufficiently clear and understandable without the need of an infallible teaching Magisterium. Roman Catholics do not.

[1] Geisler & MacKenzie, pg. 180

morals; God has ordained tradition in addition to the Bible to faithfully guide the church."[1]

Geisler & MacKenzie's Rebuttal

"As convincing as these arguments may seem to be to a devout Catholic, they fail to refute the Protestant view of *sola Scriptura.* As we shall see, they fail to provide any substantial basis for the Catholic dogma of an infallible teaching magisterium."[2]

"*The Bible teaches* sola Scriptura. Two points must be made here. First, as Catholic scholars themselves recognize, it is not necessary that the Bible explicitly and formally teach *sola Scriptura* in order for this doctrine to be true. Many Christian teachings are a necessary logical deduction of what is clearly taught in the Bible."[3]

"Second, the Bible does teach implicitly and logically, if not formally and explicitly, that the Bible alone is the only infallible basis for faith and practice. This it does in a number of ways. Scripture states that it is 'inspired' and 'competent' for a believer to be 'equipped for every good work' (2 Tim. 3:16-17). If the Bible alone is sufficient to do this, then nothing else is needed. Also, this text teaches that the Bible alone is inspired and capable of saving, edifying, and equipping believers. This is evident from several things stated in the text. First, only the Scriptures are 'inspired' or God-breathed. Second, while the reference here is only to the Old Testament (v. 15), other passages show that the New Testament Gospels (1 Tim. 5:18; cf. Luke 10:7) and Epistles were considered 'Scripture' too (2 Pet. 3:15-16). Third, the use of the word 'competent' or 'thoroughly' (KJV, NKJV), in connection with the ability to save (v. 15) and sanctify (vv. 16-17), implies the sufficiency of Scripture for faith and practice. Fourth, the total absence of reference to any other instrument or source of authority than the written Word (Gk. *graphe*) reveals that the locus of this sufficient authority is in the written Word (= Scripture). Fifth, Paul repeatedly stresses the need to cling to the Scriptures (1:13; 2:15; 3:15-16; 4:2). Finally, given that this was his last book (4:6-8), if there was some other apostolic authority other than the written Word of God the apostle surely would have mentioned it."[4]

---

[1] Geisler & MacKenzie, pg. 181
[2] Geisler & MacKenzie, pg. 183
[3] Geisler & MacKenzie, pg. 184, emphasis in original
[4] Geisler & MacKenzie, pg. 184

"Third, Jesus and the apostles constantly appealed to the Bible as the final court of appeal. This they often did by the introductory phrase 'It is written,' which is repeated some ninety times in the New Testament."[1]

"What is more, Jesus made it clear that the Bible was in a class of its own, exalted above all tradition. He rebuked the Pharisees for negating the final authority of the Word of God with their religious traditions, saying, 'why do you break the commandment of God for the sake of your tradition?... You have nullified the word of God, for the sake of your tradition' (Matt. 15:3,6)."[2]

"Further, the Bible teaches *sola Scriptura* by stressing that it is a revelation from God (Gal. 1:12; cf. 1 Cor. 2:11-13) as opposed to the words of men. A revelation from God is a divine unveiling or disclosure. Paul's contrast vividly illustrates the difference: 'Now I want you to know, brothers, that the gospel preached by me is not of human origin. For I did not receive it from a human being, nor was I taught it, but it came through a revelation of Jesus Christ' (Gal. 2:1-2)."[3]

"Finally, although written revelation was progressive, both Catholics and Protestants agree that normative revelation ended by the time of the completion of the New Testament. Indeed, Jesus told the apostles he would 'lead *them* [not their successors] into 'all truth'" (John 14:26; 16:13, emphasis added), and to be an apostle one had to have been an eyewitness of the resurrected Christ (cf. Acts 1:22; 1 Cor. 9:1; 15:4-8). But, as we will see shortly, the only infallible record we have of apostolic teaching is in the New Testament. Therefore, it follows that Jesus predicted that the Bible alone would be the summation of 'all truth' that he desired for his followers. This being the case, then, since canonical revelation ceased at the end of the first century, *sola Scriptura* means that the Bible—'nothing more, nothing less, and nothing else'—has infallible authority."[4]

Our Comments

In light of what the authors have said about the Roman Catholic position on the Scriptures, we expect a hearty denunciation of Rome. We expect to be

---

[1] Geisler & MacKenzie, pg. 185
[2] Geisler & MacKenzie, pg. 185
[3] Geisler & MacKenzie, pg. 186
[4] Geisler & MacKenzie, pg. 187

warned. We expect to have a strong conclusion drawn for us. We expect the authors to give us the implications and outworking of the Romanist position so as to protect the Body of Christ. But, alas, it is not forthcoming. This section on Holy Scripture ends by giving all evidence that Rome is indeed dead wrong. But the authors are unwilling to conclude anything from it. Incredibly, we come away from this entire section feeling that the war over *sola scriptura*, fought with blood throughout the centuries, is nothing more than an intellectual tempest in a teapot! There is no fiery conclusion. There is no fire. We are left with the impression that "Rome is very wrong, but so what?" It is as if the authors want to protect Protestant ground rather than the ultimate truth. Once again, the issue is presented as one of "difference" rather than that of "fatal error." Geisler & MacKenzie are defending Protestantism simply because they were born on the Protestant side of the street. They view this whole conflict as an intramural tussle between two guys in the same fraternity. They naturally side with the Protestant point of view but are quick to call it just that: "a point of view." They do not see this as a life and death battle between two radically opposite religions. For them, it is not a matter of truth versus error, but a matter of who has the best *perspective* on the truth. They think Protestants do, but the fact Rome does not is no big deal. It is presented as a difference in *kind* but not a difference in *species*.

We ask the reader to think through the issues with us. If the Bible is the only authoritative source of divinely inspired writing in the sense of establishing the way of salvation and sanctification, then what trust can we place in any other source? If the Bible is only one of three divinely inspired authoritative sources, then we should obey the other two as well. But if the Bible is the *only* source we can trust, Rome must be wrong in adding two more. Why no emphatic protest from Geisler & MacKenzie based on their own findings?

If the Romanist religion is right then all that has been passed down by the Popes and Councils is binding on all Christians everywhere. If Rome is right, then Geisler & MacKenzie—along with millions of others—are all wrong and need to repent and return to Rome. If Rome is wrong, then it is the very heart of anti-Christ activities. It claims authority that it does not have. It sets forth a way of salvation and sanctification that is wrong and leads to a miserable end.

If Rome is right, Christians would be wrong to think that the Bible alone has authority for faith and living and is sufficient for salvation. The authors fail miserably to arrive at even the most obvious conclusion. If Evangelicals and the Reformers are wrong, then Rome is right, and we have been wrong before God ever since the Reformation. But if Rome is wrong, as the authors rightly conclude, then Rome is lost. For in being so wrong at this point, Rome has become apostate. It is replete with man-made traditions and a religion that looks nothing like biblical Christianity. The conclusion of the matter stands. But once again, the authors have laid out the matter in detail, only to shrug their intellectual shoulders as if they were embarrassed of the natural conclusions of their own investigation. We well fear they might be!

The one absolute and necessary ingredient for apostasy is to go beyond what God has written. When once this door has been opened, there is no end to what man will do in the name of religion. Allow Rome's outrageous claims of extra biblical authority to stand as nothing more than a "difference" is tantamount to theological suicide. The authors do not seem to understand that these things matter in the realm of absolute truth. They are not mere "differences." Rome's view of authority and that of the Protestant Reformers, as well as all Christians today, is radically opposite. Ultimately, this produces a radically opposite gospel.

We must do more than say the arguments of Rome are "wanting" or "insufficient" or "poorly attested historically." We must be willing to say that Rome has departed from all of Christianity in promulgating the heresy of a threefold authority. To tolerate Rome's two alternate sources of authority without a clear and forceful rejection of Rome is to deny the essence of Christian authority and to give at least tacit consent to other authorities or religious systems. The authors have done just this.

Justification

IT IS NOT A problem to find evidence of the official Roman Catholic view on justification. It was the featured doctrine at the Council of Trent. We reproduce for you a summary statement from *Agreements and Differences* which relies heavily on Ott's *Fundamentals of Catholic Dogma*, and Denzinger's *Sources of Catholic Dogma*, to get to the heart of the matter:

The Roman Catholic Position

> "In spite of the common core of Augustinian belief in salvation by grace, Roman Catholics and Protestants have had strong disagreement over the doctrine of justification. For one thing, while Catholics believe in the primacy and necessity of grace, Protestants believe in the exclusivity of grace; that is, only Protestants believe salvation is by grace alone (*sola gratia*) apart from any good works. Likewise, while Catholics believe in the necessity of faith (at least for adults) for justification, only Protestants believe in the exclusivity of faith. The heart cry of the Reformation was 'justification by faith alone' (*sola fide*). The distinguishing salvation doctrines of the Reformation, then are grace alone and faith alone (*sola gratia* and *sola fide*) through Christ alone and based on the Bible alone."[1]
>
> "Catholic dogma states: 'By his good works the justified man really acquires a claim to supernatural reward from God.' Of course, this demand is not intrinsic; it is only because God has placed himself in this situation because of his promise to reward good works. Further, eternal life is given to us on the grounds of our good works. Thus the Council of Trent declared that 'those who work well 'unto the end' [Matt. 10:22], and who trust in God, life eternal is to be proposed, both as a grace mercifully promised to the sons of God through Christ Jesus, 'and as a recompense' which is… to be faithfully given to their good works and merit.' It adds, 'If anyone

[1] Geisler & MacKenzie, pg. 221

shall say that the good works of the man justified are in such a way the gift of God that they are not also the good merits of him who is justified, or that the one justified by the good works... does not truly merit increase of grace, eternal life, and the attainment of eternal life (if he should die in grace), and also an increase of glory; let him be anathema.'"[1]

It is necessary now to reproduce for you the excellent rebuttal which Geisler & MacKenzie construct against Rome's claim. We do so to allow the impact of Christian theology to decimate Rome's very foundation. We also wish to illustrate, once again, the bizarre ritual of Geisler & MacKenzie as they thoroughly crush an aberrant theological system while concluding that it is in fact Christian:

Geisler & MacKenzie's Rebuttal

"While Catholics wish to remind us that the whole doctrine of merit should be viewed in the context of grace, they overlook the fact that Scripture teaches that grace and meritorious works are mutually exclusive."[2]

"The Council of Trent declared clearly that 'those who work well 'unto the end' [Matt. 10:22], and who trust in God, life eternal is to be faithfully given to their good works and merit.' Even the new *Catechism of the Catholic Church* which tends to state doctrine in a way less objectionable to Protestants declares that '*the merit of good works is to be attributed* in the first place to the grace of God, then *to the faithful*' (2008, emphasis added, p. 486). Hence, it is grace *plus* good works. By contrast the Bible declares clearly and emphatically that 'the wages of sin is death, but *the gift of God is eternal life* in Christ Jesus our Lord' (Rom. 6:23, emphasis added)."[3]

"Even granting that, for infants, works are not a condition for receiving initial righteousness (= justification), nonetheless, Catholic theology makes works a condition for progressive righteousness (= sanctification). In other words, one cannot receive a right standing before God by which one has the divine promise of salvation (eternal life) without engaging in works of righteousness. But this is precisely what Scripture says is not the case: It is 'not because of any righteous deeds that we had done but because of his mercy, he

---

[1] Geisler & MacKenzie, pg. 227
[2] Geisler & MacKenzie, pg. 230
[3] Geisler & MacKenzie, pg. 231

saved us' (Titus 3:5). 'It is not from works, so no one may boast,' wrote Paul (Eph. 2:9). To repeat the apostle, 'if by grace, it is no longer because of works; otherwise grace would no longer be grace' (Rom. 11:6). A right standing before God comes by grace through faith alone! Grace means unmerited favor, and reward based on works is merited. Hence, grace and works are no more compatible than is an unmerited merit! Trent overreacted to Luther, and in so doing, obfuscated the purity and clarity of the gospel of God's grace."[1]

"Put in traditional terms, Catholicism fails to recognize the important difference between working *for* salvation and working *from* salvation. We do not work in order to get salvation; rather, we work because we have already gotten it. God works salvation *in* us by justification, and by God's grace we work it *out* in sanctification (Phil. 2:12-13). But neither justification nor sanctification can be merited by works; they are given by grace. Gifts cannot be worked for, only wages can. As Paul declared, 'when one does not work, yet believes in the one who justifies the ungodly, his faith is credited for righteousness' (Rom. 4:5)."[2]

"The New Testament verses against salvation by works are clearly opposed to the Catholic teaching that salvation can be merited. In order to counter this Roman Catholic scholars have made an artificial distinction between 'works of the law' (which they admit are not a condition for salvation) and works (which they insist are a condition of salvation). But contrary to the Catholic claim, Paul's statements against 'works' cannot be limited to only 'works of the [Mosaic] law' (such as circumcision) but extend equally to all kinds of meritorious good works, for all such works will in one way or another be works in accordance with God's law. They would not be *good* works if they were not in accordance with God's standard of goodness, namely, his law. Since God is the standard of all righteousness, it follows that all true works of righteousness will be according to his law and nature. It is only *our* righteousness (= self-righteousness) that is abhorrent in God's eyes (cf. Isa. 64:6; Rom. 10:3). It makes no difference whether these works are prompted by grace; they are still meritorious works as a condition for eternal life. They are not based on grace and *grace alone*. That is, part of the basis for obtaining eternal life is meritorious works."[3]

---

[1] Geisler & MacKenzie, pg. 232

[2] Geisler & MacKenzie, pg. 233

[3] Geisler & MacKenzie, pg. 234

Our Comments

We have reached a point in our research where we must revisit the initial question of this book. We began our investigation by asking, essentially, "Does the Roman Catholic religion qualify as a Christian denomination?" We have shown that the alleged "things held in common" between the Roman Catholic and the Christian are extremely suspect. We have labored to show a world of difference between the word *Catholic* prior to Trent and *Romanism* which came out of Trent. We have mentioned that the early Church Creeds and Councils do not speak directly to the message of the Gospel, and that commonality on some points with the Councils does not equal commonality on the *Gospel*. We have also pointed out that the Councils are frequently rewritten by Rome in order to bend and shape them to take on new Roman meanings. They are not adhered to as one might be led to believe, however.

In this section, we have given verbatim quotes showing ample testimony and evidence of what is wrong with Rome on the critical question of justification. We ask the reader to consider, "When is another gospel, another gospel?" If Rome is so entirely out of synch on the question of how a person is justified before God, then how can Rome be considered Christian?

It has been stated boldly—both by us and by Geisler & MacKenzie—that Rome misses the Gospel in its defense of merit justification. We applaud their candid portrayal of Romish views on justification. There is no better summing up of Trent than how they have done it:

> "While Catholics wish to remind us that the whole doctrine of merit should be viewed in the context of grace, they overlook the fact that Scripture teaches that grace and meritorious works are mutually exclusive."[1]

> "The Council of Trent declared clearly that 'those who work well 'unto the end' [Matt. 10:22], and who trust in God, life eternal is to be faithfully given to their good works and merit.'"[2]

In his book, *Faith Alone*, R. C. Sproul explains for us the proper conclusion of the Reformers with respect to the Protestant Reformation:

> "Since the gospel stands at the heart of Christian faith, Luther and other Reformers regarded the debate concerning justification as one

---

[1] Geisler & MacKenzie, pg. 230
[2] Geisler & MacKenzie, pg. 231

> involving an essential truth of Christianity, a doctrine no less essential than the Trinity or the dual natures of Christ. Without the gospel the church falls. Without the gospel the church is no longer the church. The logic of the Reformers is this: 1. Justification by faith alone is essential to the gospel. 2. The gospel is essential to Christianity and to salvation. 3. The gospel is essential to a church's being a true church. 4. To reject justification by faith alone is to reject the gospel and to fall as a church. The Reformers concluded that when Rome rejected and condemned sola fide, it condemned itself, in effect, and ceased to be a true church."[1]

However, after Geisler & MacKenzie devote twenty pages in protection of the Reformed and Christian *defense* of the doctrine of justification by faith alone in the finished work of Christ alone for salvation, we would expect the natural conclusions of their research to follow. But unlike the Reformers who understood that to miss justification was to miss the Gospel, there is a major and inconceivable failure here. Rome is allowed to stand. Incredibly, the distance placed between Rome's faulty view of justification and the Christian Gospel is not enough for Geisler & MacKenzie to conclude that Christianity is antithetical to Roman Catholicism. They conclude,

> "However, the Catholic view of justification, made dogma by the Council of Trent, obscured the pure grace of God, if not at times negating it in practice. Indeed, it was condemned as heretical by the Reformers. Both sacramentalism and sacerdotalism vitiated and institutionalized grace so that it was incorporated into a system of works. Nonetheless, at least officially, though not in practice, Rome has always held to the common Augustinian belief of salvation by grace. In this way they have avoided more serious doctrinal error."[2]

We notice that the Roman Catholic view, although condemned by the Reformers, is not condemned by these two men. Does this mean that the Reformers were in error? Does it mean that the authors reject the Reformers? Does it mean that Rome's views on justification are more tolerable today than they were in the 16th century? Rome has not changed its view of justification. Have these Evangelicals changed theirs? Trent still stands today as having been cast in concrete as the irreformable dogmas of the Roman Catholic religion. Yet the immense difficulty encountered with Rome on justification is softened by language which suggests that error on justification is *not* fatal to the Gospel. We ask the reader if there could be more serious error than to err on the way a person is accepted by God? Evidently, some do not see the vitiation of grace by institutionalizing it into

---

[1] Sproul, *Faith Alone*, pg. 19

[2] Geisler & MacKenzie, pg. 248

a system of works as lethal to the Gospel. We find this to be not only dumbfounding but also prophetic.

In our opinion there have been a number of attempts to reconcile Christianity and Romanism by those who simply are not aware of the vast and fatal differences which exist between Rome and the Gospel of Jesus Christ. However, when once educated of these contradictory views of salvation, there is normally a cry of warning. But we see here a different breed arising on the American Evangelical landscape. The authors have been more than adequate in exposing the error of Rome and contrasting it with the Christian Gospel. However, they desire us to believe that the differences are not deadly to the Gospel. We are entering a new age of theological enlightenment which is able to point out error in brilliant colors and then conclude that it does not make any ultimate difference. What the Reformers called heresy is today passed off only as "the obscuring" of the grace of God.

Furthermore, we notice the unavoidable conclusion—that Romanism is not Christian—is tempered by the outrageous claim that "officially, though not in practice, Rome has always held the common Augustinian belief of salvation by grace."[1] We are astounded that the same authors who quote so aptly the Council of Trent on justification can conclude that "officially" the Roman Catholic religion has always held to Augustine on justification. This would mean that Augustine would have supported the council of Trent. We remind the reader that Rome's *official* doctrines are not found in the works of Augustine, but in the Council of Trent! Why on earth would the authors resort to Augustine after quoting exhaustively from "infallible" Trent which held to a vastly different view of grace than Augustine did?

This little bit of revisionism is reprehensible and contrary both to history and theology. In our opinion, Augustine would have backed the Reformers against Trent in the establishment of a biblical view of forensic justification. The authors appear to have repeated their pet error again. They have described every characteristic of a duck and concluded that it is really a swan. They have described in Rome the very essence of apostasy, and then concluded that it is not offensive to Christ's Gospel!

---

[1] Geisler & MacKenzie, pg. 248

Sacramentalism

WE NOW WISH to examine the Roman Catholic sacramental system from the same point of view as the other dogmas of Romanism. We will first give you a summary of Sacramentalism and a rebuttal by the authors. We shall be interacting with the authors at this juncture. Keep in mind that we wish to showcase what is a distressing trend. The evidence of the Romanist position is stated clearly, followed by a convincing rebuttal, followed by a non-conclusion. This is the perturbing pattern. No matter how severely the Romanist religion strays from the Gospel, the fatal dogmas of Rome are mitigated, allayed and blunted out as nothing more than "differences" within Christianity:

The Roman Catholic Position

> "The Council of Trent proclaimed infallibly of the sacraments that 'If anyone shall say that the sacraments of the New Law were not all instituted by Jesus Christ our Lord …let him be anathema.' This excommunication includes almost all Protestants, since most affirm that there are less than seven sacraments. This condemnation has never and can never be revoked since it is an infallible *ex cathedra* pronouncement of the Roman Catholic Church."[1]

> "A Sacrament is a cause of grace. According to Roman Catholic authority Ludwig Ott, by 'its etymology the word 'sacramentum' means a sacred or holy thing.'"[2]

> "Sacraments are effective objectively, whether or not their efficacy is felt subjectively. 'Sacraments confer grace immediately, without the mediation of fiducial faith.' However, 'it is true that in the adult recipient, faith is an indispensable pre-condition or a disposing cause, but it is not an efficient cause of grace.' In order to designate the objective efficacy of a sacrament, Catholic theology coined (and

[1] Geisler & MacKenzie, pg. 249

[2] Geisler & MacKenzie, pg. 249

Trent adopted) the phrase *ex opere operato* (by the work that has been worked); that is, 'the Sacraments operate by the power of the completed sacramental rite.'"[1]

"Each particular sacrament confers a specific grace on the recipient, corresponding to its special purpose. Most Catholic theologians believe that God conveys the same measure of grace on each of the sacrament's recipients. This grace continues until the death of its receiver."[2]

"Thus, the sacraments are necessary for salvation. The Council of Trent reminded Catholics that 'If anyone shall say that the sacraments of the New Law are not necessary for salvation, but are superfluous, and that, although all are not necessary individually, without them or without the desire of them through faith alone men obtain from God the grace of justification: let him be anathema.'"[3]

"The Council of Trent proclaimed that 'If anyone shall say that the sacraments of the New Law were not all instituted by Jesus Christ our Lord, or that there are more or less than seven, namely baptism, confirmation, Eucharist, penance, extreme unction, [holy] order, and matrimony, or even that any one of these seven is not truly and strictly a sacrament: let him be anathema.' In brief, there are seven and only these seven sacraments."[4]

For the purposes of this book, let us now zero in on two of the most important sacraments within Rome: baptism and communion, or the Eucharist.

Baptism

Rome anathematizes all those who believe that baptism is to be administered *only* to those who have first expressed faith in Jesus Christ:

"But the denial of infant baptism (such as Baptists and many other Christian groups do deny) is a heresy. For Trent declared that 'If anyone shall say that infants, because they have not actual faith, after having received baptism are not to be numbered among the faithful, and therefore, when they have reached the years of discretion, are to be rebaptized ...let them be anathema.' This, of

---

[1] Geisler & MacKenzie, pg. 250
[2] Geisler & MacKenzie, pg. 251
[3] Geisler & MacKenzie, pg. 252
[4] Geisler & MacKenzie, pg. 252

> course, anathematizes all Baptists and like groups, including the authors of this book!"[1]

The authors reserve their rebuttal of Roman Catholic baptism to an eleven-page Appendix E in the last pages of their book. We urge anyone interested in a clear and precise presentation of why the Romish sacrament of baptism cannot be supported from Scripture to read that appendix in its entirety. Although there is room for minor disagreement on the treatment of some passages, the authors have done a very credible work in uncovering and correcting Catholic exegesis of passages marshalled to buttress Rome's baptismal regeneration. But the refutation of Rome on this extremely critical point is very reminiscent of the rest of the "Areas of Doctrinal Differences" section. Although Geisler & MacKenzie seem most at home in refuting Rome point by point, they fail to attach a conclusion to the data. We are left with that "something is missing" feeling. So, what is missing? Before giving the authors' presentation and rebuttal of the rest of the Romish sacraments, including the Eucharist, we take the time here to comment on what is missing from their critique of Romish baptism.

We have already heartily recommended this section on the refutation of Rome, so we jump right to the conclusion of the appendix. Herein lies our problem once again with their book and with many Evangelicals. The good news is that Rome has been thoroughly thrashed and exposed as holding an untenable position on baptism. The authors are lucid and convincing in their defense of biblical orthodoxy on the subject. Great pains are taken by them to examine every text summoned by Rome and to show Rome's error. The bad news is, as in the case of the Apocrypha, Scripture, Justification and now the Sacramental system of Rome, the authors fail to conclude that such severe theological errors are not merely "differences"! We ask, "If Rome is wrong in thinking that baptism brings about regeneration, the forgiveness of sin and the inclusion of an infant into the Church of God, *then how wrong is Rome?*" Is this view of the atonement not a different way of salvation? Is this not a different gospel? Is this not an entirely foreign way of reading the Bible? Are we to think that it really does not matter if one believes in baptismal regeneration? Picture the inquiring pagan who asks of Rome, "What must I do to be saved?" Rome answers, "Believe on the Lord Jesus Christ and be baptized for the forgiveness of sins and receive Christ through the Sacramental System and obey the dictates and dogmas of the Romish religion by being faithful to the sacraments. And, if you should marry and have children, your children will be born again and justification will begin in the waters of infant baptism. To believe any other way is a sin and you will be condemned to hell by Jesus Christ through His Church which is the Holy Roman Catholic Church."

---

[1] Geisler & MacKenzie, pg. 254

According to Geisler & MacKenzie, such a response would be "different" from what they might say to an inquiring pagan, but not fatal to the Gospel. When faced with Rome's insistence on baptismal regeneration, the authors note it as an *error,* but file it as only a "difference." We hope the reader is as weary as we are of the word "difference." It portrays only the facts of the matter but not the value of those facts. Rome *is* different. But without the "so what?" question answered, we are left with the impression that it ends with the word "different."

Here, as with justification, the authors have blown an opportunity to conclude according to the biblical mandate. Instead, the writers trail off into a discussion of how difficult it is to understand Martin Luther and his changing views of baptism. The authors further divert attention away from the obvious conclusion—that Rome teaches another gospel—by citing the many Reformed Christians who baptize babies, albeit for different reasons.

The fact that the authors are willing to point out that great tensions exist with Reformed Christians who believe in justification by faith alone but still baptize infants shows how strong the pull of Rome is on Christian communities that are inconsistent with their profession of faith. It appears the authors let pass an opportunity to exterminate Romish baptism with the Scriptures because of the corresponding slight to infant-baptizing Christian communities. It appears that there is a fear of offending those communities who persist in practicing what Rome practices. While draining away the Romish meaning, and substituting their own, Luther and Calvin, among others, did not have the clear light to see that Rome's practice and meaning of infant baptism stand and fall together. The fact that many Reformers chose to keep the practice and impact it with a different meaning or rationale does not make it any more acceptable from a purely biblical point of view.*

At any rate, after the authors labor, both in the main text of the book and in the appendix, to show how Rome errs on the sacramental issues, we do not find the announcement we are looking for in the conclusion of Appendix E!

---

* We are not able to engage in a discussion on the merits of Reformed Christian infant baptism. This battle has been waged since the Protestant Reformation. We only point out that we feel the devastating effect of the Roman Catholic doctrine of baptismal regeneration and *ex opere operato* (the thing itself brings about the thing signified) is dangerously close to the Reformed view of infant baptism. It is not uncommon for Roman Catholic exegetes to defend their practice of baptismal regeneration with Reformed Christian logic based upon the Old Testament Covenant with Abraham. The author has felt the difficulty inherent in denying Rome while affirming the Reformed Churches who still practice infant baptism. At the least, it makes it almost impossible to torpedo the Roman ship of sacramental regeneration when one is worried about taking out Luther as well. We, for this reason, appeal to the exegesis of Scripture alone and settle for its dictates without fear of offense.

Disappointment comes in waves as we seek to know if one can be Christian believing that infant baptism takes away sin, starting the process of justification culminating in Purgatory. Is this another gospel? If not, what is?

We give you the authors' summary rebuttal of Romish baptismal regeneration. We ask the reader to keep in mind that, according to the authors, these represent "differences" that are nowhere mentioned as fatal to the Gospel:

> "*Baptismal regeneration appears to be contrary to grace.* The belief that baptism brings regeneration seems inconsistent with the biblical teaching …that salvation comes by grace through faith and not by any works of righteousness, including baptism. Baptism is called a work of 'righteousness' in Matthew 3:15, but Paul declared that it was 'not because of any righteousness deeds we have done but because of his mercy, he saved us' (Titus 3:5)."[1]
>
> "*Baptismal regeneration is in conflict with the need for faith.* Throughout the Bible it is faith and faith alone that is commanded as a condition for receiving God's gift of salvation. When the Philippian jailor asked, 'What must I do to be saved?' Paul answered, 'Believe in the Lord Jesus Christ and you and your household will be saved' (Acts 16:30,31). In the entire Gospel of John belief is the only thing required to receive eternal life."[2]
>
> "*Baptismal regeneration is contrary to the teaching of Paul.* The great apostle called of God to take the gospel to the Gentiles said emphatically, 'Christ did not send me to baptize but to preach the gospel' (1 Cor. 1:17), thus putting the 'gospel' and 'baptism' in opposition. Clearly, baptism is not part of the gospel. But the gospel 'is the power of God for the salvation of everyone who believes' (Rom. 1:16)."[3]
>
> "*'Baptism of desire' proves baptism is not essential to salvation.* According to Roman Catholic theology someone can be saved who has never been baptized, providing the desire was present. Ott claims that 'Baptism of desire, it is true, replaces Sacramental Baptism in so far as the communication of grace is concerned.' Even the great Catholic theologian, Thomas Aquinas conceded that 'a person may be saved extrasacramentally by baptism of desire and therefore [there is] the possibly of salvation without actual membership …in the church.'"[4]

---

[1] Geisler & Mackenzie, pg. 260, emphasis in original
[2] Geisler & MacKenzie, pg. 260, emphasis in original
[3] Geisler & MacKenzie, pg. 260, emphasis in original
[4] Geisler & MacKenzie, pg. 261

The Eucharist

Here again, we let the authors set the stage for a discussion on the Roman Catholic sacrament of the Eucharist, or communion:

> "Few issues better illustrate the difference between Catholics and Protestants than the doctrine of communion. This is especially true with regard to the Catholic dogma of transubstantiation, which holds that, during communion, the wine and bread are transformed into the actual body and blood of Christ."[1]

> "Since in transubstantiation the elements become the actual body and blood of Christ, Catholics believe that it is appropriate to worship the consecrated elements as God. Trent pronounced emphatically that 'There is, therefore, no room left for doubt that all the faithful of Christ… offer in veneration (can. 6) the worship of *latria* [the act of adoration] which is due to the true God, to this most Holy Sacrament.'"[2]

Geisler & MacKenzie's Rebuttal

> "More important than the differences over baptism is the disagreement about communion. Roman Catholic scholars argue that Jesus' words should be taken in a physical sense when he said of the bread and wine 'This is my body' and when he said 'unless you eat the flesh of the Son of Man and drink his blood, you do not have life within you.' But Evangelicals believe there are several good reasons for rejecting this interpretation. *It is not necessary to take these phrases literally*. Jesus' words need not be taken in the literal sense of ingesting his actual physical body and blood. Jesus often spoke in metaphors and figures of speech."[3]

> "*It is not* plausible *to take Jesus' words literally*. In response to the Catholic argument, first of all, the vividness of the phrases are no proof of their literal intent. ...Neither is it necessary, as Catholic scholars suggest, to take flesh and blood literally because this phrase was used that way in many places in other contexts. The same words have different meanings in different contexts."[4]

---

1 Geisler & MacKenzie, pg. 255
2 Geisler & MacKenzie, pg. 257
3 Geisler & MacKenzie, pg. 261
4 Geisler & MacKenzie, pg. 262

"The fact that some of Jesus' listeners apparently took his words literally (John 6:52) without his explicit and immediate rebuke is not a good argument. Jesus rebuked their understanding, at least implicitly, when he said later in the same discourse, 'It is the spirit that gives life, while the flesh is of no avail. The words I have spoken to you are spirit and life' (John 6:63)."[1]

"It is not possible *to take a literal view.* In at least one important respect it is logically impossible (inconsistent) for an orthodox Christian to hold to a literal interpretation of Jesus' words at the Last Supper. For, *when Jesus said of the bread in his hand, 'this is my body,' no disciple present could possibly have understood him to mean that the bread was actually his physical body since he was still with them in his physical body, the hands of which were holding that very bread.* ...This reminds one of the medieval myth of the saint whose head was cut off yet he put it in his mouth and swam across the river!"[2]

"It is idolatrous to worship the host. As we have seen, it is an official dogma of Roman Catholicism that the consecrated Eucharist can and should be worshiped. But many Protestants believe this is a form of idolatry. For it is the worship of something which the God-given senses of every normal human being inform them is a finite creation of God, namely, bread and wine. It is to worship God under a physical image which is clearly forbidden in the Ten Commandments (Exod. 20:4)."[3]

"While, as Roman Catholics point out, the New Testament term 'remembrance' (Gk: *anamnesis*) is often used in a sacrificial context, it does not justify their contention that communion is a sacrifice. What Jesus said was that, in participating in communion, we are *remembering* his sacrifice on the cross, not *re-enacting* it."[4]

"The whole concept of re-enacting and re-presenting Christ's sacrifice on the cross is contrary to the clear teaching of Hebrews that this sacrifice occurred once for all time (Heb. 10:12-14). Thus, when the Council of Trent speaks of Christ being 'immolated' (sacrificed) again and again in the mass, it violates the clear teaching of Scripture."[5]

---

[1] Geisler & MacKenzie, pg. 262
[2] Geisler & MacKenzie, pg. 264, emphasis in original
[3] Geisler & MacKenzie, pg. 264
[4] Geisler & MacKenzie, pp. 266-267, emphasis in original
[5] Geisler & MacKenzie, pg. 267

Our Comments

We have seen that the Roman Catholic religion teaches that Christ is to be re-presented in an unbloody sacrifice for the forgiveness of sin. We have seen that, in the Catholic system, bread and wine are transformed into the actual body and blood of Christ. Not only this, but this bread and wine are then to be worshiped as true God. Perhaps we would do well to put all of this into some perspective. It has been our labor to show the reader that the authors do, in fact, understand the Romanist religion very well. The citations of Romish authorities and illumination of Romish theology is well documented and presented fairly without ridicule. Also, we have labored to show that the authors are more than aware that Rome has "differences" with the Evangelical community. The authors are brilliant at times in their zeal to show us the "differences." What is missing is a pronouncement that Rome is not a Christian religion. It would do us well to recall that the Apostle Paul had a violent reaction to those who were trying to retain the time-honored and godly tradition of circumcision in with the Gospel formula. His letter to the Galatians warns them to leave alone the addition of circumcision to the Gospel of grace. If they were to persist then Christ would be of no benefit to them. They were warned that such thinking constituted another gospel. It took away from Christ to add anything to the finished work of Christ, according to Paul's authoritative apostolic admonition!

Now comes the Roman Catholic religion with its agenda consisting in part of the doctrine of the sacrament of the mass and Eucharist. We expect that the authors will come to their senses at this point and admit that Rome truly is a religion unto itself with no affinity for the Gospel of Christ. Sadly, they do not. We allow the authors once again to speak for themselves in their conclusion to the sacramental section:

> "We have examined both the arguments from the Bible and tradition in support of the Roman Catholic view and found them wanting. In fact, some dimensions of Roman Catholic teaching on the sacraments clearly contradict Scripture, other orthodox Christian teaching, and even fact and logic."[1]
>
> "As long as Roman Catholics maintain that these are unnegotiable dogmas, we will have to find *ecclesiastical lodging* elsewhere, in spite of all the other doctrines on which we agree and the practical areas in which we can cooperate."[2]

Is the Romish mass and teaching on the crucifixion of Christ, in the sacrament of the mass, contrary to the Scriptures? According to the authors,

---

[1] Geisler & MacKenzie, pg. 269

[2] Geisler & MacKenzie, pg. 269, emphasis added

Yes. We concur. However, we must press home the point that the authors are not willing to allow the overwhelming evidence to condemn Rome. The conclusion given is that we must find "ecclesiastical lodging" elsewhere. This is very much like saying all hotels are basically the same, but this one smells like fish all the time, so we should seek lodging elsewhere. Is Rome, to push the metaphor, another Christian hotel? Or, is Rome an inner city dumpster? The comparison is rude, we agree. But the point has to be made that an elephant and a rat are not the same even though they both possess ears, legs and tails. The authors wish for Rome to be viewed as a change in *kind*, even though the evidence from their own pen points indisputably to a change in *species*! The fact that some poor miserable souls have sunk to the level of sleeping in dumpsters does not make a dumpster a hotel!

Furthermore, we are constantly put on notice by the authors that "differences" with Rome are to be likened to "differences" between other professing Christian communities. Rome is assumed to be "in the loop" of Christianity despite its horrific array of anti-biblical doctrine in the most critical aspect of Christianity, i.e., the Gospel of Christ. We wish to point out that there is no small difference between Pentecostals and, say, Calvinists. But at heart, both agree on *sola fide* and *sola scriptura*. To say that our differences with Rome can be likened to in-fighting among Evangelicals over such things as tongues, elder rule, a pre-tribulation rapture, mode of baptism and closed communion is foolishness.

We also think it unwise to call upon Luther as a bridge to help us adjust to Romish thinking and to lend an air of credibility to Rome. We must keep in mind that Luther, on his way out of Rome, is bound to rub shoulders with those who are on their way in. At that juncture, it would be wise to remember in which direction Luther was going.

Had he lived long enough, Luther would have perhaps helped to carry the Reformation to its necessary and logical end. We have the advantage over him. Luther had not the time to arrive at where we are. Also, the final judge in these matters is the Word of God. What sayeth the Word? The closer Luther is to Rome, in some aspects of his thinking, the more the light of the Word needs to be shed on him. Likewise today, it is not that Rome is closer to the Gospel because some Lutherans believe similarly to Rome. Rather, it is that some Lutherans have strayed farther from the truth in their desire to enter into affinity with the heresies of Rome.

Purgatory

OUT OF ALL the categories of Roman Catholic doctrine and dogma, the authors were correct in selecting the Apocrypha, Scripture, Papal Infallibility, Justification, Sacramentalism, Ecclesiology, Mariology and Purgatory. For our purposes we have chosen to interact with only five of the above listed. While more could be said on each of the five, it is equally true that we could have expanded our analysis to Mary, the Pope and the Church.[1] We have not done so in light of the fact that we wish to interact with other books of the ecumenical nature which are equally as perilous in attempting to lead the flock of God back to the lethal domicile of Rome. We close this section on "areas of doctrinal differences" with an analysis of the Romish doctrine of Purgatory. We have chosen Purgatory over Papal Infallibility because of its absolute relevance to the Gospel of Jesus Christ. No other single doctrine, except perhaps justification, displays the contempt for the Gospel of Christ as clearly as does Purgatory:

The Roman Catholic position

> "The belief in purgatory is an essential part of the Catholic faith. The Council of Trent declared infallibly: 'If anyone says that after the reception of the grace of justification the guilt is so remitted and the debt of eternal punishment so blotted out to every repentant sinner, that no debt of temporal punishment remains to be discharged, either in this world or in Purgatory, before the gates of Heaven can be opened, let him be anathema.'"[2]

---

[1] We have done just this in the author's own book, *Romanism, The Relentless Roman Catholic Assault on the Gospel of Jesus Christ,* available through White Horse Publications, Huntsville, AL, USA. In *Romanism*, we have endeavored to interact with Roman apologists and work in some detail to explain and evaluate all aspects of Romanism from a doctrinal perspective. We feel our purposes here are more than accomplished by the highlighting of five major categories that display the anti-Christian character of the teachings of the Romanist religion.

[2] Geisler & MacKenzie, pg. 331

> "Before discussing purgatory it is necessary to mention that only a few teachings regarding the doctrine are considered infallible by Catholic theologians. These include the fact that: (1) there is a purification that takes place before one enters heaven; (2) this purification involves some kind of pain or suffering; and (3) this purification can be assisted by the prayers and devotions of the living."[1]

Geisler & MacKenzie's Rebuttal

> "*Purgatory is a denial of the sufficiency of the cross.* Protestants reject the doctrine of purgatory primarily because it in effect denies the all-sufficiency of Christ's atoning death. Scripture teaches that when Christ died on the cross, he proclaimed, 'It is finished' (John 19:30). Speaking of his work of salvation on the earth, Jesus said to the Father, 'I glorified you on earth by accomplishing the work that you gave me to do' (John 17:4). The writer of Hebrews declared emphatically that salvation by Christ's suffering on the cross was a once-for-all accomplished fact. 'For by one offering he has made perfect those who are being consecrated' (Heb. 10:14). These verses demonstrate the completed, sufficient nature of the work of Christ. To affirm that we must suffer for our own sins *is the ultimate insult to Christ's atoning sacrifice!*"[2]

> "*Purgatory is contrary to the immediacy of heaven after death.* The Bible speaks of death as the final moment of life after which one goes immediately to heaven or hell. For 'it is appointed that human beings die once, and after this the judgment' (Heb. 9:27). Jesus said that 'a great chasm is established to prevent anyone from crossing' the border into heaven after death (Luke 16:26). Upon death a person goes directly to one of two destinies, heaven or hell. At death believers immediately 'leave the body and go home to the Lord' (2 Cor. 5:8). That Paul is not merely expressing his wish to be immediately with the Christ but a reality is evident from verse 1: 'For we know...'"[3]

Our Comments

We ask the reader now to consider how any writers, from any point of view, can wish to recognize as Christian the religion of Rome. The writers wish to include Roman Catholicism within the circle of Christianity while openly declaring that Rome's teaching on Purgatory constitutes *the ultimate*

---

[1] Geisler & MacKenzie, pg. 332

[2] Geisler & MacKenzie, pg. 338, emphasis added

[3] Geisler & MacKenzie, pg. 339

insult to Christ's atoning sacrifice! If the intellectual honesty of the authors was not in question up to this point, it most certainly is now. Geisler & MacKenzie are calling Christian an institution which formally denies the Gospel of Christ and insults His death on the Cross. We stand amazed, but we must move on.

The Treasury Of Merit

> "Another Catholic teaching associated with the doctrine of purgatory is the treasury of meritorious works for the dead. According to Catholic theology, in addition to the merit obtained by Christ on the cross, there is a storehouse of merit deposited by the saints on which others can draw for help. The concept of merit or reward involves the dispersion of mercy over and above justice, but such merit is required for salvation nonetheless."[1]

Geisler & MacKenzie's Rebuttal

> "Protestants reject the Roman Catholic doctrine of a treasury of merit by noting that it is based on a misinterpretation of Scripture and is contrary to the all-sufficiency of Christ's atonement."[2]

> "*Other Biblical Arguments against a Treasury of Merit.* The most important reason to reject a treasury of merit by which one human being can do good deeds that can be credited to the account of another is the very concept of merit. As we have demonstrated in chapter 12, salvation is not merited; it is obtained by grace through faith. ...The whole idea that one can buy an indulgence, the very reason that prompted Luther's reaction against the abuses in the Church, is repugnant. ...The most important reason for rejecting the Roman Catholic dogma of a treasury of merit by which the *good deeds of the righteous on earth* can be applied to the account of the righteous in purgatory is that it is contrary to the all-sufficiency of the atoning sacrifice of Christ on the cross. *Christ not only died for the guilt of our sins but also for their consequences, eternal and temporal.* His atoning sacrifice is both sufficient and efficacious..."[3]

Our Comments

At this point let us be reminded that these are the same authors (quoted here in rebuttal of Purgatory) who earlier in their book had these bold things to say about Roman Catholic salvation:

---

[1] Geisler & MacKenzie, pg. 340

[2] Geisler & MacKenzie, pg. 341

[3] Geisler & MacKenzie, pp. 344,45, emphasis added

"Catholics and evangelicals share a *common core* of beliefs about salvation. ...Our differences on the doctrine of salvation notwithstanding, a survey of both Roman Catholics and Protestant Reformers leads to the following conclusions regarding Roman Catholic and evangelical agreement in this area. First, both believe salvation is historical. The Old Testament view of salvation as effected through historic, divine intervention is affirmed in the New Testament. Against Gnosticism, we jointly affirm that man is not saved by wisdom; as against Judaism, *man is not saved by moral and religious merit apart from the grace of God.*"[1]

"Second, *both evangelicals and Catholics believe* salvation is moral and spiritual. Salvation is related to a deliverance from sin and its consequences and hence from guilt... from the curse of the law... from death... from judgment... from fear and finally from bondage."[2]

Hopefully, the reader can see by now that the writers have, in fact, as we labored to show in Part I, carefully crafted their words and have woven concepts of deceit. One cannot have it both ways. One cannot protect Rome with one hand while dismantling the teaching of Rome with the other. In some cases the authors are caught in a hopeless contradiction. Hence, Roman Catholicism is pictured as offering a salvation that is *related* to deliverance from sin, through a system of sacraments, culminating in a doctrine of Purgatory and the Treasury of Merit that is, in reality, an insult to the atoning sacrifice of Christ. The authors seem oblivious to all this or, worse yet, partakers in the subterfuge.

Prayers To The Dead

The Roman Catholic Position

"It is a matter of Catholic dogma *(de fide)* that 'The living Faithful on earth can come to the assistance of the souls in Purgatory by their intercessions (suffrages).' Ott explains that 'suffrages are understood not only as intercessory prayers, but also indulgences, alms and other pious works, above all the Holy Sacrifice of the Mass.' The Council of Trent pronounced infallibly that 'there is a purgatory, and that the souls there detained are aided by the suffrages [prayers] of the faithful and chiefly by the acceptable sacrifice of the altar.' They insisted that the bishops 'instruct the faithful diligently in matters relating to intercession and invocation of the saints... to invoke them and to have recourse to their prayers,

[1] Geisler & MacKenzie, pp. 81,103 emphases added

[2] Geisler & MacKenzie, pg. 103, emphasis added

assistance and support *in order to obtain favors from God through His Son, Jesus Christ our Lord.*"[1]

Geisler & MacKenzie's Rebuttal

"Protestants reject both purgatory and prayers for the dead. They find no support for either in Scripture."[2]

"There are many reasons the Scriptures forbid praying to Mary and the saints or even venerating their images. Among these several stand out as noteworthy. *God is the only proper object of our prayers*. Nowhere in Scripture is a prayer of anyone on earth actually addressed to anyone but God."[3]

"*It is an idolatrous practice*. Prayer is a form of worship, and only God should be worshipped (Exod. 20:3). It is idolatrous to pray to mere human beings or to bow down before them or an image of them or any other creature."[4]

"*It is forbidden as witchcraft*. The Old Testament condemns all attempts to communicate with the dead along with other condemnations of witchcraft.[5]

"*It is a practical denial of the mediatorship of Christ*. Evangelicals believe that to use any mere human being to mediate with God is an insult to the all-sufficient, divinely appointed mediatorship of Jesus Christ."[6]

"*It is an insult to the intercession of the Holy Spirit*. Much of the practical Catholic justification for praying to the saints is based on the seemingly plausible argument that, because of their position in heaven, dead believers may be better able to intercede on our behalf. This is a practical denial of the ministry of the Holy Spirit, whose task it is to do this very thing on our behalf."[7]

Our Comments

We come to the end of this section on the "Areas of Doctrinal Differences" in hopes of summarizing what is good in the authors presentation but with a

---

[1] Geisler & MacKenzie, pg. 347, emphasis in original

[2] Geisler & MacKenzie, pg. 348

[3] Geisler & MacKenzie, pg. 350

[4] Geisler & MacKenzie, pg. 351

[5] Geisler & MacKenzie, pg. 351

[6] Geisler & MacKenzie, pg. 352

[7] Geisler & MacKenzie, pg. 352

stern warning. In our estimation, the "Areas of Doctrinal Differences" could be cut away from this book and re-labeled: *Why the Roman Catholic Religion is not Christian*, and re-marketed as a good resource book for those who wish to better understand the reasons why Rome is apostate. We have found some very solid and extremely helpful biblical exegesis in virtually all aspects touching upon Roman Catholic dogma and doctrine. The authors are to be complemented on their diligence. Nevertheless, the warning far outweighs the accolades when it comes to evaluating the overall value of their book.

We have pointed out time and time again that the authors have failed miserably to show that post-Tridentine Rome has any affinity with the Catholic (universal) Church of the first 1400 years after Christ. The deliberate intermingling of the term "Catholic" with the term "Roman Catholic" has left us in a hopeless maze of contradiction and dilemma. The writers' insistence on trying to prove that Christianity has all things historical in common with Roman Catholicism was doomed from the start. There is a codified system of theology in Rome that cannot be squashed into the first 14 centuries of the Catholic (universal) Church. Thus, in honesty, the Roman Catholic religion should have been separated from the Catholic or universal Body of Christ rather than compressed as though the two were one and the same. We add the same assessment for the marshalling of pre-Trent theologians. The independent thoughts of stellar theologians cannot find a safe haven in Roman Catholicism, no matter how hard they are squeezed into Romanism.

We have concluded that the "Areas of Doctrinal Agreement" are not only shallow but misleading, being built upon a foundation of sand. The authors have used carefully crafted concepts in hopes of finding common ground with the Gospel of Christ. We have shown that they failed to do so. We have also allowed the authors to show us that no matter what they have affirmed in the "Areas of Doctrinal Agreement" section, they have denied it all in their "Areas of Doctrinal Differences" section. If one were to pit Geisler & MacKenzie Part I, "Areas of Doctrinal Agreement," against Geisler & MacKenzie Part II, "Areas of Doctrinal Differences," there is essentially no contest. The authors may object to this assessment of their work, but their own facts and biblical exegesis leave no room for doubt. Roman Catholicism is not a Christian religion and does not harbor the Gospel of Jesus Christ. Why the authors of *Agreements and Differences* cannot see the plain conclusions of their reasoning is quite beyond us.

The authors' conclusion to each of their sections should have ended in a grand finale appraisal of the Romanist religion as fatal to the Gospel. But the authors do not arrive at this conclusion. We shall allow their own conclusion and summary of the heretical Roman Catholic doctrine of Purgatory, Praying to the Dead and Treasury of Merit to represent in microcosm the danger of their book. As was true in each and every conclusion of these five critical areas of Roman Catholic theology, the authors have failed to protect Christianity and allowed the door to remain open, despite the evidence, for acceptance of Rome as a *bona fide* Christian community:

> "The doctrine of purgatory and its accompanying dogmas are a crucial area of *difference* between Catholics and Protestants. We have examined the biblical basis for these beliefs and found them *seriously wanting*. They are not only extra-biblical but anti-biblical, since they run contrary to fundamental teachings of Scripture, such as the all-sufficiency of the atoning sacrifice of Christ and the uniqueness of God as the sole object of all our devotion and prayer. The only real bases for pronouncing them dogma are conflicting traditions and human speculations often based on apocryphal books that have been rejected from the canon of Scripture by both Catholic and Protestant scholars. These matters were at the heart of the Reformation and continue to be *seemingly insurmountable* theological obstacle (sic) between orthodox Catholics and orthodox Protestants today."[1]

If we were to catalogue all of what the authors have found in Romanism to be anti-biblical, contrary to fundamental teaching, insulting to the Holy Spirit, denying the mediatorship of Christ, idolatrous in practice, undermining of Christ's atonement, misrepresentative of Scripture and a denial of the sufficiency of the cross, to name just a few, we would expect a conclusion from the authors that Rome is apostate. Incredibly, they do not do so. Using the analogy of a hunter, we might say the authors have carefully selected their weapon, i.e., the Word of God. They have honed and polished it as the safeguard of the Gospel. They have become intimately involved with all its wondrous intricacies and have practiced using it and caring for it until the day of the big hunt. Upon arriving at the day of the big hunt, the authors have carefully loaded their weapon (exegesis, logic, revelation, study, line upon line) and gone after a mad rhinoceros which is trampling the vineyard of the Lord's people. Upon discovering the rampaging monster, the authors have shouldered their weapon and taken careful aim. They have cocked the trigger and pointed the mighty weapon at the invader. All wait in hushed silence for the shot which will fell the behemoth. But there is none. The authors refuse to pull the trigger! Instead, they retreat and back peddle away from the monster. Ultimately, there is no kill. The mad rhino senses that the hunter has lost the resolve to defend the vineyard and begins to trample and stomp. The Lord's people begin to scatter. Who will kill the mad rhinoceros if theologians will not pull the trigger?

---

[1] Geisler & MacKenzie, pg. 355, emphasis added

We believe Mr. Geisler and Mr. MacKenzie are on the edge of apostasy in their failure to conclude that Rome is not a Christian religion. There is no safe ground to be found for them. In pointing out all that is fatal to the Gospel in Rome, the authors commit theological suicide in their failure to conclude what the evidence demands. The authors have not been faithful to the Gospel of Christ. They have done the opposite; they have betrayed it. We say this with sadness but with resolve. The authors have cleared the way to affirm apostasy by not denouncing it. Rest assured the next breed of professing Evangelicals will take these writers far beyond where they have imagined in the destruction of the Gospel. The authors are guilty of making the next step toward killing the Gospel an easy one. The authors, like a crooked judge, have found the defendant guilty of harboring a false gospel and declared him innocent. By not expressing the only possible conclusion of the data, they have expressed another devastating conclusion. They have identified Rome as anti-Christ (the evidence is undeniable), but have concluded that it is not fatal. They have given a stamp of approval to call Romanism what it is not. They have attempted to mesmerize the reader into thinking that Christianity is so elastic as to admit the repugnant doctrines of Romanism.

Ultimately, the authors have informed us that Rome is acceptable and to be condoned as an alternative worshipping community. Though this is not stated, the net result is unavoidable. The authors have changed the focus from the historical fight with Rome as an apostate religion, to a nonjudgmental explanation as to why Evangelicals and Roman Catholics find it difficult—but not impossible—to have ecclesiastical unity. This subtle shift leaves them teetering on the edge and unable to embrace the only thing which can rescue them from their precarious position: the Gospel of Jesus Christ.

The motivation which we believe drives the authors will be discussed in an upcoming chapter. We exit Geisler & MacKenzie with a better appreciation of how difficult it will be to defend the Gospel of Jesus Christ in the coming years.

Geisler & MacKenzie have done a masterful job of maximizing the alleged agreements with Rome and minimizing the devastating disagreements with her. But what is even more compelling is the ease with which the authors are able to withstand the heresies of Rome while promoting Rome as essentially Christian. As we have said before, there is a new breed of Evangelicals who are fearless in their acceptance of heresy in order to accommodate a new world order where Rome is said to be home.

Part III
The Ecumenical Mindset

The Bridge Builders

WHEN FACED WITH a choice whether to be strident with the truth of the Gospel or to relax the truth ever so slightly in favor of enlarging the circle of his followers, the Apostle Paul chose the former. We believe the Apostle had a mindset for truth and its protection. We do not believe the Apostle favored an ecumenical mindset. On the contrary, he was willing to admit that his labors would have been in vain had the struggling band of communities he established departed from the *truth* of the Gospel. We sense the Apostle was far more worried about the *truth* of the Gospel than in trying to bring together religious communities under any other guise of unity. For the Apostle Paul, *truth* was of maximum importance. All else flowed from *truth*. Unity without *truth* was not a consideration:

> "To whom we gave place by subjection, no, not for an hour; that the *truth* of the gospel might continue with you" (Galatians 2:5).

The Apostle Paul was born a Jew. He was, "Circumcised the eighth day, of the stock of Israel, of the tribe of Benjamin, an Hebrew of the Hebrews…" (Philippians 3:5). No one had a better understanding of the Law of God and more zeal for the traditions of his ancestors. By his own confession, Paul was a religious zealot. He viewed the world, in a religious sense, as composed of either Jew (God's people) or Gentile (pagans). A person was either "of Abraham" or was "of the heathen." Paul took seriously all the prophetic warnings issued by God to the Jews which strictly forbade them from intermingling with the nations. Israel was warned time and time again not to pick up the practices of the heathen nations around them, which warnings they often ignored, to their own harm. Knowing this, Paul carried that zeal into his life as a Christian. To him, a person was either of the true God of Abraham in Christ, or of the myriads of false gods from the surrounding Gentiles, be they Greek, Roman or Egyptian. The unthinkable was to blend these radically opposed religious communities together.

The mind of Paul was not framed in an environment of religious toleration and ecumenism. This would have been foreign to the teaching of the God of Israel. This helps to explain Paul's virulent attacks against the early Christian communities. Paul calls himself, "a persecutor, and injurious" to the

Church of Jesus Christ (1 Timothy 1:13). Paul did not apologize for his zeal—he apologized only for his ignorance. To him, zeal for the truth was as necessary as the truth itself. It is no surprise that God converted and used this Saul of Tarsus to become the zealous defender of the truth of the Gospel of Jesus Christ. It is equally unsurprising that Paul brought with him a zeal, albeit without violence, to protect the Gospel against dilution of any kind.

That the truth of the Gospel was preëminent with Paul is exhibited in his many defenses of it. However, we are particularly interested in his stalwart defense of the Gospel against his fellow kinsmen in the flesh. In his example, we see a lesson for the church today. We believe that Paul was subject to an appeal by his kinsmen in the flesh (Israel) to relax a little and focus on common beliefs and traditions rather than the strictness of the Gospel. The litmus test of Paul's willingness to forsake his own kinsmen presented itself in the form of those who rejected Christianity outright and those who wished to add Moses to Christ. Paul considered both equally fatal to the truth. The direct opposition to the Gospel by the nation of Israel is not our focus here. We wish rather to center in on the more subtle destruction of the Gospel from those who would dilute it with the Law of Moses. An appeal was made to allow the inclusion of circumcision as part of the Gospel of Jesus Christ.

Let us center in on two occasions where the Church responds to the suggestion that circumcision be admitted as part of the Gospel equation. We wish to keep in mind that Paul was not asked to include some sort of Egyptian love feast or Greek ritual in the Gospel equation. He was pressured by members of his own religious community. They were monotheists (one God only). They were clean (Israelites by birth). They could trace their lineage back to the Patriarchs and believed in the God of Moses. They held much in common with Paul. They rejoiced in the rich traditions. They had in common the "holding onto" of Jewish culture in the midst of Roman captivity. These were brothers and sisters of Paul, according to the flesh, "Who are Israelites; to whom pertaineth the adoption, and the glory, and the covenants, and the giving of the law, and the service of God, and the promises; Whose are the fathers, and of whom as concerning the flesh Christ came..." (Romans 9:4-5).

Apparently some had come to a faith in the Lord Jesus Christ. However, they brought with them this one small anathema which the Church knew to be fatal to the Gospel it had been commissioned to preach and protect: "Except ye be circumcised after the manner of Moses, ye cannot be saved" (Acts 15:1).

At the Council of Jerusalem (Acts 15) the Apostles were faced with an opportunity for expansion and perhaps inclusion of a great number of Jews.

They may have stood to double their ranks if only they would relax the Gospel a little bit. We notice the strong suggestion comes via professed "believers" from a sect of the Pharisees. However, were they in fact true believers of the true Gospel?

> "But there rose up certain of the sect of the Pharisees which believed, saying, That it was needful to circumcise them, and to command them to keep the law of Moses" (Acts 15:5).

The decision of the Council of Jerusalem was a victory for the Gospel. We see it as a defeat for incipient ecumenism. Rather than buckle under pressure to add a time-honored Jewish custom, which may have swelled their ranks, and apply it to those who were coming to Christ from the Gentiles, the Apostles said "No." They wished instead to protect the Gospel against the Law of Moses. They saw circumcision as being in competition with a straightforward Gospel. The Gospel was affirmed and the yoke of the Law of Moses was not put on the neck of Gentiles converts. The glorious conclusion at the Council of Jerusalem in Acts 15 is summarized by verse eleven:

> "But we believe that through the grace of the Lord Jesus Christ we shall be saved, even as they" (Acts 15:11).

The Apostle Paul, along with the others, determined that it would compromise the Gospel to add any thing to the finished work of Christ. The Gospel could not remain "the Gospel" once circumcision was admitted to the equation. Nor do we think that the council was only concerned that circumcision not be "pushed" onto the Gentile believers. It was also not to be required of Jewish converts, either.

We now move to a second episode where zeal for the Gospel again takes precedence over an inclusion of circumcision or any other aspect of the Mosaic Law. The Council at Jerusalem not withstanding, Peter himself was caught up in the pressure to conform to his kinsmen's Moses-oriented mentality. In Galatians 2, Paul recounts the story of how he had to stand for the Gospel even against Peter—the very same Peter who had stood against the Pharisees at the council of Jerusalem!(Acts 15:7). When Peter came to Antioch, Paul challenged him for eating with Gentiles until Jews came around. When the Jews arrived, Peter would hide his ham sandwich (so to speak) and ignore the Gentiles. And this from the one who had received revelation from Christ that eating such food was perfectly acceptable! (Acts 10). Yet Peter found himself compromising in order to avoid the peer pressure of the Jewish contingent that still wanted Christ *and* Moses. Paul rebuked Peter, saying that he "walked not uprightly according to the truth of the gospel" (Galatians 2:14).

The Council of Jerusalem should have settled the question once and for all. The Gospel was not to include circumcision. The Gospel was not to include the prescriptions of the Law of Moses. The Gospel was not a re-admission into a set of Jewish laws and traditions. The Gospel was not a New Law of new works to be performed. The new wine would burst the old wineskins. The new cloth would rip away the old garment. Paul therefore withstood those who would pressure him into adulterating the Gospel by mixing the Law with it. Those who persisted in this "hypocrisy" were disenfranchised from the Gospel:

> "For I testify again to every man that is circumcised, that he is a debtor to do the whole law. Christ is become of no effect unto you, whosoever of you are justified by the law; ye are fallen from grace" (Galatians 5:3-4).

We can see, when it came to the Gospel, there is not a hint of the ecumenical mindset with Paul. He does not flinch:

> "For do I now persuade men, or God? or do I seek to please men? for if I yet pleased men, I should not be the servant of Christ" (Galatians 1:10).

These words come from the apostle who, by his own testimony, was "above many my equals in mine own nation, being more exceedingly zealous of the traditions of my fathers" (Galatians 1:14). Paul felt the pressure and temptation to allow such things as common history and traditions to cloud the clarity of the Gospel. But he would not:

> "Beware of dogs, beware of evil workers, beware of the concision. For we are the circumcision, which worship God in the spirit, and rejoice in Christ Jesus, and have no confidence in the flesh. Though I might also have confidence in the flesh. *If any other man thinketh that he hath whereof he might trust in the flesh, I more*" (Philippians 3:2-4).

We point out all of this to reinforce an important, and perhaps most critical, detail when considering the Roman Catholic religion. For we see parallels between Paul and Judaism, and modern Evangelicals and Romanism. The obvious comparison is that of common traditions and monotheism. Well might the Judaizers have argued (*a la* Geisler & MacKenzie), "But we share five covenants (Adamic, Noahic, Abrahamic, Mosaic and Davidic), four millennia, three tribes (Judah, Benjamin and Levi), two witnesses (the Law and the Prophets), and one God." But the Apostle Paul was keenly aware that commonality with Israel on the fact of the existence of God, a shared world view, collective ancestral traditions, shared Mosaic Law and the fellow covenantal citizenship did not equal out to the Gospel of Christ. In fact, Paul was willing to forsake all of it in light of the greater *truth* of the Gospel. For Paul, everything centered around the Gospel—not monotheism or zeal for God or a socio-economic culture. Paul was faced with the decision of having to forsake his own people even though he knew they had a zeal for God. Paul had more in common with Israel by far than anyone else on the planet, but he was unwilling to compromise the Gospel to accommodate the dead religion they insisted on bringing to the table. Listen to his lament:

> "Brethren, my heart's desire and prayer to God for Israel is, that they might be saved. For I bear them record that they have a zeal of God, but not according to knowledge. For they being ignorant of God's righteousness, and going about to establish their own righteousness, have not submitted themselves unto the righteousness of God" (Romans 10:1-3).

Paul is praying for the salvation of his own countrymen who had a zeal for God! But having a zeal for God does not qualify one for salvation in the eyes of Paul. The reason why zeal is insufficient for salvation is because the zeal itself can conflict with the Gospel of Christ if it is not informed by the Gospel. Paul laments that Israel had not "knowledge" in its zeal for God. They did not know about God's righteousness, and instead, they established their own and did not subject themselves to the righteousness of God. In the case of Israel, they had a zeal for God and they had their own righteousness but they were lost. Israel simply could not see that Christ was the end of the Law for righteousness. They did not embrace the righteousness of Christ by faith apart from works of the Law. In fact they were unwilling to forsake their own righteousness, and were willing to anathematize all who disagreed! (Acts 15:1).

We believe Paul's firm stand for the Gospel against his religious countrymen is our example today. Evangelicals are caving in to cultural considerations, and as a result are abandoning the Gospel in hopes of forming social and religious alliances with those outside of Christianity. As Judaism was the litmus test to prove Paul's resolve to stand firm, so Roman Catholicism is our test to validate our resolve to stand firm for the truth of the Gospel.

Paul lived in a day and age where he could have used all the help he could get. One can only imagine the multitudes of religious ideologies presented to the inquiring mind of the first and second century. It is no wonder Paul was thrown out of Ephesus for preaching Christ, *and thrown out of synagogues by Jews for the same offense!* The radicalness of the Gospel Paul preached would offend any religion and certainly not make many friends among the religious elite of his day. Thus, to find a ready ally to reinforce the Gospel in the thick of the fight would have appealed to Paul. However, the reinforcement could not be "included" if it in any way mitigated the exclusiveness of the Gospel. Paul realized that to forfeit the Gospel in his fight was, in effect, to disarm himself; the message Paul preached precluded mass participation since it exposed error in all other religions. In short, the message was destined for loneliness. The reason for this resides in the heart of the Gospel which calls down the religions of men and offers only one alternative. Paul, like Evangelicals today, felt the pressure to find allies to help in the battle. The problem with Paul was that he refused to lower his admission standards to enlist more soldiers. He insisted that all fellow combatants first embrace the Gospel and then—and only then—join the foray. We believe that the pressure is so severe on the Gospel of Christ in our society that Evangelicals are looking for all the help they can get. The Romanist religion, like Judaism of its day, appears appealing under such stress, yet in order to include it, we would first have to lay down the very weapon with which the battle must be won. We believe that Paul's example of avoiding any compromise of the Gospel in favor of expanding his religious beachhead in the Middle East is our example to follow today.

We can see from Scripture that Paul's zeal for the Gospel overwhelmed the lure of diluting it. Paul refused to focus on common heritage, monotheism, the Law of God and descendency from Abraham. Paul was unwilling to distill the Gospel down to a reduction of the absurd. By this we mean that Paul was not content to find the lowest common denominator of the Gospel—"saved by Christ"—and allow it to absorb the shock of adding circumcision or customs or the laws of Israel. He was unwilling to increase the size of Christianity by rallying around a "Jesus plus" gospel:

> "But neither Titus, who was with me, being a Greek, was compelled to be circumcised: And that because of false brethren unawares brought in, who came in privily to spy out our liberty which we have in Christ Jesus, that they might bring us into bondage: To whom we gave place by subjection, no, not for an hour; *that the truth of the gospel* might continue with you" (Galatians 2:3-5).

What Has Changed Since Then?

We believe there is a redefining of the truth and a willingness to allow "outside" environments to dictate the meaning of the Gospel. This is perhaps the chief characteristic of the ecumenical mindset. Paul viewed everything from inside the Gospel out toward society and then stood rigidly inflexible to any environment that would compromise the Gospel. However, some modern professing Evangelicals are being coaxed to look at the Gospel *from* the environment and are contemplating its obsolescence. In short, Paul measured the environment by the Gospel, while moderns are in essence measuring the Gospel by the environment. As a result, there is a new gospel in the land vying for the place of preëminence.

The heart and soul of the mission of Jesus Christ was the individual reconciliation of God to man. God reconciling Himself to one person at a time, through the death of His Son, is the heartbeat of the New Testament Gospel. The primary and chief concern of Jesus Christ was to fulfill the will of His heavenly Father and die in the place of sinners. He did not come to build a political empire, much to the chagrin of some, nor did He come to set an example of selfless love, though this He did. He came to seek and to save the lost. He did not come to judge the world *but to proclaim that its judgment had been determined already* (John 3:18). He came to offer escape from the penalty and judgment that sin was due. The burden of the New Testament is to showcase the glory of God in the individual conversion to Jesus Christ Who is the Way and the Truth and the Life. No one can go to the Father except through Him (John 14:6). The world is passing away and all who come to Christ have been enabled by God to see the unseen with spiritual eyes. This emphasis on individual conversion to a heavenly city transcends all political, socio-economic and ideological boundaries. It is not restricted to a peculiar political system nor does it give rise to any one particular socio-economic structuring. The chief concern of the Gospel is the Kingdom of God. The intent of the Gospel is not to create a social and political system which is more suitable for Christians to live in. The focus of the Gospel is to "Set your affection on things above, not on things on the earth. For ye are dead, and your life is hid with Christ in God" (Colossians 3:2-3);

> "For many walk, of whom I have told you often, and now tell you even weeping, that they are the enemies of the cross of Christ: Whose end is destruction, whose God is their belly, and whose glory is in their shame, who mind earthly things. For our conversation is in heaven; from whence also we look for the Saviour, the Lord Jesus Christ: Who shall change our vile body, that it may be fashioned like unto his glorious body, according to the working whereby he is able even to subdue all things unto himself" (Philippians 3:18-21).

Naturally, there is an ethical outgrowth stemming from the reception of the Gospel in the hearts of men. When men go from rebellious God-haters at heart, to submission to God through the conviction of the Gospel of their need for reconciliation, there is a corresponding ethical transformation. Men stop lying about the truth and they begin to stop lying to each other. Honesty and integrity are restored in the heart as well as a new rule of order where Christ is the master of behavior. "For sin shall not have dominion over you: for ye are not under the law, but under grace" (Romans 6:14). This ethical transformation, *sanctification*, will filter out into society as laws become more just and Christians serve as lights in the darkness. But all of this is a *by-product* of individual conversion to Christ through the Gospel preached. It is not the Gospel itself.

What we find in the ecumenical mindset, however, is a willingness to preach the thing produced as the thing which produces it. In other words, the result of the Gospel faithfully preached has given us a Judeo-Christian culture. This culture finds its roots in the Law of God given to Israel and in the New Covenant commands given by Christ to His followers. The ecumenical mindset believes so strongly in the Judeo-Christian culture that it is willing to make *it* the gospel. Thus, the culture (the thing produced) is preached *as* the gospel (the thing which produces it). The reason we call this a different gospel goes back to why the Apostle Paul could not find help in his day. The very nature and dynamic of the Gospel precludes acceptance by those who love *only the result of the preaching of the Gospel*, but have not a clue as to the cause of the result, i.e., the Gospel itself. In short, zeal for God or a Judeo-Christian culture is no more respected by the Gospel than Israel's zeal for God was in the first century. So, in order to bring together those who have a zeal for God and the Judeo-Christian culture, the Gospel of Jesus Christ has to be changed or eliminated. In our day, we are seeing just this before our eyes. The tail has begun to wag the dog!

The efforts to bring Romanists together with Christians *as Christians* has no hope of success if the Gospel is in control. The preaching of the Word of God for individual conversion to Christ leaves no hope for the Romanist system. But if our motivation is to have a Judeo-Christian culture, then the Gospel will be the first casualty when Rome moves in to share the battle. We believe the Gospel is being set aside in favor of what the Gospel produces, i.e., a Christian-influenced culture. This, of course, is nonsense, for one cannot have the thing produced without the producer. But so strong is the delusion, and so fearful are some of losing their culture, that a new gospel of Judeo-Christian *culture* is preached throughout the land. The proponents of this will gain in appeal rather than diminish as we move into the 21st century. The new gospel is the gospel of culture, and the culture hoped for is a combination of Romanism and many other "ism's," as well. This new gospel will be called upon to save the Western world from its own decay. It will be called upon to rescue the West from the impending doom of atheism, cultism, far eastern mysticism and other religions of the world.

But it will fail in the task which has been cast upon it, for this new gospel asks only for a zeal for God while tolerating an ignorance of His righteousness in Christ. That gospel could not save the Jews, and it will not save our culture any more than an effect can bring about the cause.

Apostasy *du Jour*

Perhaps the most important ingredient in the stew of apostasy is the increasingly popular notion that Christianity is to be understood as having faith in God rather than having faith in anything about God. There is emerging within American Evangelicalism a false dichotomy which seeks to separate confidence in doctrinal propositions about God from confidence in God. Gordon Clark writes against this dichotomy and the dangers accompanying it in his work, *Today's Evangelism: Counterfeit or Genuine?*:

> "Mark 1:15 commands us to 'believe in the Gospel.' Some people make a distinction between believing a written account and believing in a person. This verse undermines such a distinction. Really, when one believes *in* a person, he believes the words the person speaks—he believes his promises and his asserted ability to perform. This is what is meant by saying that we trust a person. ...The point is particularly appropriate for the present days of apostasy. The liberals use the name of Jesus Christ, and some other historic terms, as symbols to evoke some pious emotions. The phrases often sound good. But after a little study we discover that their Jesus was not born of a virgin, never raised Lazarus from the dead, and never himself came out of the tomb. Their Jesus is an empty name without intellectual content, a mere emotional idol. Real Christians believe the truth about Jesus: that he actually was virgin-born, that he actually said, 'the Son of Man came... to give his life a ransom for many,' and that this is precisely what He did on the cross. It is the intellectual content, the message, that counts. ...For further emphasis note also this passage from Klaas Runia, in his *Reformation Today* (pg. 56): 'One of the most popular slogans in contemporary theology is that truth in the New Testament does not mean doctrinal truth about Christ but a personal knowledge of Christ. We believe that such a contrast between propositional conceptual truth (truth about) and personal truth (knowledge of) is utterly foreign to the New Testament.'"[1]

The "distinction" or the "contrast" of which Clark complains is the idea that we can experience God to the maximum but need not have any confidence in doctrinal propositions about Him, or that trusting in the Person precludes any need to trust in His message. From this platform many unfortunate leaps are made. It is suggested that one's personal relationship with God is the basis for unity. One should meet Jesus and come to know Him personally as Lord. One is urged to have a full and active faith. But while these tunes about *meeting* Jesus and *experiencing* Jesus and *loving* Jesus are strummed, there is another drum roll in the background. This drum roll beats out the steady rhythm of anti-doctrine and anti-theology.

Suppose we try to convince someone to believe in God as found in the Bible. Our first attempts may be put off by a person who says, "I already

---

[1] Clark, Gordon H., *Today's Evangelism: Counterfeit or Genuine?*, (Jefferson, MD: The Trinity Foundation, ©1990) pp. 34-36, 50-51

believe in God." We then begin to probe and ask questions about the god that is the object of this person's faith. The answer comes back that it is faith in God and a personal relationship with God that really matters, not some doctrines about God. "But," we ask, "how do you know that you are worshiping the right God?" The answer comes back, "There is only one God and I am connected with him in my own personal way. That is what really matters!" At this juncture we are left feeling uneasy. Our conversation would have to end if we had brought with us the erroneous assumption that faith itself is more important than the object of the faith, or further, that one's faith is more important than God's own doctrinal propositions about Himself. Obviously, this leaves a person in great danger of believing in a god of his imagination—that is, in an idol.

It seems obvious that faith is empty if God can be stripped of His content. His content is expressed through doctrinal propositions which He Himself has revealed. The first ingredient toward apostasy is the assertion, "It is not the truth *about* Jesus that is the basis of conversion, but rather the truth *of* Jesus that really counts." This terribly unnatural separation of the doctrinal truths of Christianity from Christianity itself has led to the ruination of the Gospel. Indeed, it has taken root in Evangelicalism already. We are being told that one is saved by coming to a person—not by believing something said about the person. This is typical ecumenical nonsense, and leads easily into the Roman error of coming to Jesus *in the Eucharist*. We are converted only when we come to the right person, believing the correct message about Him. One cannot hope to separate Jesus from the message He preached. One cannot hope to have a relationship with God except on God's terms. One cannot truly worship Him Who is not known.

When once we give up doctrinal integrity, the entire thing collapses into a mish-mash of sentiment and feelings. We have heard it said that one is not saved by any definition of salvation but rather by God. Now it is true that believing in a definition of salvation without acting on the implications and commands of all that the definition entails is hopeless. However, it is equally impossible to conjure up salvation for anyone without a definition of what salvation actually is. If faith comes by hearing, and hearing by the Word of God through the faithful preacher (Romans 10:14-17), then how will any be saved without definitions? Or without the preaching of the Word? How will one know the Gospel unless the Gospel is taught? How can one be saved unless one is told the truth about God? And how will the truth be told if truth itself is deemed irrelevant to the Gospel?

There is much at stake here. The essential thrust of all ecumenism is to eliminate all but the simplest statements about God and Jesus Christ. The first ingredient for apostasy among Evangelicals is to buy into the lie that we can separate the doctrine of God's revelation from God Himself.

When once doctrine and truth are played down, what remains is only man's experience, and taking this cue, Evangelicals are beginning to jump on the bandwagon of *experiencing* God as opposed to *knowing* about God. Yet, the fly in the ointment is that one cannot properly experience God without a proper knowledge of Him. We agree that there are many who know about Christ but never believe in Christ. But to use this as an excuse to rid the Church of knowing about God and to fail to define *what* we know about God, is reprehensible. It opens the door for an experience-based gospel void of any doctrinal integrity. It also tends to measure Christianity by the whitewash on the sepulcher rather than by faith in God's Gospel.

Ultimately, this mindset will forge ahead carrying a gospel without content, appealing to the emotions rather than to God's truth. Exit: Sin, Righteousness and Judgment—the object of this new gospel is to have an encounter with God. Enter: self-worth, behavior modification, and non-judgmentalism. Later on we shall see that the measure of conversion will be one's willingness to sign on with the "clean up the world" congregation. The litmus test of true conversion will have nothing to do with believing the propositions of Scripture, but rather with a person's willingness to alter his behavior. The new Great Commission will be a willingness to cooperate in cleaning up the moral decay of the Western world, having a nonjudgmental attitude toward other religions, living a pious life and practicing one's religion in a fair and just manner. This new order of pseudo-Christianity will, of course, include Roman Catholicism as well as all others who can confess to a similar contact with the unknown god of man's unenlightened experience.

The apostle Paul understood that there were many in his day who had a great zeal for God. He understood better than most that one can have a great zeal for God and still be absolutely ignorant of Him. Far from applauding those of his own nation who had met and accepted God in the reality of their religious experience, Paul seeks to ground his religious countrymen in proper doctrine:

> "Brethren, my heart's desire and prayer to God for Israel is, that they might be saved. For I bear them record that they have a zeal of God, but not according to knowledge" (Romans 10:1-2).

Surely the modern ecumenists would chastise Paul. They would be quick to tell Paul, "It is not faith in some doctrinal proposition about God that saves Israel, but rather faith in God that is essential. Leave them alone. We need their help against the Romans!"

So what's new? Armed with the weapon of indifference toward doctrinal propositions which might slow down the *Ecumenical Express*, we are not surprised to read this oxymoronic excerpt from an Evangelical on the edge of apostasy:

> "As Harold O. J. Brown has written, 'to the extent that a Catholic and a Protestant are orthodox, there is more by far that unites them than divides them, particularly over against the monolithic secular culture of today.' ...There are ...apparently insurmountable obstacles for orthodox Catholics and conservative evangelicals. What we make reference to here is exploring areas of personal and social cooperation, as well as evangelistic efforts, noting some of our common spiritual heritage."[1]

Such is the blindness of the ecumenist that he cannot see that within the space of a few lines he totally contradicts himself. We notice that an assumption lingers which presumes that all that unites us with Rome is vastly superior to that which divides us, especially if we compare ourselves to rank atheism and humanism. Not much of a contest. But this comparison is meaningless in light of the fact that Rome does not have anything in common with Christianity when it comes to what really matters about Christianity. Furthermore, we marvel at how any author can state boldly that *insurmountable obstacles* exist between Catholics and Evangelicals, yet go on to assert that *joint* evangelism is to be explored. Only in a world where doctrine is irrelevant can these two contradictory statements be reconciled.

The first ingredient of apostasy, therefore, is to minimize the doctrine of salvation. When this is accomplished through witty little half-truisms like, "No one was ever saved by believing in the definition of justification," or, "No one is ever saved by believing *about* God rather than *in* God," the door is open to add yet more ingredients to the apostasy stew.

"With Fear As Our Motivation, Let Us Press On!"

The above caption sums up the second ingredient of apostasy stew. We have labored to show that the differences between the religion of Rome and the Gospel of Jesus Christ are absolutely and without a doubt fatal to each other. One of these two religions has to go. They both cannot be true, as they are supremely antithetical. They both cannot have been produced by the Gospel of Christ. Yet we have also shown time and time again that modern Evangelical authors are ignoring these differences or waving them off as trifles when compared with other considerations. And what are these other considerations?

---

[1] Geisler & MacKenzie, pg. 407

Undoubtedly, the engine that drives the ecumenical train is a groveling, abject and obsequious fear of losing what is loosely defined as Western culture. This is the second ingredient of apostasy stew. If tragically overlooking the doctrinal chasm which separates us from Rome—like so many ostriches with their heads in the sand—is the vegetable of apostate stew, then cultural consideration is the meat. So dominant is the fear of losing the so called "cultural wars," that Evangelicals are willing to sell out the Gospel for a chance to promote some fuzzy ideas of a Western society.

After quoting favorably from Keith Fournier, a self-confessed "Evangelical Catholic," Geisler & MacKenzie conclude that this is the "kind of Roman Catholic with whom many wish to align themselves to face the unbelief of this culture."[1] Here in a nutshell is apostasy stew being served up for mass distribution. We will have more to say about Mr. Fournier in our next section. Let it suffice to say that Mr. Geisler and Mr. MacKenzie are on record as saying that some, like Keith Fournier, are to be aligned with to face the *unbelief* of this culture. We shall come back to this citation when we analyze the *unbelief* of Mr. Fournier and others just like him.

For now, let us get to the heart of what we are calling the second ingredient of apostasy. Keep in mind that the two ingredients are often found together in one statement or proposition, and that they mix together in a broth to complement each other in an increasingly offensive odor. The willingness to have a content-less gospel that seeks the lowest common denominator—along with a terrifying fear that the culture is being lost to secularism—is the substance of this stew. Listen carefully as the authors set the table:

> "Since evangelicals and Roman Catholics have so much in common *doctrinally* and morally, and, in spite of our significant *intramural doctrinal differences*, we believe that there are, nonetheless, many areas of common spiritual heritage and practical social and moral cooperation possible."[2]
>
> "Our common *doctrinal* and moral beliefs are too large and the need in America for a united voice on them is too great for us to dwell on our differences to the neglect of crucial cooperation needed to fight the forces of evil in our society and our world."[3]

Essentially, for Geisler & MacKenzie, it comes down to this: "What should we give up in order to have Rome as an ally?" It is, without question, the position of some modern Evangelicals that we should take the approach,

---

[1] Geisler & MacKenzie, pg. 409

[2] Geisler & MacKenzie, pg. 357, emphasis added

[3] Geisler & MacKenzie, pg. 357, emphasis added

"Live and let live" when it comes to Roman Catholicism. It is a position that forfeits the Gospel of Christ for the sake of social cooperation; it is a position that forfeits the inheritance literally for a bowl of soup!

We shall save many of our conclusions for the end of this book, but for now we need to make certain the reader knows what is really happening to the Gospel in America. At one time, there were no takers for anyone who tried to market Roman Catholicism as even an approximation of the Christian religion. The reasons were obvious. The doctrine of Rome could not pass the test of the Bible. From baptismal regeneration to purgatory, Rome was weighed in the balance of Scriptures and found wanting. That this was true was plainly evident from a simple comparison of the Dogmas of Rome with the Holy Scriptures. Cultural considerations were not even a remote factor in settling the issue. It was cut and dried. Rome was of another spirit. This was the unanimous opinion of all of the Reformers, and not one Protestant denomination coming out of the Reformation would have dreamed of accepting the heresies of Rome at any cost. Indeed, many took death over compromise with Rome. What has changed? Has Rome changed its gospel? We and everyone else (including Rome) agree that Rome is the same doctrinally as she was at the Council of Trent. In fact, Rome is actually further afield today than during the Reformation with the addition of Papal Infallibility and the Marian doctrines. So, what has changed to make her so attractive to the Protestant?

Actually, there are two major changes. The first is Rome's marketing methods. Rome has capitalized on the relative morals of the world to offer an alternative in ethics and values. Also, Rome is selling the product with new and improved packaging by emphasizing the family, wholesomeness, the right to life and other socially conservative positions. The second change is credited to Evangelicals. The Evangelical leadership of America has lost its backbone. It truly does stand on the edge of apostasy. Retreating from any hard and fast doctrinal positions, public speakers, radio and television personalities, seminaries and Bible colleges are seeking to be "user friendly" in hopes of attracting a greater following. We suspect that money is a prime motivator as we view the landscape. We are concerned that there are so many "Evangelical ministries" vying for the Christian dollar in our society. In our opinion, the Gospel and sound theology have given way to methodology and friendship with the world. This friendship is not explicitly stated but it is felt within professing Evangelicalism. More and more colleges and seminaries are using Madison Avenue methods to attract students. Doctrine and theology are considered by many to be impractical or complicated or divisive in the Body of Christ. Dilution of truth eventually leads to alliances and compacts with those who are single-issue oriented. Under the guise of the end justifying the means, certain groups become allied for a single social issue. Soon, doctrinal issues seem to be in the way of getting things done, and the rehabilitation of society becomes the goal rather than the preaching of the Gospel of Christ. Then, visible signs of societal improvement are sought among coalitions, and the Gospel is redefined and the essence of Christianity is measured by its efficiency in Westernizing the world. Social justice, democracy, feeding the poor, and voucher systems for private education become some of the rallying cries of those involved in religion. In this new world of poorly defined terms and sloppy theology, voices are raised up to put an end to the acrimony that has existed so long between Roman Catholicism and Christianity. Voices wish to exorcise the ghosts of the past and merge together to fight the cultural wars of our day. As a result, addressing the social issues becomes the gospel, and it suddenly becomes religiously correct to speak in terms of the *error* of the Protestant Reformation. A reconstruction of history begins to take place: "The radicals of the past must be seen in a new light. The Reformers must be corrected for their misguided appraisal of Rome. Terminology must be adjusted to counteract any glaring differences. Call them 'dissimilarities,' but do not call them 'errors.' Call Rome 'another worshiping community,' but do not call it 'anti-Christ.' Focus on the minimal. Press the Triune God and the Deity of Christ. Make the gospel stretch to fit in the Mass, Purgatory, Indulgences and the veneration of Mary. Stir the pot and make the stew. After all, there is a culture war to be won!"

Apostasy is a complicated process. It takes many cooks at many levels to contribute to the final stew. Apostasy generally starts at the top and works its way down. This means that the theologians go bad first, and then those whom they teach, and then those in pulpit who are before the people week in and week out. A pastor of a local church can go bad and not much is going to change. He might even find himself out of a job if the church is strong enough to dismiss him! But it is quite another story if the teachers of the pastors go bad. One seminary professor or Bible college professor could impact thousands of would-be pastors and missionaries. One popular radio or television personality could affect millions of people. If the theology goes apostate at the top, it will soon filter its way throughout the Evangelical community.

This is why we believe this book to be of vital importance; this is why we have analyzed the theologians first. It is no secret that the theologians will impact the popular speakers, who will in turn impact the rest of America. Thus, we wish to root any apostasy out at the core. Norman Geisler and Ralph MacKenzie are well respected theologians. Their book will impact students at seminaries and Bible colleges, so we have taken aim at them first. We will next move to the popular professing Evangelicals who have taken the wind from the theologians into their sails and marketed the apostasy. In many cases they have added their own spices. But before we move on to them, we wish to end this section by interacting one last time with Geisler & MacKenzie.

We focus our attention on the final page of their book. From page 502, we believe we can summarize all that has gone wrong with the gospel in America and why we feel these two men have done a great disservice to the Gospel of Christ and led a parade of theologians, teachers, popular speakers, church leaders and confessing Christians to the edge of apostasy.

The authors frame for us the burning question of the Reformation:

> "In the final analysis, then, the question is this: is Roman Catholicism (since Trent) a false church with significant truth in it, as the Reformers believed, or is it a true church with significant error in it? Since, a 'true church' must proclaim the 'true gospel' (Gal. 1:8; 2:4), the answer will depend on what is essential to the true gospel."[1]

We notice two things in the framing of this question. First, the authors concede the point that the Reformers viewed post-Trent Roman Catholicism as a false church.[2] Secondly, the authors are willing to say that in order for

---

[1] Geisler & MacKenzie, pg. 502

[2] Point in fact, the Reformers had many terse words for Rome and the amalgamation of her doctrinal heresies. We mention just a few:

"Ah, my dear brother in Christ, bear with me if here or elsewhere I use such coarse language when speaking of the wretched, confronted, atrocious monster at Rome! He who knows my thoughts must say that I am much, much, much too lenient and have neither words nor thought adequately to describe the shameful, abominable blasphemy to which he subjects the Word and name of Christ, our dear Lord and Savior. *There are some Christians, wicked Christians indeed, who now would gloss things over to make the pope appear against in a good light and who, after he does so and has been dragged out of the mud, would like to reinstate him on the altar. But they are wicked people, whoever they may be, who defend the pope and want me to be quiet about the means whereby he has done harm.* Truly, I cannot do this. All true, pious Christians, who love Christ and His Word, should, as said, be sincerely hostile to the pope. They should persecute him and injure him...All should do this in their several calling, to the best of their ability, with all faithfulness and diligence. (*What Luther Says*, II:1072)

"What kind of a church is the pope's church? It is an uncertain, vacillating and tottering church. Indeed, it is a deceitful, lying church, doubting and unbelieving, without God's Word. For the pope with his wrong keys teaches his church to doubt and to be uncertain. If it is a vacillating church, then it is not the church of faith, for the latter is founded upon a rock, and the gates of hell cannot prevail against it (Matt. 16:18). If it is not the church of faith, then it is not the christian church, but it must be an unchristian, antichristian, and faithless church which destroys and ruins the real, holy, Christian church." (*Luther's Works*, vol. 40, Church and ministry II, The Keys, p. 348)"

"In this same way the Romanists vex us today and frighten the uneducated with the name of the church, even though they are Christ's chief adversaries. Therefore, although they
continued on following page

a church to be a legitimate Christian Church, it must preach the true Gospel. So far, so good.

It is at this juncture that the stew of apostasy begins to permeate the air surrounding these two theologians. Rather than come right out with it and side with the Reformers and say that Rome is a false church, the authors introduce new categories of thought. Let us stay with them as they seek to minimize the impact of any description which might present Rome in such stark and unflinching terms as those used by our Evangelical forefathers:

> "First, there is a difference between whether Catholics can be truly saved inside their system and whether their system officially proclaims the true gospel. Virtually everyone recognizes that one can be saved by believing the gospel in spite of being a part of a system that may officially deny essential parts of the gospel."[1]

Here comes the double-speak and the theological mist of which we have spoken. Geisler & MacKenzie show themselves to be absolutely oblivious to the obvious. They ignore the reality that in Romanism, *their gospel* ***is*** *the system.* We ask, "How can a Roman Catholic be truly saved within their system when the system itself is a formal denial of the Gospel?" If the system does not proclaim the Gospel—and it does not—then salvation must come from without. Period. If the point here is that Roman Catholics can be saved despite being in a false church, we agree. That is precisely why we believe they should be evangelized. But we see a different point being made here. We see the authors fudging on the hard core truth. There is some tap dancing going on. The impression is made that since salvation *could* occur while one is within the Roman Catholic religion, then the system cannot be totally bad. Next, the impression is given that one can still remain a part of a

---

put forward Temple, priesthood, and the rest of the outward shows, this empty glitter which blinds the eyes of the simple ought not to move us a whit to grant that the church exists where God's Word is not found. Why do we willfully act like madmen in searching out the church when Christ has marked it with an unmistakable sign, which, wherever it is seen, cannot fail to show the church there; while where it is absent, nothing remains that can give the true meaning of the church? Paul reminds us that the church was founded not upon men's judgments, not upon priesthoods, but upon the teaching of apostles and prophets (Eph. 2:20). Nay, Jerusalem is to be distinguished from Babylon, Christ's church from Satan's cabal, by the very difference with which Christ distinguishes between them. To sum up, since the church is Christ's Kingdom, and he reigns by his Word alone, will it not be clear to any man that those are lying words (cf. Jer. 7:4) by which the Kingdom of Christ is imagined to exist apart form his scepter (that is, his most holy Word)? (IV:II:4) Now they treat us as persons guilty of schism and heresy because we preach a doctrine unlike theirs, do not obey their laws, and hold our separate assemblies for prayers, baptisms and the celebration of the Supper, and other holy activities. (IV:II:5)"

[1] Geisler & MacKenzie, pg. 502

false system despite being saved from without. Nothing is said about *leaving* the system. Next, the impression is given that the Roman Catholic religion only "may officially deny essential parts of the gospel." We note also that the word "official" is used in this first point. It is as if the phrase "official teaching" used of the false system excuses the membership since they are not thinking in terms of formal theology or are not *practically* believing what is *officially* taught.

It gets stickier. Listen to point number two as they try to walk the fence on the issue of whether Rome is a false church with some truth, or whether Rome is a true church with some error:

> "Second, there is a difference between what is essential to the gospel itself and what is essential for people to believe about the gospel in order to be saved."[1]

The authors give two illustrations of this assertion. The first illustration is forensic justification. The authors argue that one does not have to believe in forensic justification in order to be saved and yet, forensic justification (the imputed righteousness of Christ for our acquittal at the law bar of God's justice) is an essential part of the Gospel. The second illustration consists in the way God saves people. The authors contend that God will save someone by grace through faith alone based on Christ alone even if they do not believe that this is necessary to the way God does it. Geisler & MacKenzie have asserted that man can be saved *by* the Gospel without *believing* the Gospel! We need to carefully unwrap this preposterous assertion, because it is the door of the world's cafeteria for all to come and eat of the stew of apostasy.

We will grant that salvation consists in a supernatural experience whereby one is enabled to believe the Gospel of Jesus Christ. That Gospel may be as simple as, "Believe on the Lord Jesus Christ, and thou shalt be saved" (Acts 16:31). Depending upon the conviction and the state of the audience, the book of Acts unfolds for us the preaching of the Gospel attended by much explanation, e.g., Paul at Athens, and very little explanation, e.g., the Philippian jailor. We would agree that one does not have to be a theologian in order to be saved. Everything true about the Gospel cannot be grasped immediately. It cannot be discovered at once. But to say that one can believe in the Gospel, while holding simultaneously to beliefs which deny the Gospel, is simply ridiculous!

The apostasy here is the failure to distinguish between believing something essential about the Gospel and denying something essential about the

---

[1] Geisler & MacKenzie, pg. 502

Gospel. One can be saved without any knowledge of terminology such as "forensic justification." But are the authors willing to say that one can be saved even while denying the doctrine of forensic justification? The authors simply say that "one can be saved without believing that imputed righteousness is an essential part of the Gospel." We ask, "Can one be saved while denying imputed righteousness?" Salvation is not for those who later deny the very essence of salvation. Yes, one can be saved without a full grasp of imputed righteousness, but one cannot maintain that he is saved while denying this essential element of the Gospel. He will have only believed a caricature of the gospel and a Jesus of his own imagination. This is idolatry, not salvation.

Next, the authors wish for us to believe that people can be saved by grace alone, through faith alone by the imputed righteousness of Christ alone even if they do not believe that this is necessary to the *way* God does it! Herein comes the broth of apostate stew in full flavor. If we have read them right, these authors are saying that someone can be saved even if they do not believe *how* they were saved or what God did to save them. In short, they are saying that God has saved people who do not believe the Gospel! They are saved but they do not *believe* how God saved them. They are born from above but do not *believe* how God saved them. They are in Christ but deny that they are in Christ by grace alone through faith alone in the finished work of Christ alone. The authors are not saying that these people fail to understand *how* they are saved. They are clearly saying that these people do not *believe* that they are saved in this manner. We are at a complete loss. Incredibly, the authors assert that salvation can come to a person and that person can sit in unbelief as to the way that salvation comes to him. Is this not the classic example of experiencing Christ without having to worry about doctrine? "Forget doctrine," according to some Evangelicals, "one can be saved even while denying the way you are saved." We ask, "What on earth did the person believe when he had this alleged *experience* with Christ?" Whatever it was, it was not the Gospel. How can it be alleged that a Christian does not believe the *way* God saves him and is still a Christian? It could happen only in a world where doctrinal propositions no longer matter.

But the authors are not through just yet. The third distinction they make in trying to discern if Rome is a false church is fashioned in these terms:

> "Third, it is important to distinguish between what the Roman Catholic Church fails to affirm as essential elements of the gospel and what it actually denies is an essential element of the gospel. We suggest that the simple failure to affirm an element (say, forensic justification) is not the equivalent of affirming a false gospel."[1]

---

[1] Geisler & MacKenzie, pg. 502

Let us attempt to follow the logic of these authors:

- Question: Is Roman Catholicism a false church?
- Answer: A "true church" must proclaim a "true Gospel."
- But to answer this question, three important distinctions must be made.
    + There is a difference between whether Catholics can be saved in their system and whether their system teaches a true Gospel.
    + There is a difference between what is essential to the Gospel and what is essential to believe about the Gospel in order to be saved.
    + We believe imputed righteousness is essential to the true Gospel.
    + There is a difference between a simple failure to affirm an element of the true Gospel (say, forensic justification, i.e., imputed righteousness) and actually affirming a false gospel.
- Therefore, the Roman Catholic Church is not a false church.

The author's bottom line is that to define a "true church" it must proclaim the "true Gospel." But the "true Gospel" can, they say, be proclaimed without proclaiming the essential truth of forensic justification. Even though the writers define imputed righteousness as essential to the true Gospel, they are willing to say one can proclaim a "true Gospel" without it. We ask, "How can something which is essential to the truth of the Gospel be left out in the definition of the 'true Gospel'?" The authors commit theological suicide here. They are saying that one essential part of a "true Gospel" can be left out with the remainder preached as the "true Gospel." The authors go on to say that to preach a gospel bereft of an essential part of that gospel is not to preach a false gospel. In their own words, "Rather, it is merely proclaiming an incomplete gospel."[1] This is the only charge the authors are willing to lay at the doorstep of Rome. One gets the feeling that the realtor is marketing swampland again.

Suppose you buy an automobile without an engine. The salesman did not sell you a false automobile. He merely sold you a *mobile* which was a little short on *auto*. It is still a *car* and will still do the job.

Or suppose you are called upon to testify in the courtroom as an eye-witness to a murder. Under oath to tell the whole truth, you tell everything except

---

[1] Geisler & MacKenzie, pg. 502

who did it. You have not proclaimed a false testimony, you have merely given an incomplete testimony.

Such prevarication is becoming of politicians, but not of theologians defending the truth of God!

Let us delve deeper into this assertion that a "simple failure to affirm an element is not the equivalent of affirming a false gospel." If someone knowingly misrepresents the facts on his tax return it is considered tax evasion and is punishable by law. The Government does not view it as "not the equivalent of filing a false tax return." It would be deliberate deception. As a matter of fact, that is exactly how the government would view it. But these authors would see it differently. They are not willing to admit that the deliberate failure to tell the whole truth is, in most cases to be viewed as a lie. The reason is because the whole truth is explicitly asked for on the tax return or in a courtroom. Likewise with the Gospel, to withhold an element of truth is tantamount to affirming the lie. Rome has been withholding the essential truths of the Gospel for centuries and proclaiming a gospel that does not contain essential truths of the real Gospel—and on purpose! It is reprehensible to assert that this deliberate omission of truth is not the equivalent of affirming a false gospel. What more can one do to affirm a false gospel than to continue to affirm as true a gospel void of its essential elements?

Sadly enough, the authors know that this "word-mongering," heretical approach to defining truth would never have been given a moment's audience with the Reformers. The authors close out their book with a rather chilling assessment. They want to know if Rome has infallibly denied anything essential about the Gospel. Their own research demands an enthusiastic affirmative from them. But, so as not to rock the boat of ecumenism, and to perpetuate all brew of apostasy, the authors can do no better than conclude only that the Rome was at odds with the Reformers. But the *reason why* Rome was at odds—a false gospel absolutely empty of hope—is very carefully avoided.

Their failure to align themselves with the obvious *conclusion* of the Reformers, as well their own research, puts these men ominously close to the edge of apostasy. And, as they teeter there, they remain responsible for the popularizers who follow after them and interpret their writings in the only way they can: as a full approbation for Rome.

We turn our attention now to perhaps the strongest and most popular bridge from the theologians to the people. Mr. Charles Colson, and what seems to us an ever-growing array of popularizers, has made good use of the tongue-tied theologians to promote the deadly heresy of Romanism onto an already weakened Evangelicalism. We turn our attention to these men who are lined up at the edge of apostasy. They have picked up their clues from the theologians and fashioned for themselves idols of ecumenism. With wit, charm and personality as their tools, they have crafted bridges to Rome. *They have failed to understand that a bridge was never meant for one way traffic.*

The Popular Evangelical, The Elder Theologian, And The Roman Catholic Writer

In the fall of 1992, a group of Roman Catholic and professing Evangelicals met together under the tutelage of Charles Colson and Richard Neuhaus to draft a document which would eventually be released in the Spring of 1994 under the title of *Evangelicals and Catholics Together: The Christian Mission in the Third Millennium.* This document is now known as simply *ECT.* We have already critiqued *ECT* * in an earlier book, *Romanism: The Relentless Roman Catholic Assault on the Gospel of Jesus Christ.*

After the explosion and subsequent settling of things in the aftermath of the release of *ECT*, there has been another book compiled by Richard Neuhaus and Charles Colson. This book entitled, *Evangelicals and Catholics Together: Toward A Common Mission,* was published by Word Publishing in Dallas, Texas and was released in 1995. It is this book—a compilation of essays written by three Evangelicals and three Roman Catholics—which will be used as a backdrop in exposing what some authors have already labeled as "The Coming Evangelical Crisis." Our method shall be to interact with only three of the contributors. We feel they are the most suitable representatives to explain a document of the magnitude of *ECT.* We believe that these men have spoken with clarity and purpose. Each one gives a generous portion of rationale from his own point of view. Together, they cover the spectrum well enough for our purposes. Accordingly they are: the popular Evangelical speaker and writer, Mr. Charles Colson, the older and widely respected Evangelical theologian and teacher, Dr. James I. Packer, and finally the well respected thinker and Roman Catholic writer, Mr. Richard John Neuhaus.

In their own words, we let the principal framers of *ECT* explain the relevance of it to our discussion in this book.

> "After all, ECT is an invitation to reexamine stereotypes, prejudices, and conventional ideas that have been entrenched, in some cases, for almost five hundred years."[1]

---

* The follow-up document, entitled "The Gift of Salvation" was released on November 12, 1997. A critique of that document is contained in Appendix I of this book.

[1] Colson, Charles, and Neuhaus, Richard John, editors, *Evangelicals and Catholics Together Toward A Common Mission*, (Dallas, TX: Word Publishing, ©1995) pg. ix

Part of the impetus for *ECT* came from the observation that Roman Catholics and Evangelicals were encountering each other in social settings such as the pro-life movement and in the political arena. This, along with the fear of growing conflicts between Evangelicals and Roman Catholics in Latin America, spawned a concern to bring the two communities together. Mr. Colson and Mr. Neuhaus have expressed that the *ECT* statement is only the beginning. We do not doubt this for a second. Indeed it is *only* the beginning. This second treatise of theirs has grown out of a concern to further explain the goals of *ECT* and press on with the task of bringing Evangelicals and Roman Catholics together:

> "A beginning has been made. This book builds on that beginning. The authors offer it to you, the reader, in the spirit of ECT's concluding affirmation that 'this is a time of opportunity—and if opportunity, then of responsibility—for evangelicals and Catholics to be Christians together in a way that helps prepare the world for the coming of him to whom belongs the kingdom, the power, and the glory forever. Amen.'"[1]

---

1 Colson & Neuhaus, pg. xiv

The Popular Evangelical

ONE OF THE distinctives of the *ECT* statement is that it assumes to be true what 500 years of theological history has denied. By the mere force of assertion, it has proclaimed the Roman Catholic religion to be part and parcel of the Body of Christ on earth and a full member of the Household of God. It assumes, without prejudice, that Roman Catholicism, with all its bizarre and Gospel-denying heresies, is to be naturally thought of as Christianity. This is the legacy of the theologians. It is not surprising that popularizers have taken their kernel of thought and run with it to the ends of the earth. So strongly and methodically is Romanism breathed in the same breath as Christianity that one now risks his entire reputation among the religious elite to question the assertion. It is a *fait accompli*. Who could dare question whether Roman Catholicism is Christian, especially in light of the cultural wars?

We want to spend some time interacting with Mr. Colson and his band of popularists on this issue of culture wars. For, as we have shown, it is the engine that has driven Evangelical theologians to abandon the entire notion of presenting the Gospel of Jesus Christ in terms of propositional truth.

Colson is not concerned about theology *per se*. He takes the hand-off from the theologians who have left to return to their ivory towers of thought. It is not that Colson does not think. It is simply that his thoughts have been loosened by the theologians from the restraints of any strict theological accuracy. Colson has been cut loose to take the implications of a Rome-including gospel and run with it throughout the land. This he does both with the *ECT* accord, and with *Toward A Common Mission*. The theologians have run interference for him, and have cleared for him the broad path of apostasy.

A gifted writer who has shown a propensity to capture the emotion of the moment with vivid stories and illustrations, Colson begins this compendium of essays with what he calls: "The Common Cultural Task." We wish to walk along side and follow the thinking of this popular professed Evangelical as he follows the theologians in a death march toward the edge of apostasy.

When The Gospel Doesn't Matter Any More

In a moving account of prisoners being held hostage by fanatic Muslim extremists, Colson opens his essay with a Catholic priest blessing a piece of bread and some water and offering communion to his fellow captives. The fellow captives included a Presbyterian minister. We are told that the Presbyterian and the Catholic have a vastly different understanding of whether those elements were the real body and blood of Christ or symbolic,

> "...but at that moment, such a theological distinction was not their concern. They took the elements and experienced what they later described as one of their most profound moments of intimacy with Jesus Christ their risen Savior. And this intimacy enabled them to endure horrifying months of captivity and eventually to emerge with their faith deepened and strengthened."[1]

We pause for a moment and reflect on what has been stated. Can we not see the same elements of apostasy which we saw in the professional theologians? We see here the dichotomy between proper theology and the experiential. There is also a disregard for precise theological language and meaning. For instance, the issue of communion within Catholicism is not only that the bread is the actual presence of Christ but also that the Mass is a propitiatory sacrifice for the forgiveness of sins. According to Rome, when the Catholic priest blessed the bread and water,* he was transubstantiating the properties into the body and blood of Christ. He was then presenting Christ's body and blood, according to Rome, as a reenactment of Calvary for the remission of his sins. It is the height of absurdity to say that such theological distinctives are meaningless at this moment just because both men fear for their lives.

This is the problem in miniature. Cultural considerations are said to be the guide and rule for theological considerations. In Colson's world, the cultural situation determines the reality and validity of the religious expression. Any decent Presbyterian minister would have turned down the priest and given him the true Gospel of Jesus Christ, and no self-respecting Catholic priest would have allowed for the administration of the Eucharist to a professed non-Catholic. Colson tells us that the "theological distinctives" of the two captives were kept intact, but his deliberate oversight is not lost on us, for each of the captives' "theological distinctives" declares that the other's is an unholy abomination before God! Let the reader consider the following for himself and see if the Council of Trent or the Westminster

---

[1] Colson & Neuhaus, pp. 1,2

* In Colson's account, water was used by the priest because it was the only liquid he was able to collect for the celebration of communion.

Divines believed that there was any room for any commonality in their two completely different beliefs about the communion table:

The Council of Trent on the Lord's Supper:

> "First of all, the Holy Council teaches and openly and plainly professes that after the consecration of bread and wine our Lord Jesus Christ, true God and true Man, is truly, really and substantially contained in the august sacrament of the Holy Eucharist under the appearance of those sensible things. ...it is a most contemptible action on the part of some *contentious and wicked men to twist them into fictitious and imaginary figures of speech* by which the truth of the flesh and blood of Christ is denied, contrary to the universal sense of the Church which, as the pillar and ground of truth, recognizing with a mind ever grateful and unforgetting this most excellent favor of Christ, *has detested as satanical these untruths devised by impious men.*"[1]

> "...the Holy Council teaches that this is truly propitiatory and has this effect... For, appeased by this sacrifice, the Lord grants the grace and gift of penitence, and pardons even the gravest crimes and sins."[2]

The Westminster Confession of Faith on the Lord's Supper:

> "In this sacrament, *Christ is not offered up to His Father; nor any real sacrifice made at all,* for the remission of sins of the quick or the dead; but only a commemoration of that one offering up of Himself, by Himself, upon the cross, once for all: and a spiritual oblation of all possible praise unto God, for the same: *so that the popish sacrifice of the mass (as they call it) is most abominably injurious to Christ's one, only sacrifice*, the alone propitiation for all the sins of His elect."[3]

We see not the least bit of commonality, which means that Colson's captives, instead of celebrating a richer, deeper meaning of communion with Christ, made the celebration mean nothing at all. This means that their perceived "most profound moments of intimacy with Jesus Christ their risen Savior" were nothing more than an emotional experience. This is what happens when two radically opposite and mutually exclusive beliefs are

---

[1] The General Council of Trent, Session XIII, (1551):DS 1651, emphasis added

[2] The General Council of Trent, Session XXII (1562):DS 1743

[3] Westminster Confession of Faith, XXIX.II, emphasis added

declared to be actually the same thing. The result is an empty ritual, empty of meaning for both of them.

But Colson has convinced himself that the theological nuances of the Bible need to be adjusted in order for us to get along with the real work of saving Western culture. It appears not to have dawned on Mr. Colson that God does not allow for the Roman Catholic view of the Eucharist and all it entails. Whether the elements of the Lord's table serve as a memorial to the death and coming again of Christ or whether they are His body and blood to be adored, worshiped and ingested to gain grace and forgiveness of sin are not puny little theological issues. They cannot be so easily discarded because of the social condition of the time or the moment. We must also make mention that Mr. Colson is under the fatal impression that Roman Catholicism is Christianity. This underlying unyielding presupposition makes it easy for him to describe heresy as merely dissimilarity. In this appraisal, Colson has been deeply aided and influenced by the theologians. Listen to the echo of the theologians as Colson taps out the rationale of his agenda:

> "Both evangelicals and Catholics are offended by the blasphemy, violence, and sexual promiscuity endorsed by both the artistic elite and the popular culture in America today. On university campuses, evangelical students whose Christian faith comes under frequent assault often find Catholic professors to be their only allies. …This new ecumenism bears no relationship to liberal ecumenism, which seeks unity by disregarding doctrinal differences. Conservative evangelicals and Catholics understand and maintain the distinctive of their respective traditions. All the same, they take united stand on the common ground of Scripture and the ancient confessions—what C.S. Lewis called 'mere Christianity.'"[1]

What Colson calls "distinctives of their respective traditions," we call fatal differences. Would Colson rather us swallow the blasphemy of a propitiatory sacrifice of the Mass so that we can defeat the blasphemy of our culture? Would he have us suffer the injurious violence Rome does to Christ's Gospel in their Mass in order to tame the violence of popular culture? We have shown in the first section of this book that theologians have a severe credibility gap when they prove something to be anti-Christian and label it as a mere difference. We find nothing new here with Colson. He is right that the new ecumenism does not seek to have a unity by disregarding doctrinal differences. But this new ecumenism is worse. It boldly states the doctrinal differences and doctrinal contradictions in fine theological detail, and then declares that they are *not relevant to the Gospel.*

---

[1] Colson & Neuhaus, pg. 2

Yet if the gospel is not doctrinally relevant, then we have truly lost the Gospel. This is the price Colson has paid to get his terms redefined.

We find it to be highly ironic that Evangelical ecumenists redefine their terms in such a way to out-do the liberals in justifying their activities. One argument which captures our attention is that the new ecumenism is not political in nature because those fighting the cultural wars against pornography and abortion do so from a deeply moral base centered around the moral order God has established. Thus, they flatter themselves that their movement is theologically motivated and energized. Perhaps they have forgotten that the entire Muslim world, where abortion is outlawed and pornography is illegal, is motivated by moral principals given to them by their god, too.

So incredibly ingrained is the notion that Roman Catholicism is a Christian religion, that Colson simultaneously insists on cooperation with Rome (because it is, he believes, Christian), while refusing to be identified with Mormons and Muslims (because they are not). Though these two religions—Mormonism and Islam—come from a highly moral base stemming from faith in their god, Colson rejects such a coalition. He says the problems are too deep. He thinks that the nation needs to be evangelized with Christianity. Here he takes his cue from the theologians who have compared Rome to Augustine, Aquinas and the Reformers, but refused to compare Rome to the Bible. Colson takes it to the next step, and compares Rome to Mormonism and Islam, rather than to the written Word.* The following statement contains Colson's analysis. He thinks that Mormonism and Islam are political alliances, at best, but Rome is Christian and hence, our real ally:

> "This is not merely a political necessity, as though evangelicals and Catholics should form a coalition (perhaps with the aid of Mormons

---

* We see this as a steady march of undiscerning lemmings toward the cliff of apostasy, and the next obvious step on this slippery slope will be to compare Mormonism and Islam against the backdrop of atheists and agnostics to declare *them* Christians, and finally atheists and agnostics against a backdrop of an ungodly culture in order to proclaim *them* Christian as well. We cite Peter Kreeft as a fine example of this. Regarding his own perception of the ecumenical efforts toward getting fallen men to honor God with their lips, he writes, "Nothing in the Jewish Scriptures contradicts Christianity, but some things in the Qur'an do. Yet even here, an 'ecumenical jihad' is possible and is called for, for the simple and strong reason that *Muslims and Christians preach and practice the same First Commandment*; Islam, total surrender submission of the human will to the divine will. We fight side by side not only because we face a common enemy but above all because *we serve and worship the same divine Commander*. ...Finally, even atheists and agnostics, if they are of good will and intellectual honesty and still believe in objective truth and objective morality, are on our side in the war against the powers of darkness. *Perhaps they can be called 'anonymous Christians.'*" (Peter Kreeft, *Ecumenical Jihad*, ©1996, Ignatius Press) pp. 30, 31, emphases added

> and Muslims) to elect better candidates and enact better laws. Our culture's sickness is far too deep for mere political remedies. *Our contemporary culture needs to be reevangelized. The Christian world view* must be brought to bear in new form and forcefulness on the intellectual and moral framework of contemporary life. This is a task for all true Christians, whether evangelicals, Catholics, or members of other traditions."[1]

At this point we will briefly point out a key concept to which we shall return a few pages hence: Colson emphatically denies at the outset that his desire is for Protestants and Catholics to be merely cobelligerent, i.e., merely cooperative in effecting a moral change in our society. Colson goes further and says that beyond mere cobelligerency, Protestants and Catholics must co-evangelize. We will return to this important distinction later on, but for now, we wonder out loud and continue to ask the obvious questions. What gospel shall be used to evangelize this country? Will it be baptismal regeneration, confirmation, sacrificial mass, penance and purgatory along with indulgences and papal infallibility? Will it be *sola fide* and *sola scriptura,* or the Magisterium of Rome? Will it be the imputed righteousness of Christ, or congruent merit? Will it be "All hail the power of Jesus' name," or "All hail Mary, queen of heaven"? Will it be "Believe and be saved," or "*Join* and be saved"?

Taking their cue from theologians who have already laid the groundwork for acceptance of Rome and a willingness to forgo doctrine in favor of experience, modern ecumenical writers and speakers now ask us to run to the arms of Rome:

> "The task is urgent. Make no mistake: The cultural war is real, and we who believe in the Bible are losing it—largely, I believe, because of our failure to understand the true nature of the forces arrayed against us. For the real assault is coming at the deepest and most dangerous level."[2]

Indeed, we agree with Mr. Colson. However, we find a level of assault deeper than even he can envision.

Mixing The Apples And The Oranges

The strange battle cry of modern Evangelical ecumenists is that "truth matters." This theme has been picked up and carried to the front of the battle lines to serve as a banner in the aforementioned cultural wars. The thinking

---

[1] Colson & Neuhaus, pg. 3, emphasis added

[2] Colson & Neuhaus, pg. 3

is that liberalism, modernism, relativism and intellectualism have abandoned all vestiges of absolute truth and moral standards. It has been rightly pointed out that post-modern thinkers are confounded by their own axiom, "The only truth is that there is no truth." Evangelical ecumenists, however, are making a worse mistake. They pick up the sword of Judeo-Christian traditions, put on the armor of Roman Catholicism and the helmet of Orthodoxy, and run headlong into battle to wage warfare with the secular world. The trouble is, they are missing the only weapon which can win the battle: the Gospel of Jesus Christ.

In so doing, Evangelical ecumenists have shown a remarkable affinity for being highly selective in determining *which* truth matters. In the blink of an eye we are told that abortion is wrong, euthanasia is wrong, pornography is wrong, and that man needs the moral law. But slipped in beside these reflections of "truth that matters" comes also the cacophonic sound of theological truth-bashing. For instance, Colson has this to say while lamenting the loss of truth in our society:

> "Christians of different traditions—Catholics and Protestants, Calvinists and Arminians—could argue theology, but they could take for granted their common worldview."[1]

Evidently, "truth matters" only in some arenas of thought. We notice here that disputes within countries (intramural affairs) such as Calvinism and Arminianism are thrown in with disputes between countries, such as Catholic and Protestant. The truth of the matter is that Roman Catholicism is a universe away from Protestantism. Whereas the dispute between Arminians and Calvinists emerged from within Protestantism itself. Mr. Colson has deliberately garbled the categories in hopes of engendering the thought that Catholic vs. Protestant equals Calvinist vs. Arminian. This is tantamount to saying that people of different nations—Germany and Russia, Munich and Berlin—should argue the speed on the Autobahn. Everyone knows that any such dispute between Munich and Berlin is an in-house discussion. What on earth does Russia have to do with it? Russia is an entirely different country. Try this one on for size: "Christians of different traditions—Catholics and Mormons, Jehovah's Witnesses and Moonies—could argue theology, but they could take for granted their common world view." This is no more strange to the Christian than Colson's ghastly assertion. We observe that truth *does* matter. It matters in all spheres, but especially in theological worlds. We are rapidly coming to the conclusion that *all* truth matters with the Evangelical ecumenists *except* the truth of the Gospel of Jesus Christ.

---

[1] Colson & Neuhaus, pg. 4

We do not deem it inappropriate to apply the same strict exactness of truth to the field of theology and the gospel that the Evangelical ecumenists have applied to the secular culture. If truth matters, then *all* truth matters. Let's apply the same standard to every aspect of thought. Indeed, let us take all thoughts captive to the obedience of Christ. We are told by Colson:

> "But if the consequences of the postmodern condition are all-encompassing, they also are incurable—except by a culturewide rediscovery of the foundations of our civilization in the *Judeo-Christian tradition.* Even a cursory examination of the intellectual cul-de-sac in which postmodernism has captured our cultural elite demonstrates the validity of this assertion. For the first consequence of postmodernism is the loss of belief in the existence of truth itself. And *without a belief in truth,* any culture inevitably descends into decay and disorder."[1]

However, we must stand fast and examine the categories and see how they relate to the Gospel of Jesus Christ and the Bible as our source of truth. We are not comfortable with the terminology "Judeo-Christian tradition." It appears to us that this is a catch basin for all that is washed through the history of Western Europe since the Protestant Reformation. Getting back to a Judeo-Christian tradition is not the Gospel of Jesus Christ. It is not the goal or the essence of the revelation of God in Christ. Neither is it a good phrase to describe a desired cultural rediscovery. We are further uncomfortable with mixing the phrase "Judeo-Christian tradition" with belief in the existence of truth itself. They take the Gospel out of the land who set their goal to reclaim an undefined "Judeo-Christian tradition." It is deep error indeed to mix the apples of Roman Catholicism and Judaism with the oranges of Christianity. If all truth matters, then let the truth be said plainly. Judaism is not Christianity. It holds to absolute values and a shared view in monotheism but rejects the Trinity and the Gospel of Jesus Christ. Roman Catholicism is not Christianity. It too shares absolute values while embracing the Trinity but rejects the Gospel of Jesus Christ. Some may argue for joint *political* endeavors between these three world-wide religions. Our regard for truth in the *theological realm*, however, will never allow us to throw them together as though we shared a common Gospel.

Fire Hoses Without Water

It is necessary, before continuing, to step back and look at the big picture. We are arguing that Evangelical ecumenists are running headlong into theological suicide by selling out the Gospel of Jesus Christ. They insist on recognizing Roman Catholicism as a *bona fide* Christian worshiping

---

[1] Colson & Neuhaus, pg. 7, emphasis added

community. The pot of apostasy stew is being prepared with two main ingredients. The first is the theological vegetables where doctrine is diminished and radically opposite gospels are said to be the same at heart. An army of professing evangelicals is exercising a deliberate indifference toward the fatal differences. Theological precision is determined to be an archaic impediment to the realization that differences must exist within the larger Body of Christ. Flat out contradictions are waved off as "distinctives of worship." The *sine qua non* of Christianity has been reduced to the litmus test of being able to walk, chew gum and say, "God is good and God is great!" all at the same time.

The second ingredient, what we have called the meat of the stew, is found in the stampede to wipe out the cultural enemies that have given us the moral decadence of the west. The fear of losing the cultural wars has encouraged popular writers to warn Evangelicals to circle the wagons and enlist the aid of all who merely call themselves Christians, regardless of the anomalies of their worship, practice and confessions. Out of sheer terror, Evangelicals are asked to give up the Gospel of Christ to Roman Catholicism in hopes of recruiting Rome to fight the cultural wars together.

The time has now come to set up some parameters of thought in hopes of stemming the tide of apostasy and gather some back from the edge. In order to do this we must engage in an honest appraisal of the cultural dilemma and then focus on the only real solution.

We liken the situation in the West, particularly in America, to a fire. There is a fire in the land, and the land is on fire! Any way you look at it, morality is down and crime is up. Relativists, radical feminists, radical alternative lifestylers including—but not limited to—the homosexual communities, are forcing their agenda on main street America. Politicians are liars, and criminals live in overcrowded conditions. New prisons cannot be built fast enough. Promiscuity and pornography are on every corner and are laced throughout the electronic communications network. Abortion mills grind up babies in a steady and chillingly methodical fashion. Teenage pregnancies are up and high-school drop-outs are not far behind. Tensions exist in large racially integrated cities and terrorism has become the buzz word of the nineties. American schools are falling behind academically and the homeless in the streets are increasing in numbers. Large corporations are moving jobs overseas for cheap labor and scandals continue to rock the White House and the Congress. The possession of hand guns in America has become the line of first defense against murder and rape. Evolution and relativism are taught as fact in our universities, and addictions to drugs, gambling and nefarious activities are on the incline. There is an attitude of cynicism toward, and an open display of mockery of, traditional family values by an array of occultic groups. The financial security of our elderly is suspect and the nation continues to tumble into personal debt. The trade deficit remains too high and the willingness of the American consumer to save remains too low. All morality seems to have been abandoned as the right to die by assisted suicide takes center stage. Hospitals have become models of modern moral schizophrenia striving to save overdosed drug addicts while killing babies in the womb and drugging the elderly to death. Lawsuits are at an all time high and personal peace and affluence remain the goals of our disenfranchised youth. Indeed, there is fire in the land and the land is on fire! We agree with the apostate ecumenists who state,

> "The only real solution to the increase in senseless violent crime is a recultivation of conscience. And throughout the history of our own society, the cultivation of conscience, both among individuals and within social and political institutions, has been provided in large measure by men and women of Christian faith."[1]

The aggravating issue that continues to undermine any attempts to put out the fire in the land, however, is the *identity* of "men and women of Christian faith." Who are they and *what* do they believe? If we cannot agree on this, there is the real danger of running to the fire with empty water hoses. We believe the ecumenists have done just this. For example, no one has done a better job of analyzing the fire than Colson:

> "In this much-discussed 'culture war,' Christians are losing. With the forces arrayed against us—a contemptuous media, unrestrained consumerism, sexual libertinism, a hostile academia, and an omnipresent hedonistic entertainment industry—Christians are both surrounded and outnumbered."[2]

Sadly, however, no one has done a *worse* job than Colson in defining the Christianity which is called upon to influence the West away from the moral, spiritual, economic and social decay. Astoundingly, Charles Colson fills in all the letters of the popular game show, but still cannot guess the phrase to win the prize. Listen to his wonderful insight on the role of Christianity in our culture, but keep in mind in all of this that Mr. Colson is including the religion of Rome as part of his definition of Christianity:

> "Where does this leave evangelicals, Catholics, and other Christians who believe in objective truth and a transcendent morality? What can the church do to renew American culture? Ironically the Church must first remember that its principal obligation is *not* to renew the culture. The task of the Church is to be the Church, to proclaim the gospel of Jesus Christ, and to make disciples. The Church is called

---

[1] Colson & Neuhaus, pg. 13

[2] Colson & Neuhaus, pg. 15

> to be faithful to God, to live out his Word, to proclaim his truth, and to assist men and women in growing spiritually as part of a holy, righteous community."[1]

Mr. Colson goes on to conclude that we "must always guard the independence of the Gospel from secular ideologies."[2] What we find so ironic is the absolute failure on Colson's part to see that the Roman Catholic religion *does not have this Gospel* with which he is so eager to defend against the in-roads of secular ideologies. We wish Mr. Colson could be as enthusiastic in protecting the Gospel against *religious* ideologies. Perhaps then Mr. Colson could understand our dilemma. Christians are waging war on the fire in America, as well, but not at the expense of losing the Gospel either to secularists or to Roman Catholic religionists, no matter how hard their stand is against the cultural evils of our day.

We shall continue to press the point. With which gospel shall we proclaim Jesus Christ throughout the land? With which gospel shall we make disciples? What truth shall we proclaim? These things are said by Colson to be the essence of the role of the Body of Christ in our land. We agree. But in the absence of any theological definitions and precise theological language, what possible good can come of it? Can we be faithful to God by preaching a gospel that is anti-*sola scriptura* (the Bible alone for faith and authority) and anti-*sola fide* (justification by faith alone apart from the works of the law, any law including the Roman Catholic laws)? Can we submit the rule of Scripture to the rule of Rome? We answer "No, not now and not ever!"

Which Church Shall It Be?

One can only speculate on what God may do within a culture. But one thing is for sure: God will have His elect interspersed among the rank and file of the world's various cultures. It seems highly gratuitous to assume that Christians can turn a culture around. This does not mean that Christians are to disappear and be silent. But we cannot say for sure that God is going to regenerate enough people unto faith in His dear Son to give us a majority of Christians in America. It seems that the Bible is fundamentally illustrative of Christians remaining a small minority on the world scene. The gate is small and the way is narrow that leads to life and few are they that find it. However, the gate is wide and the way is broad that leads to destruction and many are those who enter by it (Matthew 7:13-14). This is to say that the true Church of God is small, relatively speaking. But, however small, Christians are vocal and sensitive to the cultural problems wherein they live.

---

[1] Colson & Neuhaus, pp. 15-16, emphasis in original

[2] Colson & Neuhaus, pg. 16

How could they not be? One cannot be a Christian, holding to the Word of truth, living within the Christian Community, reading one's Bible and not be aware that non-Christians rule the roost. Having said this, we have come in a roundabout way to yet another disturbing element of Evangelical ecumenism which aids and abets the cause of theological suicide and drives them ever closer to falling headlong into the pit of apostasy, right behind the theologians.

Let it be said loudly and clearly that all Christians do in fact fight against culture. They have to. It is part and parcel to the experience of being born again that God puts within His new creation a desire to please Him and to resist the world and the devil. One cannot be a Christian and *not* be fighting the culture at many different levels. To be Christian is to fight. It goes with the territory. No Christian approves of his own or any one else's sinfulness. This does not mean that every Christian is on the picket line, and most certainly not that everyone on the picket line is Christian. It does not mean that every Christian stops sinning, nor that everyone who seeks to stop sinning is Christian. It simply means that God's elect know the difference between the ways of God and the ways of the world.

But the ecumenical Evangelicals have done much more than merely ask Christians to resist the advance of an ungodly culture. They have opened the door and declared Roman Catholicism to be Christian, and have seriously questioned the credibility of anyone who disagrees. Having put Rome into the fold of Christianity, these ecumenists have now begun to label Rome's troubles as though they were Christianity's troubles. Incredibly, the ecumenists have dragged in a non-Christian religion—with all of its afflictions—and used it as an occasion to assail true Christianity. But Christians do not want any part of Rome and will not be defined according to Rome's problems. The ecumenists have re-defined Christianity, imported a non-Christian religion full of errors, compromises, and a false gospel, and now have begun to address these problems as though they were the fault of the Church which has fallen asleep at its post. The fly in the ointment is that Christianity is not Roman Catholicism and Roman Catholicism is not Christianity. The heretical hierarchy of the ecumenical movement has declared the deadly viruses and diabolical diseases of Rome to be simple maladies within the Body of Christ. Nothing could be further from the truth. Listen to Mr. Colson. Notice how he casually uses the word "Church" to describe what is either patently Roman Catholic in nature, or simply the unbelief of those polled. It is definitely not Christianity:

> "The Church faces a series of daunting challenges. First, it must disciple its own members. A 1994 poll by George Barna found that 72 percent of Americans do not believe there exists an absolute truth about God, the origin and nature of the human race, or standards of moral conduct. An even more frightening statistic is that 62 percent

> of Americans who identify themselves as evangelical Christians do not believe in absolute truth. In other words, postmodern intellectual skepticism has infiltrated the Church. Other polls find that only 37 percent of Christians know what the word *gospel* means; only 40 percent know that Jesus gave the Sermon on the Mount; only 9 percent can identify the Great Commission."[1]

From the above citation we can see Colson's willingness to accept as Christian a sampling of testimonies that have no connection to Christianity. One of the insurmountable problems with Rome is that it defines the Church as "all who are baptized" and then marvels at the rampant unbelief within the "Church." It is entirely possible that 72 percent of Americans do not believe there exists absolute truth about God. But this is not Christianity. It is entirely possible and most probable that a high percentage of those polled attend a religious community. But it is not Christian. It is an oxymoron to say that one is an evangelical Christian and simultaneously that one does not believe in absolute truth. This is not Christian, either. One could, however, easily say one is a Roman Catholic and not believe in absolute truth. It is *ludicrous* to believe that only 37 percent of Christians know what the Gospel means. If someone does not know what the Gospel means, they are not Christian. They do not need to be "discipled," as Colson asserts above. They need to be *evangelized*! Only in Rome and in the sheer lunacy of Colson's brave new ecumenism can it be asserted that a *Christian* does not know what the *Gospel* means. It is part and parcel of the non-Christian religion of Romanism and Mr. Colson's ecumenism to make such audacious claims.

Mr. Colson, and other ecumenists, use these kinds of polls to frighten and scare people into believing that there is a crisis *within* Christianity. But it is not true. All Christians believe in absolute truth. All Christians understand and believe the Gospel of Jesus Christ. All Christians know that Jesus preached the Sermon on the Mount. All Christians can identify the Great Commission. There is no alarm over these things in the Body of Christ. But if we allow Colson to redefine Christianity and let in Romanism then we have a problem. We end up saying contradictory things like, "Christians do not understand the Gospel."

The ecumenicals err greatly in their definition of the Body of Christ and Christianity. In so doing, they corrupt the real Church and give a false hope to those who have never been born from above. Sadly, some Evangelicals have been taken in by Rome. This poll, relied upon by Colson to prove the sorry state of Christianity, really serves to give a false hope to those who are caught up in practical atheism or Romanism.

---

[1] Colson & Neuhaus, pg. 18, emphasis in original

So, who are these people who say they are of Christ but have a practical and intellectual denial of the Lord Jesus Christ? To the real Christian they are not Christians at all. They have not been born from above. They are cultural religionists. However, it is quite a different story in the world of Roman Catholicism. We would venture to say that those polled would be considered part of Rome's Church. The Roman Catholics do this because they are used to defining Christianity according to *birth* as opposed to *being born again*. When faced with a poll that showed 83 percent of Roman Catholics interviewed believed that premarital sex is morally permissible,[1] Colson can only wonder at their nominal faith. We ask the reader to ponder the significance of this. The poll did not ask who *engaged* in premarital sex. The poll asked if premarital sex was *morally acceptable*. 83 percent of Catholics *believed* it was morally acceptable. Though many Christians may in fact have engaged in premarital sex, how many Christians would *believe it was morally acceptable*?. Not one! Herein lies the difference between a state religion empty of Gospel content, and the genuine article of "Christ in you, the hope of glory"! (Colossians 1:27).

Colson thinks the remedy to rectify the abysmal results of this poll is to better educate Christians as to what it means to be a Christian. Colson thinks that Christians must be trained to think biblically so they can understand their faith and can defend it against doubt, drift and intellectual attack. We wonder if we should institute two Bible classes in Colson's "church" to do this. One could teach Roman Catholics to defend the gospel of baptismal regeneration, purgatory, penance, extreme unction, papal infallibility, the immaculate conception of Mary, the sacrifice of the Mass, confession to a priest for forgiveness of sin, penance to pay the price for earthly sins committed and how to buy a Mass for the dearly beloved now departed. Then we could have another Bible class on how to witness the Gospel of Jesus Christ to all those who actually believe these false doctrines and false hopes of the Romish religion. Hopefully, the reader can see that the new Evangelical ecumenists are very selective with their use of "truth matters" as their slogan. Those who wield this slogan are committed to taking absolute values to a valueless society. They are not, however, committed to taking an absolute Gospel to a dying and lost world which is full of both atheists and religionists.

We let the reader ponder what is on the mind of those who preach Christianity and Romanism as one. Exactly what is meant by the following statements?

> "The Church *must* put its own house in order. Otherwise, it will have nothing to offer postmodern culture."[2]

---

[1] Colson & Neuhaus, pg. 18

[2] Colson & Neuhaus, pg. 19, emphasis in original

"All Christians need to cultivate a comprehensive biblical world-view—a view of all of life informed by Scripture."[1]

This is music to the Christian's ears. Putting the Christian house in order means putting out the leaven of unbelief. It means not suffering aberrant views of the Gospel. It means not participating in tables where sacrificing to false gods is a habit. It means preaching the truth in love. It means elevating the message of salvation and keeping it away from contaminants found in worldly religions. Cultivating a biblical world view means measuring all things by the Bible and not the traditions of men. It means being satisfied to live our lives under God, having our own Bibles to read and continuing our walk with the Person of Christ. It means taking the Word of God to the streets and stressing the comprehensive revelation of God as unfolded in the text, and not in the philosophies of men.

But we find a different agenda in the above words taken from Charles Colson. Mr. Colson would have us put our house in order by importing Romanism as a permanent fixture in the living room. He and others think that we can learn from Rome among other things a high view of the Church. This is nonsense. The only proper view of the Church is found in Scripture and it does not include the ornaments of the Roman Catholic religion. It is said that we can learn from Rome how to think better philosophically. This, too, is nonsense since we are warned about philosophical meanderings and speculative theology. A vain attempt is made to "get our house in order" by realizing that even Luther was an "Evangelical Catholic":

"For example, he [Luther] held a high view of the sacraments and insisted on the baptismal regeneration of infants and the Presence of Christ in the Eucharist. But Luther believed that the gospel—the good news of salvation by grace through faith alone made possible by Christ's death and resurrection—had become obscured in the medieval and late-medieval Church (specifically: (1) apostolization of extra-biblical traditions, (2) divinization of papacy, and (3) obscuring of the doctrine of justification)."[2]

Anyone who thinks the house of Rome belongs in with Christianity because of Luther did not know Luther and does not understand the Reformation. In the first instance, we would surely object to baptismal regeneration on the grounds that it is found outside of the Bible. Secondly, we have not been given the best picture of Luther on the Lord's supper. He did not believe in "actual presence" as do the Roman Catholics. Also, the Roman Catholic absolutely denies that we are *justified by faith alone*. Nothing has changed

---

[1] Colson & Neuhaus, pg. 19

[2] Colson & Neuhaus, pg. 25, brackets added for clarity

of this anti-Gospel doctrine of Rome. And finally, Rome still holds to the Traditions of its religion as being on par with Scripture, and has not departed from Papal infallibility.

It is apparent to the Evangelical ecumenists that part of getting the house in order is coming to grips with their assertion that Rome belongs in the house. It appears to us that when one lacks the will to see things as they really are, there is nothing quite so mysterious as the obvious.

Hear No Evil, See No Evil, Smell No Evil

We close this portion of our investigation by examining the attempt by Mr. Colson to convince us to reach across boundaries. By this he means building bridges to Rome. The foundation of this bridge-building is said to be firm and readily plausible because it attempts to avoid the ill-fated liberal ecumenism of years gone by. Whereas previous ecumenicals sought unity by eliminating all doctrinal distinctives, the new Evangelical ecumenicals seek unity while taking doctrine very seriously. Or so goes their empty boast:

> "But the deepening alliance between groups of evangelicals and Catholics that is occurring today is wholly different, because it is a cooperation among Christians who take doctrines very seriously indeed. The new cooperation is possible because of what C. S. Lewis called 'mere Christianity'—the essential elements of Christianity upheld by all theological traditions."[1]

Borrowing from C. S. Lewis' analogy of a hallway, i.e., Christianity, and many rooms off of the hallway—the various denominations—it is presented that the new ecumenism is good. It is one that allows different shades of doctrinal perspectives to remain intact, i.e., the rooms off of the hallway, while being connected to one Christianity, the hallway itself.

The fly in the ointment is the almost cavalier, "take it for granted," "no hesitation" approach that Roman Catholicism is just another room off of the hallway. In part one of this book, we showed beyond any doubt that Roman Catholicism exists as its own house with its own hallways. It is not part of the structure of Christianity. It forfeited that right at the Council of Trent and continues to do so on and on with all of its bizarre anti-biblical doctrines. It is not enough to say that one believes in Jesus Christ. What of the *Gospel* of Christ? It is not enough to say that one is committed to the Trinity. What of the *Gospel* of the Trinity? It is not enough to say one is committed to the deity of Christ. What of the *message of salvation* from the

---

[1] Colson & Neuhaus, pg. 34

lips of the Savior? We bristle at the inherent contradictions which seem to fall with such ease from reputed Evangelicals. Listen again to the contradictory nonsense:

> "I became a convinced Baptist. But I know others who first learned about Christianity through C. S. Lewis's writings who then became Episcopalians, or Lutherans, or Catholics."[1]

> "This is because Lewis proclaimed the core beliefs shared by all Christians—not at all to minimize the disagreements among believers, but in the correct conviction that nonbelievers need first to hear and understand *the basic elements of the Christian gospel.*"[2]

> "'Evangelicals and Catholics Together' seeks to continue the legacy of C. S. Lewis by focusing on the core beliefs of all true Christians so that adherents of both major traditions can work together in the common task of evangelizing the nonbelieving world."[3]

At the risk of sounding redundant, we ask, "With what will we evangelize the world?" According to Colson and others, we will evangelize them with the mighty gospel that God exists and that Jesus Christ is the Son of God. We will convict the world of sin and convert them with the Apostles' Creed. We will then send them off to various worshiping communities to hammer out what it means to be saved and what it means to believe in the gospel.

But is this the Gospel of Jesus Christ? Hardly. When once the Gospel of salvation by faith alone in the finished work of Christ alone is not a part of the core belief of Christians, there is no more Christianity. Earlier, we read the theologians who sought to convince us that forensic justification was essential to the core of the Gospel, but we could have a Gospel without it. Now comes the logical follow-up. We can now be saved by believing in a core of Christian truth that does not include the propositional truth of the Gospel. Regardless of the intentions of C. S. Lewis, he proves to be a hindrance to the Gospel if he can be marshalled to support a Christianity without the Gospel. There may be many differing practices within a true Christian community such as, elder rule versus deacon rule, whether to speak in tongues or not, whether to believe in a pre-tribulation or post-tribulation rapture, or to believe there is no literal millennium to come, etc., etc. There is much liberty as the apostle Paul points out in Romans 14. But being "fully persuaded in one's own mind" (Romans 14:5) does not entail

---

[1] Colson & Neuhaus, pg. 35

[2] Colson & Neuhaus, pg. 35, emphasis added

[3] Colson & Neuhaus, pg. 36

the leaving off of the Gospel when defining Christianity. This kind of tradition without truth is nothing more than error grown old.

Rejection Of Another Way

We mentioned at the beginning of this work that the agenda of the ecumenists goes very much deeper than mere cobelligerency on social, moral and political matters. So radical are the framers of a new ecumenism that they summarily dismiss the notion that cobelligerency can work to win the culture wars. The call has gone out that cobelligerency must give way to *co-evangelization*. That is why the apostasy is so perilous to the Gospel, and must be exposed.

The new ecumenists anticipate the objection of Christians who do not want a religious alliance with Rome. Wise Christians instead opt for a working together on common social and political goals. Wise Christians want nothing to do with allowing the Christ of Scripture and His Gospel to be confused with Roman Catholicism. One would think this had some merit. But it is summarily dismissed by the new ecumenists. Why? Because they want a deep-seated loyalty on the level of religious fervor. In short, they want the house and control of it, too. We are told that the very notion of mere cobelligerency undercuts the ideal of having one united religious front. We are also told that Catholics and Christians all believe the same thing when it comes to the transforming power of the Holy Spirit and the authority of Scripture:

> "In sum, those who are committed to Jesus Christ as Lord and Savior, who have experienced the transforming power of the Holy Spirit, who affirm the authority of Holy Scripture—each and all, though they understand and in worship respond to these realities differently—share more than a political or cultural agenda. They share the 'one faith, one baptism, one Lord' of the Christian gospel."[1]

Do we really? We have 500 years of history behind us and the Bible in front of us that say we do not share the faith with Rome. How utterly fatiguing to read such contemptible nonsense coming from the new ecumenists. We neither share the faith of the Roman Catholic nor the baptism of the Roman Catholic, and most certainly not the gospel of the Roman Catholic.

It remains then to answer the modern ecumenist on one final point. It is often suggested that Evangelicals have more in common with conservative Roman Catholics than they do with liberals. Colson uses this argument and rustles up some support for this by quoting J. Gresham Machen and

---

[1] Colson & Neuhaus, pg. 38

Abraham Kuyper. Both Kuyper and Machen were stalwart Reformed theologians who had little use for the Romanist religion. They did, however, find some common enemies with Rome. Colson concludes:

> "Both Kuyper and Machen believed that devout Catholics and devout Protestants have more in common with one another than with liberal theologians within their own churches or secular modernists in American culture."[1]

But what is to be made of this? We have seen that the modern ecumenists reject the notion of mere cobelligerency as too superficial. Yet, the essence of Kuyper and Machen was cobelligerence *only*, and not an ounce more. Neither of these men would grant to Rome what is demanded here by the new ecumenists. It is one thing to say one has more in common with a chimpanzee than a walrus, but this does not elicit the deduction that humans and chimpanzees are the same. Should our nation be invaded by another nation, I might find myself in a fox-hole with a known murderer who is also a drug addict and child molester. Because we are fighting the same common enemy does not make his lifestyle any less repulsive. Nor am I to be inclined to trust his character any more because we are both trying to survive a common enemy. Likewise with the Roman Catholic religion. It may be an ally against some of what Christianity opposes. However, it is also a deadly enemy of what Christianity affirms and espouses.

Popieluszko And Tokes

Before leaving Mr. Charles Colson, we need to respond to two very moving stories told by Colson at the end of his contribution to *Evangelicals and Catholics Together: Toward a Common Mission.* The story is told of a young Catholic priest who would not give in to Communist threats, and continued to preach to thousands of people in Poland at the start of the fall of Communism in 1980. The story goes that this Catholic priest preached often on two themes. The first theme was, "Preach the Truth, Defend the Truth, Stand for the Truth." The second theme was, "Overcome evil with good." His preaching eventually cost this young priest his life. The net result, at the end of the day, was that thousands marched in the streets of Poland chanting, "We forgive. We forgive." Mr. Colson asks,

> "Is there an evangelical who does not think this Catholic priest was witnessing for Christ?"[2]

Our answer seems to hit at the heart of what is wrong with Mr. Colson and all those who rim the edge of apostasy. Father Jerzy Popieluszko may have

---

[1] Colson & Neuhaus, pg. 40

[2] Colson & Neuhaus, pg. 41

been a brave man. He was, no doubt, sincere in his beliefs. We would share many of his concerns for political, social and humanitarian changes in the world. We too would detest living under a Communist state. We too would speak out for the dignity of the unborn and the right to pursue peace and happiness without state interference. We could champion many of the causes of this young man. However, Jerzy Popieluszko did not preach the Gospel of Jesus Christ. He may have picked up one of the principles enunciated in the Sermon on the Mount. But so have many unbelievers. Many pacifists and freedom fighters from non-Christian religions have been inspired by the teachings of Jesus. But this does not make them Christian and we cannot substitute non-violence and social reform for the Gospel. Neither can we substitute someone's notion that Christ came to preach alleviation of social injustices for the Gospel itself. Poland may have been freed of the tyranny of Communism, *but it remains enslaved to Romanism.* Father Jerzy preached "Defend the Truth, Stand for Truth." What was the truth that he wished to defend? We suspect it was the gospel according to Rome. If not, then we suspect it was equality for all and an end of suppression and repression. It does not matter. Either way, the true Gospel does not consist of these components. If we are going to die, let it be with a clear witness of what God has done in Christ. Let us preach Christ crucified and salvation freely offered through believing in Him and trusting His finished work on the cross for the assurance of eternal life. Any other martyrdom is noble, but is categorically *non*-Christian.

In another country, not far removed from Poland, lived an Evangelical pastor named Laszlo Tokes. According to Colson, this man was like the Polish priest in that he too preached the message of truth. We are not told in what his message of truth consisted. We wonder if this is deliberate. If Laszlo Tokes preached the real message of truth that faith in Christ alone for salvation was the only hope for the individual and the nation, then his message was quite a bit different than that of the Roman Catholic priest. This seems lost on those only concerned with setting human injustices straight and running in fear of losing the culture. We are given a hint that Tokes may have been a preacher of the true Gospel as he held up a Bible while taking refuge from police brutality.

We know from first-hand experience that Romania is open to the mission of the Gospel of Jesus Christ. The obstacles of communism and totalitarianism have been set aside for at least a window of time. We ask the readers to consider which country is closer to the kingdom of God? According to Colson, the Romanist Poland is sitting pretty. No need to evangelize Poland. They are safely tucked into the bed of Roman Catholicism. How about Romania? At last glance, missionaries carrying the real Gospel of *sola scriptura* and *sola fide* are carefully going about their business of taking God's precious message to individuals one at a time. We wonder if they are joined by the likes of Laszlo Tokes. We hope so.

The Elder Theologian

DR. J. I. PACKER rarely needs much of an introduction among Bible-believing and openly confessing Evangelicals. His two books on evangelism and knowing God have been extremely popular and one can scarcely find a Christian who has not read and admired Jim Packer's works. He is a role model for all up and coming Evangelical theologians. At least he was. This has begun to change now that the shock of our decade has reverberated throughout the Evangelical community. This shock, of course, is the fact that J. I. Packer affixed his signature of approval to the *ECT* document. So severe was the dismay among Evangelicals upon hearing the news that many sat in stark unbelief or went into abject denial that it was true. Some thought that Dr. Packer must have been either sick (due to senility) or duped (having been tricked by the Catholics) or confused (by loyalties to old friends). People were, and perhaps still are, looking for a reason. Why would such a preëminent theologian, who knows the Gospel upside down and backwards, ever sign such a document?

The consternation was felt throughout religious circles as well. Stunned by what appears to have been an absolute about face, many close friends and relatives have called Dr. Packer to find out if he was in his right mind. It is one thing for some popular Evangelical to sign the *ECT*, but quite another for someone of Dr. Packer's status. So severe was the backlash that Dr. Packer defended himself and his signing publicly in *Christianity Today* in an article simply entitled, "Why I signed it." No one had to be told who the "I" was or what the "it" stood for in the article.

Evidently, the article in *Christianity Today* was not a totally satisfactory response. He sought to respond in more detail, and that brings him to the front as we must interact with Dr. Packer regarding why he signed the document and if he, too, has wandered off the edge of apostasy. We fear he has done just that, but we must be careful to consider all that he has to say.

At the outset, we are somewhat taken aback at the appraisal of *ECT* offered by Dr. Packer. He does not diminish the impact of *ECT* in so far as it promotes clearly that Evangelicals and believing Roman Catholics are both in acceptable worshiping communities and that proselytization of one community to another is imprudent. He correctly summarizes:

> "The document urged that Protestant evangelicals and believing Roman Catholics act together as far as possible in both the societal and the evangelistic tasks of the Christian mission, which is in truth the mission of the Triune God, carried out through God's people."[1]

Notice that there is no shrinking from the assertion that Roman Catholics and Protestant Evangelicals should act together in both societal *and* evangelistic tasks. It is assumed here by Dr. Packer that there is nothing inherently wrong enough with the Roman Catholic gospel to preclude it from being considered a part of a common task of evangelism which is the mission of the Triune God. This is precisely what *ECT* has said, and more.

However, we do see in the opening remarks of Dr. Packer some divergence and perhaps a contrary understanding of *ECT*. As we recall, Chuck Colson was dead set against using the term "cobelligerence" to identify the way in which Evangelicals and Catholics are to work together because he wanted them to "co-evangelize," as well. Notice Colson's insistence that to view *ECT* as merely a contract of "cobelligerence" undermines its true purpose and content:

> "This is the view, widely held among evangelicals, that Christians can work with anyone—not only evangelicals and Catholics, but evangelicals and Jews, Mormons, or Muslims—in behalf of a just society and government. In this view, evangelicals and Catholics are only cobelligerents in a common cultural war, or allies solely for tactical purposes in the face of a common challenge. This argument, I submit, *undercuts* the very ground on which we stand in today's cultural struggle."[2]

We compare this *denial* of cobelligerency as the theme of *ECT* with the following from Dr. Packer:

> "Grass-roots 'cobelligerence,' to use the late Francis Schaeffer's term, is ECT's theme. It identifies common enemies (unbelief, sin, cultural apostasy) and pleads that the Christian counterattack on these things be cooperative up to the limit of what divergent convictions allow."[3]

---

[1] Packer, Dr. J. I., "Crosscurrents among Evangelicals," pp. 147-174 of Colson & Neuhaus, pg. 149

[2] Colson & Neuhaus, pg. 37, emphasis added

[3] Packer, in Colson & Neuhaus, pg. 149

It may be said initially that Dr. Packer has in mind at least the concept of cobelligerence. This may give some hope that he has not gone as far as Colson and others. However, Dr. Packer is clear enough on the issue. He has accepted the Roman Catholic gospel as a *bona fide* expression of Christianity. Though he may like the idea of cobelligerency, Dr. Packer makes it crystal clear that either Protestant Evangelicals or what he calls believing Roman Catholics can get the job done when it comes to both the social *and* religious agendas:

> "The assumption [of the ECT]—indeed, the argument—throughout is that those whom, with apologies for the patronizing sound of my phrase, I shall call good quality evangelical Protestants and good quality Roman Catholics have enough in common to make this agenda both realistic and wholesome."[1]

Odd, isn't it, that Dr. Packer would single out quality Roman Catholics and quality Evangelicals? We can only assume by "quality" he means those who are consistent and hold to the teachings of their religion faithfully. The same question we asked of Colson, we ask here: "What is the gospel of the good and quality Roman Catholic? Is it any different than the Gospel of the good and quality Evangelical?" If they are not the same, then how can they both be effective in the assignment of societal evangelistic tasks?

Why Can't We See It?

Dr. Packer knows that his signing of the *ECT* does not sit well with the Evangelical community. This is why his article of explanation is resident in the Colson & Neuhaus book. In typical systematic fashion, Dr. Packer defends his signing of *ECT* and offers a bewildering array of explanations and qualifications which will take some effort to untangle. To start out, Dr. Packer identifies those who have protested his signing of *ECT*:

> "Those who protest are evangelicals who have an informed commitment to a traditional Protestant vision, heritage, and policy. That statement, however, needs a good deal of analysis before its meaning is clear."[2]

Dr. Packer then gives a brief summary of what constitutes an Evangelical:

> "Theologically, evangelicalism defines itself against naturalistic Pelagianism by affirming the need for radical renewing of our sinful hearts by the Holy Spirit and against mechanical sacramentalism by affirming the directness of the Spirit's regenerating work in our

---

[1] Packer, in Colson & Neuhaus, pg. 149

[2] Packer, in Colson & Neuhaus, pg. 150

> hearts with and through the gospel Word. In the Christian world, evangelicalism is recognized by its proclaimed and practiced adherence to the seven principals that follow."[1]

Dr. Packer goes on to set out seven principles of Evangelical adherence. Before we get to these seven points, we need to spot check the above definition. We find nothing inherently wrong with Dr. Packer's analysis. We are pleased that he has included a rejection of both Pelagianism (*autosoterism*, or self-salvation apart from the aid of God) and Sacramentalism (*ex opere operato*, or 'the thing signified is brought about by the thing signifying it,' i.e., baptismal water brings about what it represents). However, we need to stop right here and challenge the context in which this is framed. Dr. Packer uses the phrase, "In the Christian world, evangelicalism…". By couching Evangelicalism in such a context, Dr. Packer assumes as true what we categorically deny. His assumption is that there is Christianity (whatever that is), and within Christianity there is "evangelicalism" (whatever that is). By so doing, Dr. Packer makes "evangelicalism" a subset of a larger group. Evangelicalism becomes a *kind* within a *species*. His definition of Evangelicalism is framed in such a way that the description given pertains to a *kind*. An analogy from nature could be taken from the animal kingdom. One might say, "In the animal world, a giraffe is recognized by its proclaimed practices and long-held habits as evidenced by the following seven distinctives." When such a statement is given, it is understood that the giraffe is one of many animals in the animal kingdom. Everyone understands that the writer wishes to only describe one of many animals making up the animal kingdom. The same can be said of Dr. Packer. He appears to give away the store at the very beginning by asserting that those who hold to, believe, and preach the truth of the Gospel (i.e., Evangelicals), *are only a subset of Christianity!*

We are strong on this point because we believe that everything said about Evangelicals in the seven points he provides does not describe a *subset*, but rather the domain itself. Those described as "Evangelicals," by Dr. Packer are also the only people who the Scriptures would call Christians. If we allow the seven distinctives of "evangelicalism" to define only a *subset* of Christianity, the battle is over before it starts. It opens the door to set aside the peculiar traits of this one subset in order to bring along another subset that may not share the tenets described in the first. It is our contention that the seven points of Dr. J. I. Packer *define* Christianity. Period. Anything falling short of, or adding to, the essence of these points is not Christian. It goes without saying, and Dr. Packer would agree, that anything short of, or added to, these tenets, so as to defeat any one or all of the tenets, is simply not *Evangelical*. But that is not our burden. Our burden is to safeguard a

---

[1] Packer, in Colson & Neuhaus, pg. 150

description of Christianity. We think so highly of these points that they are worthy of reproduction. Though not the totality of Christian faith, they nevertheless define the Christian experience. They cannot be relegated to a subset called "evangelicalism." Such a restriction opens Pandora's box.

- 1. The Supreme authority of the sixty-six book canon of Holy Scripture as the self-authenticating, self-interpreting Word of God. This is sometimes expressed as the sufficiency of Scripture to mediate all of God's guidance for faith, life, knowledge of Christ, and securing salvation, and it is sometime abbreviated into the reformation slogan *sola scriptura* ("by Scripture alone"). Views claiming biblical warrant are respected while their credentials are examined, but any that appear to go beyond or fall short of scriptural teaching are rejected as mistaken and dishonoring to God.

- 2. The majesty of Jesus Christ as God incarnate, mediator of the new covenant of grace, substitutionary sin-bearer, perfect Savior, risen, reigning and returning Lord, head of his Church, and director of his disciples. Christ is the immediate focus of the faith, hope, love, and loyalty that in a more inclusive way acknowledge and rest on the grace and saving work of the Father, the Son, and the Spirit together. Typically, this redemptive Christ-centeredness leads to a strong insistence that our present justification through faith in Christ—that is, our acquittal from the guilt of sin and acceptance as heirs of glory—is grounded entirely on his righteousness—that is, his law-keeping, sin-bearing obedience—now imputed to us. This is referred to as *sola fide* ("by faith alone").

- 3. The lordship of the Holy Spirit as source and sustainer of all spiritual life and communion with God. The Spirit works in us understanding of the gospel, conviction of sin, regeneration of heart, faith in Scripture and its Christ, assurance of salvation, love and obedience, worship and prayer, giftings and ministry, the bondings of fellowship, and the fruit of holy and Christlike character.

- 4. The necessity of personal conversion, in which recognition of one's helplessness in sin leads to total trust in Jesus Christ as Savior, Lord, God, lover, brother, and friend, with consequent joyful assurance from the Holy Spirit of the reality of one's new life. Conversion (the subjective side of being "born again") brings eternal life and adoption into God's family, and it sets the pattern for the daily discipline of repenting of sin and finding the forgiveness of one's heavenly Father.

- 5. The priority of evangelism in the Christian life is a way of obeying and glorifying God and practicing love of our neighbor. Christians should share the gospel.

- 6. The need for community in the Christian life. The Church is essentially a fellowship of believers in Christ with Christ; it manifests its reality in local churches (gatherings committed to do all the things the Church does) and also in parachurch bodies (associations committed to do some of the things the Church does). Such bodies may be small, large, national, institutional, denominational, or transdenominational—indeed, ecumenical.[1] Since no Christian is spiritually self-sufficient and coming together is the revealed will of God, every Christian should join a local church and will ordinarily benefit from parachurch involvements as well.

- 7. The practice of administering the ordinances or two sacraments[2] that Jesus instituted, i.e., baptism and the Lord's Supper. Many, if not all, see these two rites as means of grace, conveying and confirming the benefits they signify, through the active exercise of faith that they evoke. The Lord's Supper, in particular, becomes an event of spiritual refreshment through thankful, intentional remembering of Christ's cross and self-offering to him in gratitude for it.[3]

---

[1] We will assume here that by "ecumenical" Dr. Packer means the getting along in the common task of the gospel by those who may have some differences between them but yet are in the household of God via *sola fide* and *sola scriptura.*

[2] Sacraments are defined by Rome as "actions of Christ and his Church (itself a kind of sacrament) which signify grace, *cause it in the act of signifying it*, and confer it upon persons properly disposed to receive it. *They perpetuate the redemptive activity of Christ*, making it present and effective." (*Catholic Almanac*, 1994, pg. 223). We shall give Dr. Packer the benefit of the doubt regarding his use of the term "sacrament." Many Evangelicals, however, prefer not to use this term for baptism and the Lord's table precisely because of the erroneous teaching of the Roman Catholic religion which loads up the term with its anti-biblical doctrine of baptismal regeneration and transubstantiation. Packer here finds commonality with Rome in *terminology* when there is none in *meaning*. This is the ground of our objection. Christians do not understand either baptism or the Lord's table to confirm grace, cause grace, convey grace or call grace out of heaven. Christians do not perceive of grace as an immaterial substance infused from heaven upon those who participate in Christian baptism or the Memorial of the Lord's supper. The Bible is refreshingly clear that Christian baptism is a picture of the believer dying with Christ and being raised in newness of life. Likewise, the Lord's table is a remembrance of Him, declaring His death until He comes again. There is not one shred of evidence in Scripture that either Christian ordinance creates or signifies or conveys regeneration or the reception of an alleged immaterial substance erroneously called grace.

[3] Colson & Neuhaus, pp. 150-152. As much as we like these seven points, this last point and the one previous referring to ecumenicalism should be highlighted. In our opinion, Dr. Packer takes some liberties that will lead to confusion if not straight out false teachings. We do not believe that Christian baptism of confessing believers conveys and confirms the benefits it signifies. Neither do we believe that the Lord's Supper conveys and confirms the benefits it signifies. The Christian does not believe, for

continued on following page

Dr. Packer is quite aware that those adhering to these seven points have worked toward the break-up and dissolution of the Roman Catholic religion. Those who do are convinced that Rome became heretical at the council of Trent and has done nothing but add to its heresies in the centuries since. Packer is quick to point out a number of problems Protestants[1] have had with Rome. He mentions some of the biggest difficulties: the Marian dogmas of the immaculate conception and the assumption of Mary along with papal infallibility, transubstantiation, the mass, Mariolatry and the council of Trent's definition of justification. Everything mentioned by Packer is a violation and contradiction of his seven points of Evangelicalism (Christianity). Because of the doctrinal chasm which separates the Christian Gospel from Rome, Dr. Packer takes a moment to sum up the sentiment of Evangelicals when they hear Rome being endorsed by a respected Reformed theologian:

> "Inevitably, therefore, some now feel that by commending a pattern of cooperation with Roman Catholics, however limited, Protestants like myself are implicitly sanctioning and so strengthening the Roman church system, and thus betraying, or at least frustrating, the essential Protestant purpose."[2]

But has Dr. Packer *only* "commended a pattern of cooperation with Roman Catholics"? The evidence does not suggest this at all. Dr. Packer has done

---

example, that the benefits of the crucifixion are applied to the believer through participation in the Lord's Supper! We are hard pressed to find such "convey and confirm" language in the New Testament. Also, we are more than a little leery of the concept that baptism and the Lord's Supper are "a means of grace." We are hard pressed to find any biblical correspondence to the idea that God deals out grace. Grace is God's disposition toward us, *His kindness toward us*, in Christ Jesus (Ephesians 2:7). It is the disposition of God toward His own. Grace is not dispensed as though it were a commodity. Nowhere in the New Testament are we asked to take part in rites, rituals, ordinances, sacraments, or the like, to "get grace." What exactly is meant by "means of grace" is not clarified by Dr. Packer. We only wish to warn the reader of Romish tendencies even in Packer's articulation of evangelicalism.

[1] We have seen throughout the writings of those who are addressing this issue the use of the terms Protestant and Catholic. This is extremely misleading. There are many who call themselves Protestants because they do not want to be called Catholics. However, they are not Christians. Likewise, the term Catholic can describe those who are faithful to Catholicism and lost as well as those unfaithful to the Roman Catholic religion who are nonetheless lost as well. The battle of terminology must be won by using the word Christian. Christians have trouble with Roman Catholicism because it is not Christian. Thus, every Christian is a Protestant (protests the use of the word Christian by the Roman Catholic religion) but, not every Protestant is a Christian. One need only take a small excursion to North Ireland to find out the sobering fact that the word Protestant, when used there, carries this double meaning.

[2] Packer, in Colson & Neuhaus, pg. 154

far more than commend a pattern of cooperation. He has commended an acceptance of the gospel of Rome as a *bona fide* expression of the mind of Christ and the Christian gospel, and has done so in almost uncontaminated contradiction to himself and all that he has written. Before closing this section with a response to Dr. Packer's six-point rebuttal to his critics, we shall inquire into our accusation that Dr. Packer wishes to have it both ways and ends up in hopeless contradiction.

The Good, The Bad And The Ugly

At times Dr. Packer backs way off the *ECT* statement as though he did not really know how it would be taken:

> "When I put my name to it I did not expect it to be read as implying that its evangelical supporters thought fit to end the historic war with Rome about gospel doctrine and to start treating Rome as we treat evangelical congregations and denominations other than our own—not, of course, as perfect, but not as convictionally or ecclesiastically off-limits for church communion purposes."[1]

We wish that Dr. Packer had stated things a bit stronger here. The gist of this carefully worded "back off of *ECT*" statement is that Dr. Packer did not think that *ECT* opened the door for an end to the war with Rome about Gospel doctrine. Nor did he expect an opening to treat Rome as if Rome were *not* convictionally and ecclesiastically off-limits, as we might treat another Evangelical (Christian?) Church.

So concerned that *ECT* was being read in such a way as to imply as much, Dr. Packer signed a clarification statement drafted in part by Michael Horton of CURE (Christians United for Reformation) ministries. This led to what has become known as the CURE statement of 1994. It's official title is, *Resolutions for Roman Catholic and Evangelical Dialogue*.

That Dr. Packer took the time and energy to sign a document that clarifies the concerns over *ECT* is a positive sign. But it does not help us to live with *ECT* itself. The good is that many of the declarations made subsequently by Dr. Packer, as evidenced by the CURE Statement, serve to attenuate the damage caused by *ECT*. The bad is that one has to labor to put it all together, and even then one is not actually sure of anything because the documents serve to confute each other. The ugly is that Dr. Packer stands behind *ECT* even though all that is in the CURE statement undoes *ECT* theologically.

---

[1] Packer, in Colson & Neuhaus, pp. 156-157

The only way to get to the bottom is to start out with the confession of Dr. Packer. He laments that he did not realize that *ECT* would be read in such a way that Gospel doctrine wars would cease with Rome, and that Rome would be viewed as just another Gospel-preaching church on the block. We ask, "How can Dr. Packer have missed it?" Listen to *ECT*:

> "That we are all to be one does not mean that we are all to be identical in our way of following the one Christ. Such distinctive patterns of discipleship, it should be noted, are amply evident within the communion of the Catholic Church as well as within the many worlds of Evangelical Protestantism."[1]

> "…as much as we might believe one community is more fully in accord with the Gospel than another, we as Evangelicals and Catholics affirm that opportunity and means for growth in Christian discipleship are available in our several communities. …in view of the large number of non-Christians in the world and the enormous challenge of our common evangelistic task, it is neither theologically legitimate nor a prudent use of resources for one Christian community to proselytize among active adherents of another Christian community."[2]

It is conceivable that Dr. Packer might miss it the first time around, although this is difficult to believe, but he has defended his allegiance to this document several times and continues to do so. We must allow the evidence to speak for itself. Any Christian reading even just these two quotes would understand that Rome is *in* and *evangelizing* Rome is out, according to the *ECT* document that Packer signed. We believe that Dr. Packer is deceiving himself and perhaps has fallen prey to a bad case of stubbornness. In either case, the *ECT* statement is the end of gospelizing Rome if it is taken as seriously as its framers clearly state.

Let us show yet another glaring example of supreme contradiction within the mind of one man. The *ECT* statement is absolutely clear in its assertion that Roman Catholics and Evangelicals are brothers and sisters in Christ. It is certain that each are distinct in their patterns of worship but nevertheless equal as Christians. Any doubt we may have that this is the theme of the entire document is soon eliminated upon a cursory reading:

> "All who accept Christ as Lord and Savior are brothers and sisters in Christ. Evangelicals and Catholics are brothers and sisters in Christ. We have not chosen one another, just as we have not chosen Christ.

---

[1] *ECT* Accord, Colson & Neuhaus, pg. xxix

[2] *ECT* Accord, Colson & Neuhaus, pg. xxx

He has chosen us, and he has chosen us to be his together (John 15). However imperfect our communion with one another, however deep our disagreements with one another, we recognize that there is but one church of Christ."[1]

"Those converted—whether understood as having received the new birth for the first time or as having experienced the reawakening of the *new birth originally bestowed in the sacrament of baptism*—must be given full freedom and respect as they discern and decide the community in which they will live their new life in Christ."[2]

Dr. Packer read these words, signed the document, stood by the document in public and still stands by the document in print. He also signed the CURE statement, which says the following:

"We deny, however, that in its present confession it [the Roman Catholic Church] is an acceptable Christian communion, let alone being the mother of all the faithful to whom every believer needs to be related."[3]

"While both Evangelicals and Roman Catholics affirm the ecumenical Creeds, we do not see this catholic consensus as a sufficient basis for declaring that agreement exists on all the essential elements of the Gospel."[4]

"Also, we deny that visible unity has been or can be achieved where a common confession of the Gospel in all its essential elements is lacking."[5]

We submit that Dr. Packer has spoken out of both sides of his mouth and has attempted to be all things to all men by compromising his own positions. Incredibly enough, Dr. Packer concedes the point that he cannot affirm Rome as an acceptable Christian community:

"So, as the Horton-Packer document states, I am not able to affirm of the Roman Catholic Church that 'in its present confession it is an acceptance (sic) Christian communion.' What I mean by that is that Rome's official doctrinal disorders, particularly on justification,

---

[1] *ECT* Accord, Colson & Neuhaus, pg. xviii

[2] *ECT* Accord, Colson & Neuhaus, pg. xxxi, emphasis added

[3] the CURE Statement of August 1994, Colson & Neuhaus, pg. 159, brackets added for clarity

[4] the CURE Statement of August 1994, Colson & Neuhaus, pg. 157

[5] the CURE Statement of August 1994, Colson & Neuhaus, pg. 159

> merit, and the Mass-sacrifice, so obscure the gospel that were I, as a gesture of unity, invited to mass—which of course as a Protestant I am not, nor shall be—I would not feel free to accept the invitation."[1]

We point out that the same man who speaks above of the doctrinal weaknesses and failures that obscure the Gospel in the Roman Catholic religion, signed—and still defends—a document in which he agrees not to do just that:

> "Also to be rejected is the practice of comparing the strengths and ideals of one community with the weaknesses and failures of another."[2]

Dr. Packer has broken his own pledge. We are happy that he has, but sad that all this inconsistency has to be pointed out to the reader, and sad that Packer still does not own up to his glaring contradictions. We take no joy in disclosing the consistent error of one who has meant so much to the cause of God and His truth. We can only hope that Dr. Packer will recant with the great enthusiasm which has marked his earlier writings. We do not look for this, however, in light of what Dr. Packer insists on promoting.

Some natural questions to ask Dr. Packer are these: "If Rome is not an acceptable worshiping community as evidenced by your signing of the CURE statement, why do you still call it Christian?"; "If Rome distorts the Gospel, as you have stated clearly, why do you still call it Christian?"; "If Rome is not suitable for you to become involved in, to the extent that you will not even take in a Mass, then why do you still call it Christian?"; "If Rome violates all of the seven distinctives of the Evangelical (Christian) belief system, why do you still call it Christian?"; "How is it that those who are in Romanism, including Pope John Paul II, should be considered as Christians when they continually defend and promote Romanism as the gospel?"

Dr. Packer's answer to these question places him firmly on the edge of apostasy. He joins Charles Colson and is closely followed by Geisler & MacKenzie. Dr. Packer redefines Christianity so as to include Rome. It is as simple as that. Listen to his answer to these questions:

> "Despite the shortcomings of Rome's official teaching, there are many Roman Catholic Christians: *believers* in the Trinity, the Incarnation, the Atonement, and the historic Resurrection, present heavenly reign, and future personal return of Jesus Christ…"[3]

---

[1] Packer, in Colson & Neuhaus, pp. 162-63

[2] *ECT* Accord, Colson & Neuhaus, pg. xxx

[3] Packer, in Colson & Neuhaus, pg. 163, emphasis added

We are at a critical juncture in this book as well as Christianity and all of Christian history. The assertion made here by Dr. Packer is monumental in its implications for Christianity and world history. If Dr. Packer is right, then the Protestant Reformation was indeed a grievous sin of disunity. What Dr. Packer is saying is that belief in the Trinity, Incarnation, Atonement, Resurrection, Heavenly Reign and Personal Return of Jesus Christ is enough to constitute Christianity. Our work is cut out for us.

To begin with, we give every benefit of the doubt that Dr. Packer means "wholesale trusting consent" when he uses the term "believer" in the citation above. We are all aware that Satan himself *believes* the facts of the matter. To believe something to be historically accurate and undeniable is what the Reformers called *assensus* faith. It is solely intellectual. This kind of faith is useless because it lacks the fiducial, or element of trust. All would agree that many have only a solitary intellectual apprehension of these things of historical record and prophetic prediction, i.e., the resurrection and the second advent, respectively.

Also, we are convinced that Dr. Packer is persuaded that this is no dead faith of the James 2:26 variety ("faith without works is dead"), but rather a lively and active faith as evidenced in humility and self-despairing conduct. So here we have it. Dr. Packer has come in contact with a group or groups of people who believe in the above six aspects of the Christian faith. Their faith is trusting and vibrant without any doubting on these matters. The evidence of their faith has been seen in lively confidence of these things mentioned and exhibits itself in a joyful manner. We wish not to quibble that the faith or belief of the "believers" mentioned in this citation is real and honest. We concede the point.

However, even given all these benefits of the doubt, the question is still before us, "Is faith in the reality and expectation of these things enough to warrant the assumption of Christianity?" Dr. Packer and perhaps millions like him on the Catholic side, and more and more from the "confessing Evangelical" side, are saying "Yes." We say "No."

And we say "No, not now and not ever." We say so with firmness and resolve. We say "No" with certainty and sober reflection on what this answer means to Christianity and the way it is perceived in the world. We say "No" at the risk of being extremely unpopular and branded as cultist. We say "No" at the expense of all reputation and honor of men. We say "No" because *our Lord* has said "No."

We have argued from the beginning of this book that a content-less message is being manufactured by ecumenical apostates who seek to separate doctrinal propositions from the Gospel in order to produce a new gospel of the lowest common denominator. The motivation behind such dilution is an intellectual fascination with cultural wars and a genuine fear of losing Western culture to any number of evil empires ending with "-ism." But the Scriptures will have none of this.

To believe that God exists in three persons of one essence, in the mystery of the Triune God, is part and parcel of the Christian faith. But, because all Christians believe in a Triune God does not mean that all who believe in a Triune God are Christians. All elephants eat peanuts but not all who eat peanuts are elephants. Further qualifications are demanded by Scripture before we can be reasonably sure that Christianity is present. Also, the fact that a denial of the Trinity ends all hope of Christianity being present does not lead to the converse: that affirmation of the Trinity guarantees Christianity is present. Christianity is not defined by faith in Trinitarianism. Belief in the Trinity is indispensable but it is not telling. The same may be said of the Incarnation, Heavenly Reign, Resurrection and Future Return of Christ. All of these are component parts that mark the faith of a Christian but none alone, or taken all together, constitute the presence of Christianity.

It is on this point that our frustration with Packer reaches its peak. Packer, like Geisler & MacKenzie, succeeds in defining the true elements of true Christianity over and over and over again. And then, like the bull in the china shop, they rush in and demolish the goods with their panicked stampede of reductionism, ambivalence and vacillation on precisely what the key elements of the Gospel are. Thus, like a dead fish, their real agenda always floats to the top. When these men wish to defend the Gospel, they spell it out plainly and defend it staunchly. For this, we applaud them. But when the time comes to include Rome, they never attempt to offer support for Rome's gospel, lest they be found guilty of defending a false one. Instead, they reduce the Gospel, lest they be found guilty of excluding Rome! This pattern is repeated again and again because in their hearts, these men know that the two gospels are completely incompatible; only one can be left standing. The Gospel which they earlier defended so staunchly is then transformed into a minimalist sort of heartfelt, yet undefined, faith in a set of facts which anyone can believe without being Christian. They know that this is the only way that Rome can stay inside the circle. We find it very telling indeed that it is Rome's place setting—and not the Gospel's which emerges unscathed from this stampede through the ecumenical china shop.

If we were to play a game entitled, "How many things about Christianity must I believe to be a Christian?" and "How many things about Christianity can I deny and still be a Christian?", it would be a short game indeed if on both questions the proper item was listed first. What Dr. Packer leaves out—so that Rome can stay in—means everything. What Roman Catholics deny means everything. What is left out here and denied there is the Gospel of Jesus Christ. But the Gospel of Jesus Christ cannot be distilled and presented as confidence in some or even most of its component parts. The

Gospel of Jesus Christ is dependent upon the Trinity, but it is not "belief in the Trinity" that constitutes the propositions which the Gospel entails. Nor can belief in the Trinity bring about the desired demand of the Gospel. The Gospel of Jesus Christ is certainly dependent upon the Incarnation, the Atonement, and the Resurrection, but it is not "belief in the Resurrection," or "belief in the Atonement" that constitutes the propositions which are entailed in the Gospel.

As indispensable as these component parts are to the revelation of what God has done in and through Jesus Christ, they do not constitute the Gospel message. Rather, they serve the message. They are the backdrop for the message. Obviously, without the credibility of the Trinity, Christ would have been a liar, for He predicated His authority on being one with the Father. Obviously, without the Atonement there would be no sacrifice for sins and all hope of the Gospel would be lost. But belief that Christ died on the cross only serves the credibility of the Gospel message. Belief in the Atonement without the message for which the Atonement was appointed gets us nowhere. Everything funnels down to the message to be believed stemming from the credibility of the historical facts of Christianity. But the historical facts themselves do not constitute the Gospel.

One may have a vibrant trust in the Trinity, Atonement, Resurrection and Return of Christ but have never come to grips with the message of the Gospel. "Precisely what has been believed about the Atonement, the Incarnation, the Resurrection, the Second Advent and the Reign of Christ?" is the critical question. Without the message that draws the component parts together, the parts fall like tin ash trays on a marble floor. The "So what?" of the Atonement and the Trinity is absolutely fundamental. If the Gospel message is not included in the set of ideas to be believed, then Christianity is not present. Everything channels into the message itself. Get the message wrong, or dismiss the message, or deny the message, and Christianity is not in attendance.

First on the list of things *to believe,* in order to become a Christian is the Gospel itself. It is the Gospel that takes the component parts and puts them in proper meaning and perspective and then calls for a response of belief in the hearer. First, as well, on the list of things *to deny* in order to eliminate the attendance of Christianity, is the Gospel. Take away the finish line, and there is no race. Take away the bottom line, and there is no profit. Take away the ending, and there is no story. Take away the Gospel, and there is no Christianity. There would be nothing to make of the facts if there were no explanation of the value of the facts. The Atonement, the Trinity, the Resurrection, the Reign and the Return would be void of meaning without the "What for?" The Gospel message not only gives us the "What for?", but also carries with it an invitation, command, request and demand that we are to respond to the "What for?" Taking away the Gospel imperatives, or denying the Gospel explanation of the component parts, or nullifying it through tampering with the meaning, kills Christianity. The Gospel is our only hope. The Gospel carries within it a coming together of the meaning of the events, a promise of other events, and a solicitation to benefit from the events.

What is conspicuous by its absence in the list of things believed by Roman Catholics, Mormons, Jehovah Witnesses and Moonies, to name a few, is the Gospel. We are quite certain that we can find enthusiasm for God (Muslims), piety for God (Tibetan Monks), and social polish absolutely vibrating with good deeds (Mormons), but where is the Gospel? It certainly is not left out of the New Testament:

> "So, as much as in me is, I am ready to preach *the gospel* to you that are at Rome also. For I am not ashamed of *the gospel* of Christ: for it is the power of God unto salvation to every one that believeth; to the Jew first, and also to the Greek. For therein is the righteousness of God revealed from faith to faith: as it is written, The just shall live by faith" (Romans 1:15-17).

> "We give thanks to God and the Father of our Lord Jesus Christ, praying always for you, Since we heard of your faith in Christ Jesus, and of the love which ye have to all the saints, For the hope which is laid up for you in heaven, whereof ye heard before in the word of the truth of *the gospel*" (Colossians 1:3-5).

> "In whom ye also trusted, after that ye heard the word of truth, *the gospel* of your salvation: in whom also after that ye believed, ye were sealed with that holy Spirit of promise" (Ephesians 1:13).

> "I marvel that ye are so soon removed from him that called you into the grace of Christ unto another gospel: Which is not another; but there be some that trouble you, and would pervert *the gospel* of Christ. But though we, or an angel from heaven, preach any other gospel unto you than that which we have preached unto you, let him be accursed. As we said before, so say I now again, If any man preach any other gospel unto you than that ye have received, let him be accursed" (Galatians 1:6-9).

It is our contention that no matter what you believe to be true about various aspects of the Christian faith, you cannot have Christianity present in your heart or in your community of worshipers unless there is belief in *the Gospel* of Christianity. This, of course, is *the Gospel* of Jesus Christ and *the Gospel* of God. What then is this Gospel? What does it reveal, demand and promise?

The Gospel reveals not only the Trinity, but also the importance of the Trinity. God was in Christ reconciling the world unto Himself and Christ *was* God incarnate revealing the will of the Father and serving as a complete propitiation for sin. The Gospel reveals not only the Incarnation, but also the importance of the Incarnation. God's love is manifested in the humble estate of Jesus Christ, the God-man taking abode with mankind. Jesus is the lamb of God, without spot, Who was sent to fulfill the requirements of the law of God as the representative head of all those whom the Father would be pleased to give to Him. The Gospel explains that Christ was the second Adam and all in Him are given the free gift of life stemming from His death. The Gospel explains the Resurrection as a down payment on what God has promised all in Christ. The gates of death will not hold the Christian, and the sting of death has been eliminated. Christ is the first fruits to be followed by all who are His own. The Gospel explains the reign of Christ after having presented Himself to God as both priest and sacrifice. Christ reigns at the right hand of God as the long-awaited prophet, David's Son, yet David's Lord. He reigns by right and by appointment. Worthy is the lamb that was slain. The Gospel explains to us the importance of Christ's return as the consummation of the present heavens and earth and the final judgment of mankind. Christ will come for His own that they may be eternally with Him where He is in the new heavens and earth.

But the Gospel does more than explain. It offers a promise based upon the explanations. It offers eternal life based solely on the finished work of the atonement. It offers the promise of God that all sins are and will be forgiven *for the sake of Christ alone*. It offers the end of all personal sacrifices for personal sins. It offers the promise of all guilt removed on the basis of Christ alone, and that through faith alone. It offers the security that all those in Christ will live protected with Him forever and will not lose this standing with God. Furthermore, the Gospel offers an end to all of man's vain attempts to do enough to warrant salvation. The Gospel explains that Jesus has paid it all and that there is no "our share" or "our part" involved. The Gospel explains how God gives us Christ and His righteousness for our right standing with God. The Gospel is the power of God for salvation because it holds the truth of all that God has done for mankind.

It is not enough to believe the various component parts which set the stage for the Gospel and not believe the Gospel itself. We have in mind an imaginary conversation with a Roman Catholic:

Question: "Do you believe in the Triune God of the Bible?"

Answer: "Yes"

Question: "Do you believe in the Atonement of Christ for the satisfaction of sin along with the resurrection of the dead and the current reign of Christ followed by His return to earth to judge the living and the dead?"

Answer: "Yes"

Question: "Do you believe the Gospel of Jesus Christ is summed up in the call to an individual to have a simple trust and faith in His finished work alone, whereby all sin is forgiven by grace through faith alone through which His righteousness becomes our own as a free gift of grace apart from works, sacraments and religious rituals, and that by so believing one is assured of eternal life?"

Answer: "No"

Question: "Why do you answer no?"

Answer: "Because the Triune God of the Bible who came in the Incarnation, was crucified in the Atonement, Resurrected by God almighty, and Who Reigns on high until He should return has told us the way to heaven is through faithful observance to the Sacramental system and obedience to His will as expressed in His Church—the Holy Roman Catholic Church."

Question: "What does this entail?"

Answer: "This entails faith of the highest sort and grace to do His will. The faith given by God understands that original sin is forgiven in my infant baptism whereby I began the process of justification. This faith also gives me grace for more faith as I have my soul cleansed from sin every time I attend Mass and eat the body of Christ and drink His blood after it has first been re-presented to God. This faith allows me to believe that God will allow me to suffer the penalty of unconfessed sins in Purgatory as I fill up that which is lacking in Christ's death. With the aid of Christ and Mary, His immaculate mother, and all the saints, I shall one day be purified to such an extent that God will receive me. For by His grace I will finally be saved should I persevere."

Question: "It sounds like you have a lot of work to do and a lot of confessions to attend and a lot of penance to perform. Do you have any assurance that when you die you will go to heaven?"

Answer: "I am called to work out my salvation with fear and with trembling. This is the gospel of Jesus Christ. I will let Him decide. If we say we know for sure, we sin the sin of the presumptuous."

Question: "In a nutshell, what is the Gospel?"

Answer: "Listen to Christ through His Church and strive to obey Christ through His Church and all will turn out well. Never reject the means of grace for your own purification: penance, purgatory, indulgences, the merits obtained for us by Christ, His mother and the saints. Never deny the mercy to be found in returning to Christ by surrendering to His will as expressed in His Church."

Hopefully, upon reading this—a compilation of actual responses from actual conversations with actual professing and believing Roman Catholics—the reader can see that the *way* of salvation cannot be omitted in any definition of Christianity. This hypothetical Roman Catholic had it all right as far as Trinity, Incarnation, Atonement, Resurrection, Heavenly Reign and Personal Return of Jesus Christ were concerned, but absolutely missed the Gospel itself. Leaving out the way of salvation while preserving its vocabulary imperils the very Gospel in which we stand. The apostle was not insensitive to the zeal for God among his compatriots. But it only served to frustrate him all the more. While embracing God, they rejected God's message:

> "Brethren, my heart's desire and prayer to God for Israel is, that they might be saved. For I bear them record that they have a zeal of God, but not according to knowledge. For they being ignorant of God's righteousness, and going about to establish their own righteousness, have not submitted themselves unto the righteousness of God" (Romans 10:1-3).

We suspect, at heart, Dr. Packer knows that Roman Catholicism falls under the same condemnation as the Israel of Paul's age. We hear the echo of Paul's lament in his first hand experience of those Jews who wanted God but could not hear His Son. "It was necessary that the word of God should first have been spoken to you: but seeing ye put it from you, and judge yourselves unworthy of everlasting life, lo, we turn to the Gentiles" (Acts 13:46).

Tied To The Idol

We now summarize the folly of Dr. Packer by interacting directly with his rebuttal of those so opposed to him. Dr. Packer has lifted out six objections to his favorable stance toward Rome and given his answer:

Point 1. In answer to the criticism that it is wrong to call Roman Catholics our brothers and sisters in Christ, Dr. Packer responds: "…some Catholics do accept Jesus as Lord and Savior in a fully personal way…"[1]

---

[1] Packer, in Colson & Neuhaus, pg. 168

We answer that it means nothing to say this. One can have Jesus in a personal way as a tyrant or a slave master or a puppet or as a philosopher. And for some Roman Catholics, the most "fully personal way" to receive Christ is by eating Him in the Eucharist. But one cannot know the Savior without embracing the Gospel of the Savior. What King would claim as servants those who do not believe Him or show any inclination to tell others the good news about Him?

Point 2. The objection was made that living by the infallible Scriptures cannot mean the same for Evangelicals as it does for Roman Catholics. Dr. Packer responds that since Rome only has a few magisterially expounded texts with which we would dispute leaves the Catholic free as we are to let the Bible interpret itself.

We answer that it means nothing to say this. The few texts that Rome has expounded saddle Catholics with a false gospel. The texts interpreted to teach justification by faith plus works, the existence of Purgatory, the veneration of Mary, the sacrifice of the Mass and the divinity of Christ in the bread, along with the infallibility of both the Pope and the teaching Magisterium leave Romanists trapped in a system well entrenched. If even one erroneous interpretation of the text altered the Gospel, then it would be a bogus religion. Besides, the infallible Scriptures are second fiddle in Rome in light of their trust in infallible Tradition, Magisterium and Pope!

Point 3. It is objected that the formula, "We are justified by grace through faith because of Christ" masks the radical disagreement with Rome so as to express two different gospels, one of which is not a true one. Dr. Packer responds that the Council of Trent (Tridentine) assertions of merit cannot be harmonized with the Reformational assertion of imputed righteousness. But it is not of overwhelming consequence. According to Dr. Packer:

> "But surely ECT's insistence that the Christ of Scripture and the creeds is faith's proper object, and that 'Christian witness is of necessity aimed at conversion,' both as an initial step and also as a personal life-process, constitutes a sufficient account of the gospel for shared evangelistic ministry. Evangelism seeks to lead people into salvation, *and what brings them salvation is not any theory about faith and justification, but trusting Jesus himself as Lord, Master, and divine Savior…*"[1]

We answer that this is the same old same old. All the errors are here. The *ECT* left out the word "alone" when defining justification by grace through faith. It also gave no attention to the way that "through faith" and "by grace"

---

[1] Packer, in Colson & Neuhaus, pg. 168

is interpreted in the Roman Catholic system. The "by faith" to a Roman Catholic means faith in what the Church tells them to do. It does not mean faith in the finished work of Christ alone. In the Roman Catholic system, "by grace" does not mean an absolutely free gift of the righteousness of Jesus Christ, but rather the infusion of the ability to perform well. This ability is brought about through fidelity to the sacramental system.

We answer that Dr. Packer has walked away from the Gospel when he asserts that the principle elements which describe the contents of salvation can be pushed aside as merely some *theories* about faith and justification. The apostle Paul did not labor to illuminate salvation so as to encourage confidence in a theory of faith. Nor do we find the clarification of true faith, as distributed throughout the Bible, to be nothing more than theories of description. Nor do we find the formulas of justification in all their explication to be a hindrance to understanding salvation. If we are to throw out definitions of the things revealed in the Scriptures as "only theory," then with what level of confidence do we conclude that we have presented the proper Jesus and the proper Gospel? Dr. Packer insists that evangelism seeks to lead people into salvation. But he does not want to shoulder the responsibility of assigning actual definitions to the terms. However, to not do this undermines the very content of the Gospel, even if it preserves the Gospel's vocabulary. Packer insists that we direct people to the Christ of Scripture. How will we know that we have pointed to the correct Jesus? Over the centuries many have twisted the Scriptures to create a Jesus of their own imagination. These false mental images of Jesus have been alleged to be the "Christ of Scripture." What words would we use to describe the Atonement and the ground of our justification? What words do we use to evangelize? Why evangelize if the words you use are only some conjecture of what happened to Christ? In the end, Dr. Packer is convinced that the essence of the Gospel is not the imputation of the righteousness of Christ through faith alone, however imperfectly stated and understood by the early Church. He goes beyond even Geisler & MacKenzie here (men not known for their reformed theology) in his undermining of the Gospel and betrayal of the Protestant Reformation and all foundation of solid biblical exegesis.

In his book, *Faith Alone*, R. C. Sproul comments perceptively:

> "Packer argues that it is faith itself in Christ himself that brings salvation, not any theory about faith in Christ, justification, or the church. This is a red herring. What Reformed person ever asserted that justification is by faith in the doctrine of justification by faith alone? Who has maintained that doctrinal theory ever saved anyone? The sole point of sola fide, which Rome categorically rejects, is that we are saved by faith in Jesus Christ alone. The issue is not, Does

> Christ save or does doctrine save? The issue is, What is the gospel that must be the basis of any shared mission of faith?"[1]

Point 4. It is objected that *ECT* accepts the Roman Catholic dogma of baptismal regeneration which will ruin souls by giving them a false hope. Dr. Packer has a somewhat surprising response:

> "But ECT's real logic here, as the careful reader will see, is that agreement on the necessity of personal conversion to the Christ of the Bible and the creeds makes evangelistic cooperation fully viable despite Catholic belief about baptism, inasmuch as any thought that baptism without personal faith will save anyone is hereby ruled out."[2]

To refresh our memory, we reproduce what the *ECT* has to say about the issue of baptism:

> "For Catholics, all who are validly baptized *are born again* and are truly, however imperfectly, in communion with Christ... Those *converted*—whether understood as having received the new birth for the first time or as having experienced the reawakening of *the new birth originally bestowed in the sacrament of baptism*—must be given full freedom and respect as they discern and decide the community in which they will live their new life in Christ."[3]

And in the section of *ECT* that purposely points out the differences between Evangelicals and Roman Catholics, we read a simple yet profound sentence on whether we should view "Baptism as a sacrament *of* regeneration or testimony *to* regeneration."[4]

We cannot fathom a theologian of Dr. Packer's immense insight and erudition to be so blind that he cannot see that the careful reading of *ECT* which he prescribes yields the very thing that he asserts is not there: the undeniable fact that Roman Catholic baptismal regeneration is to be sanctioned as one way to be born from above and made a member of the household of God. The difference between the "of" and the "to" in the above sentence is an eternal difference. Both cannot be right. By allowing baptismal regeneration, Dr. Packer ends the Gospel. He also ends all understanding of regeneration and salvation as taught in the Bible. He is saying regeneration takes place by baptism and that the regenerated may fail

---

1 Sproul, *Faith Alone,* pg. 185

2 Packer, in Colson & Neuhaus, pg. 169

3 *ECT* Accord, Colson & Neuhaus, pg. xxx-xxxi, emphases added

4 *ECT* Accord, Colson & Neuhaus, pg. xxi, emphasis added

at being saved if they do not have faith. This is rank Roman Catholic sacramental salvation. We are aghast that Dr. Packer fails to understand the rudiments of the faith and the domino effect of selling out the significance of being born from above. In Christianity, all those born from above have faith as the first fruit of rebirth and never stop believing. They all are of God's elect and will certainly go to heaven. In Christianity, being born from above is not initiated, brought about, or conjured up in the cauldron of Romish baptism. Neither can it be invoked by any other man-made religious ritual including all other baptisms, be they of water, oil, vinegar, blood or desire! Incredibly, Dr. Packer has endorsed "born from below" and all of its ugly entailments. We stand amazed!

Point 5. It is objected that it is irresponsible to let Roman Catholics who have been converted choose to go back to their churches, since they will not be nurtured there. Dr. Packer answers that there is nothing in the *ECT* that prevents someone from being encouraged to attend a church that puts him under the faithful ministry of the Word where truths are being taught. Having said this, Dr. Packer adds the following caveat:

> "All that is ruled out is associating salvation or spiritual health with churchly identity, as if a Roman Catholic cannot be saved without becoming a Protestant or vice versa, and on this basis putting people under pressure to change churches."[1]

There is a popular hymn which we often sing in our church which starts out with the lyrics, "What more can He say than to you He has said?" We have that same song running through our mind as the evidence mounts up against Dr. J. I. Packer. As elusive as Geisler & MacKenzie have been, they at least held out for some kind of snow fence between Christianity and Rome called "ecclesiastical union." Dr. Packer makes no such attempt. The issue is settled. Rome is in. Dr. Packer would have thousands of missionaries to France, Italy, Mexico, Brazil and Central America—not to mention Italy—give the new gospel: "Go, and return to your Roman Catholic churches and get serious about Romanism!" According to *ECT,* Colson, Packer and all those signing and supporting this dreadful document, missionaries the world round should put an end to pressuring Roman Catholics to change churches. What more can we say than Dr. Packer has said?

Point 6. In this final point the objection is made that church planting evangelism in Roman Catholic parts of the world would have to stop if *ECT* went ahead. Dr. Packer responds that church planting is always legitimate. He reminds us that free association for religious purposes is a recognized human right.

---

[1] Packer, in Colson & Neuhaus, pg. 169

In light of all that has already been said and given away by Dr. Packer, this is a hollow and meaningless point. He is really saying that anyone who would like to spice up the neighborhood with an Evangelical church is welcome to it. He is also handing the Roman Catholic evangelists a key to the city and rolling out the red carpet for their evangelism teams. The idea is to "live and let live." The underlying assumption of course is the same as that of Colson. "Rome is in; Rome is Christian." The Reformation, in the eyes of these men, gave us another point of view but only to show that *theories* abound on issues of salvation. We speak as if insane! The Gospel is very flexible in the mind of Colson, and now has been stretched beyond our recognition due to the efforts of Dr. J. I. Packer. How times have changed since the great preachers and teachers of the Gospel of Jesus Christ from another era departed:

> "Essence of lies, and quintessence of blasphemy, as the religion of Rome is, it nevertheless fascinates a certain order of Protestants, of whom we fear it may be truly said that 'they have received a strong delusion to believe a lie, that they may be damned.' Seeing that it is so, it becomes all who would preserve their fellow-immortals from destruction to be plain and earnest in their warnings. Not in a party-spirit, but for truth's sake, our Protestantism must protest perpetually. Dignitaries of the papal confederacy are just now very prominent in benevolent movements, and we may be sure that they have ends to serve other than those which strike the public eye. A priest lives only for his church; he may profess to have other objects, but this is a mere blind. Our ancient enemies have small belief in our common sense if they imagine that we shall ever be able to trust them, after having so often beheld the depths of Jesuitical cunning and duplicity. The sooner we let certain Archbishops and Cardinals know that we are aware of their designs, and will in nothing co-operate with them, the better for us and our country. Of course, we shall be howled at as bigots, but we can afford to smile at that cry, when it comes from the church which invented the Inquisition. 'No peace with Rome' is the motto of reason as well as of religion."[1]

[1] Spurgeon, Charles Haddon, *The Sword and the Trowel,* January 1873

The Roman Catholic Writer

WE CANNOT LEAVE this section without interacting with a professed Roman Catholic.[1] Richard John Neuhaus is mentioned as "president of The Institute on Religion and Public Life. Editor-in-chief of *First Things: A Monthly Journal of Religion and Public Life*."[2]

He and Charles Colson are the chief architects of the *ECT* statement. Neuhaus' contribution to *Evangelicals and Catholics Together: Toward A Common Mission* is entitled, "The Catholic Difference."

Neuhaus champions the *ECT* statement with measured enthusiasm. He believes it reflects a historic reorientation in our understanding of the Christian mission. He assures us:

> "And it is not too much to believe that it is for this moment that God is bringing evangelicals and Catholics together to present to the world its promised future in Jesus Christ."[3]

Neuhaus' guarded optimism follows on some commentary of the world scene whereby Neuhaus is triumphant in his enthusiasm over the fall of destructive political eschatologies and what he calls the "hegemony of a

---

[1] We say "professed" Roman Catholic because we have been severely chastised by some members of the Catholic community as being much too liberal in our attributions of Catholicism to those who claim to be in the fold of Romanism. On more than one occasion, we have been stopped dead in our tracks, having quoted a Catholic authority, only to be told that the person was not *really* a Roman Catholic. This stings a little but it also serves the point. Not any of the Roman Catholics with whom we have debated publicly or privately would be comfortable with *ECT*. We are certain that there are many who would not think Neuhaus *is* a real Roman Catholic. We have a hard time keeping the players straight without a score card, but we do give the benefit of the doubt to Richard Neuhaus that he is a Roman Catholic.

[2] Colson & Neuhaus, pg. xxxv

[3] Neuhaus, Richard John, "The Catholic Difference," pp. 175-227 of Colson & Neuhaus, pg. 177

secular Enlightenment, a scientism disguised as science…" [1] We wonder aloud if the *ECT* statement and all that is packed into the Evangelical romance with Rome might far exceed the devastation wreaked upon mankind by the failed enlightenment of human reason. We sense the dawn of an *old* age, i.e., a religion disguised as Christian.

As in the case of Colson and Packer, Neuhaus finds in the social issues the occasion for the awakening of a consciousness among Evangelicals and Roman Catholics that they really believe in the same things at heart:

> "Behind the political agreement was the discovery of agreement about moral truth, expressed in terms of common grace or natural law. Undergirding it all was the discovery of a shared allegiance to the Author of truth and a shared faith in the One who is the way, the truth, and the life."[2]

We notice that there is no word here of a shared gospel. It is a shared allegiance. But this is meaningless terminology if the One to Whom allegiance is due has spelled out His terms of fidelity. Jesus has done just that. Jesus defines the way of the Way. We believe that Jesus Christ is not only worthy of allegiance but only deems worthy *loyalty* on His terms. One does not come to Christ in *ways* of his own making. One comes to Christ in the *way* of God's revelation. All other *ways* are man's ways. To dress them up as the tenacious perceptions of zealous men is to do nothing more than create religions. When Jesus says that He is the *way,* the *truth* and the *life*, He means it. He is not the way which admits of many procedures. He is the only means. This singularity of method expresses both the His unique Personhood and the fashion of contact with Him. In short, Jesus is not just the Way; He signifies the Way, e.g., "If any man serve me, *let him follow me*; and where I am, there shall also my servant be: if any man serve me, him will my Father honour" (John 12:26).

We are not surprised by two observations early on in Neuhaus' contribution to *Toward a Common Mission.* The first observation is that he thinks the most important affirmation of *ECT* is that Evangelicals and Roman Catholics are brothers and sisters in Christ. Neuhaus has the most to gain by such an assertion. Evangelicals are the only ones on the face of the earth telling Roman Catholics they are not Christians; Neuhaus would like to see this last pocket of resistance to fall. The second observation is that all those who are concerned that Rome is seducing Evangelicals in order to convert them are just paranoid:

---

[1] Neuhaus, in Colson & Neuhaus, pg. 177

[2] Neuhaus, in Colson & Neuhaus, pg. 178

> "Some promoters of this conspiracy theory evidence a mindset that is aptly described as paranoid."[1]

The conspiracy spoken of in full is the betrayal of the Reformation as well as the return to Rome by Evangelicals. Aside from the fact that any return to Rome would be, by definition, a betrayal of the Reformation, the motive for condemning *ECT* is far more noble than this. The document needs to be condemned because it elevates the Roman Catholic apostate religion to the same status as Christianity and drags down the name "evangelical" to the same level of Rome. The fear is not conversion—the fear is assimilation and distortion of the Gospel. These fears have been already substantiated in an earlier portion of this book.

Neuhaus finds himself in a self-described historical moment of time for the propagation of the sentiments expressed in the *ECT* statement:

> "As for our historical moment, it is enough that, after four centuries of suspicion and hostility, we have found one another; it is enough that we are able to address our differences with candor and clarity; it is enough that we are learning to engage one another in mutual respect for the institutions, traditions, and patterns of discipleship that have developed over the years of our separation; it is enough that we discern together and embrace together the great challenges of moral and cultural renewal; it is enough that we witness to the world, and witness to one another, the saving gospel of Jesus Christ; it is enough that, toward that great end, we can admonish and encourage one another, always speaking the truth in love (Eph. 4:15)."[2]

Our question is ever the same: "What is the saving Gospel of Jesus Christ?" "Who has it to share?" "What does it entail?" Rome is on record and so are the Reformers. What has changed? What is meant by the sentiment that "we have found each other"? Are there really different ways of becoming and being a Christian? We may grant that there are different expressions of worship. Some sing more than they pray. Others are more vocal and exuberant than the quiet crowd. Some churches meet more often together than others. Some share the Lord's table more often than others. But all these superficial differences do not spell out different ways of *becoming* a Christian. We are convinced if one thinks he became a Christian through a novel way not revealed in the Bible, he is likely to defend the way he thinks he has *become* a Christian by asserting there are many ways of *being* a Christian. But this is meaningless language if there is only one way of

---

[1] Neuhaus, in Colson & Neuhaus, pg. 179

[2] Neuhaus, in Colson & Neuhaus, pg. 180

entering Christianity, and that one way is ignored. We think Romanists genuinely believe that they can *become* a Christian through novel contrivances and continue in their bizarre religious rituals under the excuse that there are many different ways of *being* Christian.

We cannot allow the word "difference" to be the white paint on rotted-out fence posts in our modern era of ecumenists. We heard this word over and over again from Geisler & MacKenzie. Now comes the Romanist writer as if on cue:

> "The ways in which the terms *catholic* and *evangelical* have been appropriated and employed in the last four centuries of Christianity in the West are not without importance. Words are never mere words. Their uses represent distinctive accents and sensibilities that give a recognizable form to different ways of being a Christian."[1]

The grand assertion is repeated like the relentless drum beat of some ancient funeral march. Notice that the word Evangelical is being passed off as a term of distinction to differentiate two different ways of being a Christian. Say it long enough and in many different ways, and the only conclusion must be that Roman Catholicism is a "different" worshiping community, but is not "wrong." We have already shown the folly of using the word "different" in this manner. Let it suffice to say that we see it again and again. Here it pops up as the first line of defense with Neuhaus. He first declares that Roman Catholicism is the Gospel and then declares it is merely a "different way of being Christian" than Evangelicalism. We shall next see that the "difference" is absolutely necessary to really understand Christianity. We are not surprised. We wonder how in the world Neuhaus and Packer could have even been in same room, let alone sign the same *ECT*. Let us juxtapose their contradictory and muddled thinking for you:

- **Neuhaus:** "Catholics insist that they are equally *devoted to the good news of the gospel*, that there is no Church apart from the gospel, and therefore they, too, are evangelical. [2]

- **Packer:** "So, as the present Horton-Packer document states, I am not able to affirm of the Roman Catholic Church that 'in its present confession it is an acceptance (sic) Christian communion.' What I mean by that is that Rome's official doctrinal disorders, particularly on justification, merit, and the Mass-sacrifice, *so obscure the gospel…*"[3]

---

[1] Neuhaus, in Colson & Neuhaus, pg. 181

[2] Neuhaus, in Colson & Neuhaus, pg. 181, emphasis added

[3] Packer, in Colson & Neuhaus, pg. 162, emphasis added

Both men endorse this hopeless *ECT* document. It is beyond our ability to write just how bizarre things have become.

If You Cannot Join Them, Declare Them Joined!

Through carefully selected terminology and finely honed subtlety Dr. Neuhaus wanders around a bit at the beginning of his article. He probes and pinches. He is much like a doctor taking the measure of a fallen athlete on the playing field. He firsts sees some things that are right and then tests some things that may be wrong. But his unmistakable theme is ever before us: Roman Catholicism is the same as Evangelicalism in essence, and only differs in expression. Both are, in his estimation Christian, yet too long separated by 16th century theological considerations that should not have lasted this long:

> "Surely there is no reason to think that the forms of division that came into being in the West in the sixteenth century of the Christian era are intended to be forever, or even for the next hundred years."[1]

If we are to understand Neuhaus, then we must conclude that the differences of the 16th century have either been eliminated or have been a mistake all these years. If a mistake, then on whose part? Who were right: the Reformers or the Council of Trent? Who should change? Should the articulation of the Gospel and the theology of the New Testament as exhibited by the Reformers or the Council of Trent be changed? Dr. Neuhaus fails to point out that the differences have lasted this long because they are radically opposite at heart. If "2 + 2 = 4" has been the same since Adam, then what makes us think that directly opposite statements on the content and nature of truth will go away simply because someone says they should? While Dr. Neuhaus says we must be open to any surprises that the Holy Spirit may have for us, he begins to go about his business of joining all to Rome by *fiat*. The surprise would be if Rome stopped being Rome; we do not look for this to happen. What we do look for is an all out attempt to validate the gospel according to Rome. All subtlety aside, Neuhaus seizes the language of Vatican II and solves the problems of 500 years by simply declaring unity to exist:

> "'Those who believe in Christ and have been properly baptized are in a certain, although imperfect, communion with the Catholic Church.' In the Catholic view, the problem posed by the division between Catholicism and evangelicals is not that we are *not* united. *The problem, indeed the scandal, is that we are united but live as though we were not.*"[2]

---

[1] Neuhaus, in Colson & Neuhaus, pg. 187

[2] Neuhaus, in Colson & Neuhaus, pg. 187, emphasis in original

Part IV
Unity, O Unity, Wherefore Art Thou?

Unity, Falsely So-Called

IT IS THE CONTINUED siren song of the ecumenists that God has not given us a divided, fractured and split-up Church. We agree that the gift of God is a united Body of believers. Fragmentation is nothing less than sin to be repented of and resisted strenuously. We acknowledge this, but cannot make the fatal error of placing unity ahead of truth. Only truth brings about a trustworthy unity in the Body of Christ. In reality, the Church is united. In reality, all those in Christ Jesus share the same faith and are individual parts of the Body. But there are many wolves in sheep's clothing. There are many who are enemies of the Cross of Christ. There are many who say, "Lord, Lord!", yet they are not members of the Body of Christ because they do not believe the Gospel of Christ. They reject the revelation of God as it pertains to salvation.

There is indeed one Lord, one faith and one baptism. The question is, "Which Lord, which Faith and, which Baptism are we going to accept as the genuine article?" It will do no good to cry "Unity, unity!" until the basis of solidarity is established, and Rome comes to grips with the Gospel of Christ. When we hear, "One Lord, one Faith and one Baptism," we need to ask the appropriate questions. When we hear, "A new commandment I give unto you, That ye love one another; as I have loved you, that ye also love one another" (John 13:34), we must temper it with: "For I know this, that after my departing shall grievous wolves enter in among you, not sparing the flock. Also of your own selves shall men arise, speaking perverse things, to draw away disciples after them" (Acts 20:29-30). We would also add the cautionary words of the apostle John: "Beloved, believe not every spirit, but try the spirits whether they are of God: because many false prophets are gone out into the world" (1 John 4:1). If the train of love and unity is not propelled by the engine of truth, it will never capture the citadel of satanic opposition, but will meander hopelessly through the valleys of opinions, feelings and emotions until, out of steam, it comes to rest on the edge of apostasy.

The modern ecumenists, with their insistence upon unity at the cost of the Gospel of Jesus Christ, appear to have believed their own publicity. It goes something like this, "If we are the only ones who really care about unity, then we must be the true Body of Christ." What is neglected in this assumption is the much overlooked fact and understated reality that there is an absolute homogeneity in the Body of Christ which abhors unity for the sake of unity. There already exists an accord founded on the person of Christ and the message of the Gospel of salvation to all who believe. If one were to travel the world over, one would find the Church of Christ in just about every place. There is already existing a unity that cannot be manufactured. It is the heartfelt unity brought about by the same belief system given to God's own people. This unity is not founded on the principle of unity but rather on the person and message of the Gospel. As Peter writes:

> "Simon Peter, a servant and an apostle of Jesus Christ, *to them that have obtained like precious faith with us* through the righteousness of God and our Saviour Jesus Christ" (2 Peter 1:1).

This is lost on those who push the gospel of unity without the reality of biblical theology and sound doctrine.

Sleight Of Hand, Sleight Of Word

When Jesus spoke the little parable of the piece of new garment sewn on an old garment and the new wine put in old wineskins (Luke 5:36-39), He did so to make a dramatic point. The point is that the old and new do not do well together. The new fabric shrinks and tears the old. The new wine ferments and bursts the old wineskin. The point is that the two are incompatible and ruin each other. The best thing to do is to sew new on new and put new in new. Jesus Christ came to fulfill the old and to establish the new:

> "In that he saith, A new covenant, he hath made the first old. Now that which decayeth and waxeth old is ready to vanish away" (Hebrews 8:13).

He did not rearrange the old and make it new. He said it is now the time for a New Covenant, for the old is ready to vanish.

We have always viewed Roman Catholicism as the counterpart to first century Judaism. We have always seen the parallels. As a committed first century Jew could not break with the customs of the old, but sought rather to legitimize them within the greater light of Christ, so does the Roman Catholic. The Lord knew that a complete break was necessary if one was not to spoil the other. A blend was not possible. The Lord knew that certain things about old cloth and old wineskins would ruin the new. He knew that they could not exist together on the same shirt or in the same container. Neither can Christianity be stretched to include both the Gospel and Romanism. The two are mutually exclusive and cancel out each other. They are incompatible no matter how hard one tries to sew them together or to pour the wine of the Gospel into a Roman wineskin.

This is painfully obvious as we linger over Richard John Neuhaus speaking out of both sides of his mouth while trying to hide and protect the old shirt on which he has sewn a new patch. Neuhaus uses sleight of hand and word to pour the New Wine of the New Covenant into the musty bags of Romanism. But we hear the tearing of the cloth and the cracking of the vessel, as well as the bleating of the sheep for that matter! Roman Catholicism is very much like an old shirt which seeks for legitimate space in the Lord's wardrobe despite its incompatibility with the new fabric. Roman Catholicism is like the old wineskin that begs to hold the new wine but is constitutionally unable and will only destroy it. No matter how many patches one puts on an old shirt, the old cannot be improved. No matter how many repairs are made to an old wine skin, it is still the old wine skin and will ruin the new wine. The essence of the materials involved cannot sustain the new. It is that simple. The old must go and the new must come to replace it. All the patchwork in the world is not going to legitimize or hide the fact that the garment is unsuitable for new cloth and the wineskin is unsuitable for new wine.

Imagine someone trying to hide the fact that they are wearing an old garment by putting new patches on it every time it tears. It is pure folly, for the cause of the tearing is the new patch itself. Not only is the old seen for what it is, but the new looks positively ridiculous on it. Such is the case with Rome. No matter how hard Neuhaus tries to hide old Rome with patches of Evangelicalism, the old is always there in substance and looks grotesque with Evangelical patches sewn here and there. Is it any wonder that the rank and file knowledgeable Roman Catholic thinks the *ECT* statement is offensive as well? Let us eavesdrop on Neuhaus, busy in his sewing room. See the garment he wears:

> "All the saving and sanctifying grace that is to be found outside the visible boundaries of the Catholic Church has built into it, as it were, a God-given gravitation toward unity with the Catholic Church. But the gravitational pull, of course, works both ways. Thus Catholics are drawn to unity with other Christians. This in no way weakens or calls into question their communion with the Catholic Church; indeed they are drawn precisely because of their communion with the Catholic Church, for it is here that they have learned to recognize as brothers and sisters those who are 'truly but imperfectly' in communion with the one Christ and the one Church." [1]

[1] Neuhaus, in Colson & Neuhaus, pp. 195-196

Explicit in this statement is the opinion of Neuhaus that Roman Catholicism, at heart, is not the problem. Rather, he tacitly asserts that the problem lies with those who would dare to disagree, or in his words, those for whom the gravitational attraction seems to be having little effect. Let it be understood that for the past 500 years Rome has represented the "old" garment of ancient Judaism. It remains so now. Also, explicit in this statement is the recognition that other Christians are in imperfect communion with Christ. This would be the Evangelical community. Let it be understood that for over 500 years the doctrines and belief system centered around the *solas* of the Protestant Reformation were considered as nothing less than the Gospel of the New Covenant of Jesus Christ. It is the same now. It is only in the imagination of Richard John Neuhaus that there is anything whatsoever attractive about Rome that would cause anyone born from above to be drawn to it. Rome gives off a scent which the living find repulsive.

Explicit and implicit in Neuhaus' statement is that both belief systems can be compatible. With sleight of hand and word, Neuhaus in this one paragraph, sums up the mind-set of the modern Roman Catholic ecumenist. We have selected this quote because it is so revealing. Notice that Rome is still to be looked at as the gravitational center of Christianity. Notice that the doctrinal beliefs of the Roman Catholic religion are accepted as Gospel. Notice that the Catholic is now free to recognize the imperfect communion of non-Catholics with Christ. Notice that unity is the engine that runs the entire train. But notice something much more dangerous and much more subtle. As we have mentioned in our previous writings about Romanism, there is inherent in all of this a double-speak manipulation for credibility. The genius of the Roman Catholic religion in our age is that it has succeeded in putting itself in the seat of judgment over all other religions. Historically, Rome has always assumed this posture. What is new, and altogether surprising, is that Rome is now being granted this permission by Evangelicals. Rome seeks legitimacy. She finds a score of Evangelicals who will grant legitimacy and then begins to determine the role and place of all those who legitimize her. The biggest—and most ironic—patch on the oldest garment is the patch wherein Rome legitimizes Evangelicalism! If we are credentialed by Rome, then how can we ever speak back? How does the one seeking accreditation discredit the accreditation committee? The answer is that it cannot seek to correct that from which it seeks approval. Incredibly, Rome is parading around in, and even flaunting, its old garment with all these new patches, and precious few are willing to address this hypocrisy in the Christian community. We hasten to say that the Vatican knows exactly what it is doing and will not tolerate the Evangelical patches at all in the future. They will be ripped off by Rome herself in the name of Roman unity. As with Geisler & MacKenzie's opening section, Neuhaus reeks with Romanism even in his conciliatory remarks on Evangelicalism:

"The local church is understood, first of all, as the priests and the faithful gathered around their apostolically ordained bishop in a particular place. Thus each diocese is a local or particular church that is fully and rightly ordered by virtue of its communion with another particular church, the church of Rome, which, in the words of Saint Ignatius, 'presides in charity' over the entire Christian people."[1]

"Mary from her conception (by virtue of anticipating in faith her Son's redeeming work) and the saints in their heavenly perfection are like him also in his sinlessness."[2]

"The Catholic claim is that the Catholic Church is the fully and rightly ordered expression Christ's Church through time. That claim rests upon many considerations, very important among them being what many Protestant as well as Catholic scholars recognize as Christ's intention for a continuing 'Petrine ministry' in his Church."[3]

"In the Catholic view, Protestant theories of the Church, whether advanced by liberals or conservatives, seem woefully inadequate. Such theories do not take with sufficient seriousness the New Testament witness to the inextricable and intimate union between Christ and his Church, the Head and the body, the Bridegroom and the Bride."[4]

If one cares to listen, one can always hear the drum beat of Rome in the background. We also hear the never-ending lecture to come home to the one true worshiping community. We also hear another gospel!

The Article

As in previous theological discussions, we must now turn our attention to what Luther called *articulus stantis et cadentis ecclesiae* or, the article upon which the Church stands or falls. This article is the Christian doctrine of justification by faith alone apart from all works of law, be they Jewish, Romanist or pagan works. Neuhaus is eager to enter the discussion. We shall hear him out.

In typical Romanist fashion, Neuhaus makes a bombastic statement by mixing in a few truths to hide the error. Neuhaus rightly notices that

---

[1] Neuhaus, in Colson & Neuhaus, pg. 193

[2] Neuhaus, in Colson & Neuhaus, pg. 191

[3] Neuhaus, in Colson & Neuhaus, pg. 196

[4] Neuhaus, in Colson & Neuhaus, pg. 197

justification by faith alone is central to 16th century Lutheran and Calvinistic theology. But he makes an unwarranted leap in saying that the great majority of Evangelicals in America would not accept the Lutheran or Calvinistic schools of theology as normative for their understanding of the Christian faith:

> "Wesleyan, Arminian, Holiness, Pentecostal, and other evangelical traditions are much closer to the Catholic understanding of the connections between faith and the converted life, between justification and sanctification."[1]

While it is true that many of these Evangelicals would differ with *some* of the teachings of John Calvin and Martin Luther, it is a *non sequitur* to say that therefore, they do not believe in justification by faith alone. If any do not, then they have no right to claim the name of Jesus Christ and His Gospel. Their gospel would be as faulty as Rome's. We lament that there may be some truth to the assertion that some professing Evangelical communities are closer to Rome than they ought to be. But it is to the discredit of their leaders and has nothing to do with the truth of the Gospel.

We must point out that Neuhaus, like all Roman Catholic apologists, likes to speak in terms of traditions and historical communities. This paves the way for minimizing Protestant teaching down to a novelty which emerged in a particular historical setting. Neuhaus narrows down the resistance to the *ECT* as coming from a rigorous band of Calvinists. By separating the so-called Calvinists from the mainstream of Evangelicalism, Neuhaus hopes to show that the language of the *ECT* is perfectly compatible with Roman Catholicism and with Evangelicalism as well as the Bible itself.

Neuhaus defends the language of the *ECT* statement by trying to convince us that the formula *ECT* used for justification has more biblical warrant. First, let us review the formula of the statement.

> "We affirm together that we are justified by grace through faith because of Christ."[2]

Realizing that the framers of *ECT* deliberately left out the important word "alone" from this formula, Neuhaus defends the statement:

> "A merit of the formula chosen by ECT—'we are justified by grace through faith because of Christ'—is that all the parts of that formula are actually found in the New Testament. The advocates of

---

[1] Neuhaus, in Colson & Neuhaus, pg. 199

[2] *ECT* Accord, Colson & Neuhaus, pg. xviii

> 'justification by grace alone through faith alone because of Christ alone' may well believe that it most adequately reflects the teaching of the Bible, but the formula itself is in fact a sixteenth-century theological construct that is not found in the Bible."[1]

Note well the fact that the formula decided upon by the framers of the *ECT* i.e., "we are justified by grace through faith because of Christ," does not present itself as such a formula in the Bible either. But more importantly, we notice that the formula, "justification by grace alone, through faith alone, because of Christ alone," was deemed to not have all of its parts found in the Bible according to the document signers. Despite this, Neuhaus does in fact concede, as we shall see, that as a Lutheran this very formula was instrumental in powerfully forming his theological understanding and spiritual life. However, in the citation above, he reduces it to a mere "sixteenth-century theological construct" that does not have all of its parts in Scripture. Such assertions notwithstanding, Neuhaus is convinced that the formula, "faith alone, grace alone because of Christ alone" is fully sufficient to protect the *truth* of the Gospel. Finally, to add to the complete mystery of Catholic double-speak, Neuhaus believes the formula is compatible with the *ECT* (which omits it) and the Catholic religion (which denies it). Listen to him once again:

> "As a Lutheran Christian, my theological understanding and spiritual life were powerfully formed by the formula of 'justification by grace alone, through faith alone, because of Christ alone.' The truth of the gospel that that formula was intended to protect is, I am convinced, entirely compatible with ECT and with the authentic teaching of the Catholic Church."[2]

All of this is to say that Neuhaus thinks "faith alone" and "grace alone" are quite all right if one is inclined to talk about protecting the Gospel. It is also somehow compatible with a statement on salvation which deliberately omits the word "alone" from the formula. It is also prudent to omit the word "alone" from the formula because all the parts (presumably the word "alone") are not found in the Bible. And yet, if one really wants to know, says Neuhaus, the "faith alone, grace alone, Christ alone" formula is really what the *ECT* statement means, and is the official teaching of the Catholic religion as well. Welcome to *Theology 101*, Roman style.

When asked, "Why does not the Catechism of the Catholic Church speak more clearly to the great issues of the Protestant Reformation especially as it touches on how a person is justified before God?", Neuhaus answers in

---

[1] Neuhaus, in Colson & Neuhaus, pg. 200

[2] Neuhaus, in Colson & Neuhaus, pp. 199-200

perhaps the most masterful bit of straight-faced foolishness and double-speak we have quoted yet:

> "While not pressing a comparison between the two, the *Catechism* and ECT are alike in this respect: both attempt to bring together in a positive form what can and should be said as Christians prepare themselves for the challenge and promise of the future. The desire is to move on, not to get bogged down in past disputes, and yet to do so in a way that is scrupulously faithful to the truth."[1]

Here, much is revealed. How does one go on in scrupulous faithfulness to the truth without treating the issue of justification? Could it be that Neuhaus understands that this one article is important enough to bring down the entire house of Rome? Could it be that the Catholic Catechism knows full well that this one article, if accepted in terms of the biblical data and articulated in the "faith alone" formulas, will end all of Rome? We think so. We think this is why *ECT* assiduously avoided the clearer statement. We think this is why the Evangelical world is allowed to have its "incomplete" formula on the condition that Rome's formulas are left uncontested.

In an effort to exonerate the Catholic Catechism for its lack of attention to the issue of justification by faith alone, Neuhaus gives us this startling statement on the value of justification for the formulation of the Gospel of Jesus Christ:

> "The arguments surrounding the *sola fide* formula are the preserve of a relatively small number of professional theologians, mainly Lutheran and Calvinist, in North America and Western Europe. That does not mean the arguments are wrong; *it does mean that they are not, and cannot be,* at the center of the global proclamation of the gospel and the Christian mission in the third millennium."[2]

We sincerely hope the signatories of the *ECT* are listening. We hope that all of Christianity is listening to the efforts of this Romanist to kill the life-changing message of hope and salvation delivered once and for all to the saints by Christ and His faithful followers. We hope all the Evangelicals who are flirting with Rome and leading their sheep into the slaughter house will ponder these words carefully. According to Neuhaus, silly little arguments over how a sinner is justified in the eyes of God cannot possibly be important enough for the Roman Catholic Catechism to contemplate. The way a man is justified is hardly the centerpiece of the Gospel, according to Neuhaus. And this from someone who holds that Rome is *the* God-

---

[1] Neuhaus, in Colson & Neuhaus, pg. 201

[2] Neuhaus, in Colson & Neuhaus, pg. 204, emphasis added

ordained guardian of the Gospel itself! We wonder aloud, "What then is the centerpiece of the gospel of Rome, or of anyone else that is interested in global evangelism?" But Neuhaus goes on:

> "Entering into these disputes over all the necessary distinctions and qualifications lands us right back where Protestants and some Catholics were four hundred years ago. One is inclined to believe that that is not where the Holy Spirit intends to lead the Church at the end of the twentieth century."[1]

> "As for those who insist that the theological wars of the past are the wars of the present and must forever be the wars of the future—or at least until one side unconditionally surrenders—it is to be feared that they are demanding something other than unity in the gospel."[2]

The Roman Catholic publicity machine is in high gear, and Evangelicals are in it up to their collective earlobes. Together they have beaten a path to the edge of apostasy. "Rome is not apostate," they say. "Rome is simply an alternative worshipping community." …"Rome is not fatal to the Christian Church. Rome simply views the Body of Christ differently." …"Rome does not harbor false doctrines. Rome is simply full of interesting and peculiar doctrines which when viewed rightly enhance the Body of Christ." …"Rome does not preach another gospel. Rome simply teaches a gospel that embraces a number of concepts in a fuller expression of the message of Jesus Christ." …"Rome does not define Christianity in an unbiblical manner. Rome has discovered that there are many ways to express justification and is not limited to sixteenth century formulas." …"Rome is not the progenitor of all auto-soteric (man-made religions). Rome is the last bastion of moral rectitude and an example for all to follow on their road to heaven." …"Rome is not dogmatic and autocratic in her ecclesiology, emptying the biblical demand of *sola scriptura* and *sola fide* for our only source of authority and salvation. Rome is the depository of Petrine authority and magisterium infallibility which protects the Church from error and confusion."

The stew of apostasy is gathering the herbs and seasonings of theological language contributed by Romanists and Protestants alike. To the ecumenical mind, the gospel is much too mysterious to be entrapped in definitions. The gospel, for Rome, is like the mysterious person of Mary. Like the Mary of Romish devotion, Rome's gospel is forever shrouded in myriads of sayings and abstract speculations. All this is done under the rubric of heightened faith. For Rome, there can be no one theological formula that captures the

---

[1] Neuhaus, in Colson & Neuhaus, pg. 204
[2] Neuhaus, in Colson & Neuhaus, pg. 205

essence of the momentous truth of God's word. Or so we are told. There can be no doctrinal limitations on the mysteries of Christ. Stir, stir, stir. As with the wicked witches of the Scottish Highlands who concocted a brew of deceit to capture the soul of Macbeth, this brew too must be made ready. Richard John Neuhaus need not fear of sending Rome back to the 16th Century. Rome has never left. We, as Christians, will meet them where they are.

The Spin Doctor

In political circles when a candidate gives a speech that has no obvious meaning, or has an obvious meaning which needs to be toned down or massaged, they call in the "spin doctors." These professional political pundits and wordsmiths put a more palatable spin on what was said. They do this to bring out the best possible image and picture of the candidate. The Romish religion is not without its own such doctors. Neuhaus is one of them. We devote the remainder of this section to catching up with the spin that Neuhaus puts on for the theologians, magisterium, popes and councils of Rome.

There are three ways in which Romanism is given the good spin by the spin doctor Neuhaus.

SPIN #1

The first spin is to assure the Christian community that God is much too big to be understood by the use of one formula or one theological system. Listen to the doctor:

> "There is no one formula or theological system that can catch all the dimensions of the momentous truth that 'God was in Christ reconciling the world to himself, not counting their trespasses against them, and entrusting to us the message of reconciliation' (2 Cor. 5:19 RSV). There are many ways of saying that."[1]

We ask, "There are many ways of saying *what*?" When we are told that there are many ways of saying *something*, we expect the *something* to be identified. If Neuhaus has 2 Corinthians 5:19 in mind, then how many ways are there of saying, "not counting their trespasses against them"? Evidently not enough, since one of the pillars of the Roman Catholic religion is to do penance, attend mass, confess sins to a priest and suffer in Purgatory, by which means Rome actually teaches that God *counts* men's trespasses against them!

---

[1] Neuhaus, in Colson & Neuhaus, pg. 205

The spin doctor wants us to buy into the Romish nonsense that God cannot be put in a thimble, and therefore we cannot say anything for sure about Him. His ultimate point is that everyone who reads the Bible or contemplates God comes away with a little piece of truth. Neuhaus thinks there is no one way to believe the truth, or to have the truth, or to catch the truth. Different people in different communities have different pieces of the truth and it is foolish to say that one is more truthful than another. Or so we are told. Neuhaus then introduces the reader to something called the "rule of faith" which is said to control all of the various ways of articulating the Gospel so that it does not get out of control:

> "There is, as the early fathers taught, a rule of faith in the Great Tradition to which all these worthies [those who have articulated the gospel differently] belong, and that rule of faith, that orthodoxy, precludes some ways of saying the gospel while including diverse ways of articulating and living the wonder of Christian truth."[1]

This sounds more like an American Indian seance than any solid biblical exegesis or exposition. We are never told what this "Great Tradition" consists of, or where it comes from, or how we can get a hold on it. One thing we suspect is that it is located within the confines of the Romanist religion. The bottom line here is that Rome teaches a different gospel than the early Church and the Reformers. To get around this, we are expected to understand that there are many expressions of the Gospel. God cannot be limited to just one. Listen to the baby spin that complements this big spin:

> "At different times and places in Christian history, there have been different controlling concepts in how the message of salvation is expressed."[2]

This is just plain heretical. We know of only one "controlling concept" in how the message of salvation is expressed. The Word of God, i.e., the Scripture, with its clear and unambiguous statements, timeless in its straight-forwardness and timeless in its life-changing effects, is our only controlling concept. Furthermore, the Gospel does not consist in a myriad of controlling devices which change throughout history depending upon the winds of man-made theological systems. We may talk all we will about loving God, being married to God in soul, living for Christ and transforming the world in the name of Christ. But there is only one Gospel. These things are not the Gospel. Only in Rome are the effects of the Gospel turned around to equal the Gospel. That is why Rome spins hard to get her gospel included as one of many controlling concepts that differ in the

---

[1] Neuhaus, in Colson & Neuhaus, pg. 205, brackets added for clarity

[2] Neuhaus, in Colson & Neuhaus, pg. 206

expressing of the Gospel. Rome confuses "many ways of saying the same truth" with "many truths to be said that mean the same thing." Rome also exposes to us what we have known all along: her real gospel, which acts as the mother control panel, is something absolutely unidentifiable and outside of Scripture. This so-called "rule of faith" is none other than Rome herself. But Christians are not bound by any mystical or magical rule of faith. We are bound by the tangible Word of God. We are not bound by alleged limitless cultural expressions of the Gospel. We are bound by the Gospel itself. It has not changed in nearly two thousand years. It stands eternal as the very utterance of God. Any attempts to bring in religious ideologies that are not accountable to the Scriptures and the Gospel revealed therein serve only to dilute and compromise the Gospel rather than express it in a "different way."

SPIN #2

The second spin of the spin doctor is no less ingenious. The essence of it is that theology is to be reckoned as either good or bad by a historical poll. The idea is that systems of theology must be judged by their capacity to hold the various ways that the Gospel has been taught and lived throughout history:

> "Theological schools produce theological systems. When theologians refuse to test a system by its capacity to comprehend the variety of ways in which the gospel has been thought and lived, the temptation is to found a 'true church' in order to maintain what is claimed to be the true system."[1]

We urge the reader to pause and contemplate the essence of what is being put forth here. There are two elements of this statement that we must address. The first element is *historical* in nature. History is no safe judge for the rightness or wrongness of any theology. It is impossible to reconstruct the systematic theology of any of the Church Fathers to such an extent that we can say for sure where they would stand on all issues of modern theology. Augustine, for instance, has been used and abused throughout history. Virtually all the Reformers appealed to Augustine against Rome. Rome counts Augustine on their side in some of their peculiar doctrines. Besides, who will decide how much of and which variety of ways the Gospel has been taught in an acceptable reconstruction of the Gospel? Is it any wonder that the cry of the Protestant Reformation was *sola scriptura* (Bible Alone) for our guidance? Thousands of bits and pieces of theology come to us from the early Church. Shall we decide our Gospel on the basis of which one contains the greatest diversity of expression? We think not.

---

[1] Neuhaus, in Colson & Neuhaus, pg. 206

The second element is *theological* in nature. We are constantly told in the spin that there are and always have been a "variety of ways in which the Gospel has been thought." This is supposed to free Rome from having to seek the truth about the Gospel. What it does in reality is obliterate the Gospel. The Romanist spin doctor has subtlely changed categories on us. He has gone from "saying the Gospel" to "dominant motifs in understanding the Gospel." We are back to the same old Roman nonsense. The thing produced is put forth as the thing itself. Rome wants to sell us a package deal. The package is that there are many ways to understand the Gospel according to motif. The Gospel is to be understood as the deity of Christ (motif one), or as friendship with God (motif two), or as marriage of the soul (motif three), or as union with Christ (motif four), or as righteousness before God (motif five), or as human participation in the drama of God's redemptive program (motif six) etc., etc., etc. Rome believes that Luther's motif of righteousness before God is simply another motif that has a place but is not *the* central piece of theology upon which the Gospel (church) stands or falls. Listen very carefully:

> "But to declare it to be the article by which the Church stands or falls in a manner that excludes other ways of saying the gospel is to turn it into a sectarian doctrine."[1]

Here is where Rome misses it altogether. Because Rome's theology prevents it from separating the cause and effect of salvation, it wanders around confusing the "saying of the Gospel" with the results of the Gospel. It is impossible for Rome to talk about *how* one becomes a saved person because Rome does not have this as a category in its collection of motifs. In Rome, no one can say for sure that they are saved. Hence, Rome cannot see the difference between how one is saved and the results of that salvation in a person's life.

The Reformers did not have this problem. Neither have Christians throughout history. Rome cannot grasp that the "saying of the Gospel" of salvation, i.e., that one is justified by faith alone in the finished work of Christ alone, cannot be said any differently and still retain the essence of the message. To speak of the Gospel in any other terms ruins the Gospel. The very nature of the Gospel excludes all other ways of saying it. Rome cannot see this. Jesus and Paul did not say the Gospel in a variety of ways as though there were a variety of ways to be saved. There is one central theme that is say-able and it excludes all others. That say-able Gospel is none other than justification by faith alone in the finished work of Christ alone for our salvation.

---

[1] Neuhaus, in Colson & Neuhaus, pg. 207

SPIN #3

The third spin set out by the spin doctor is that the formula, "justification by faith alone in the finished work of Christ alone," was devised sixteen centuries after the historical facts of Christianity. The Reformers were constantly chastised for being unable to produce early church councils which articulated salvation in the precise terms of the Reformers. To counter such an attack, the Reformers appealed to the Bible and exhausted every avenue of remedy within the Roman Catholic religion until it became apparent at the Council of Trent that Rome had anathematized *sola fide* (salvation and justification by faith alone). In appealing to the Bible, the Reformers appealed to the fact that all of the Councils of the Church appealed to the Bible for their final deliberations on matters of faith and practice. Rome would have none of it and has not changed one bit. Happily, the concept of justification by faith alone is not foreign to the Church Fathers.[1]

Which Came First: The Church Or The Word?

We would remind the reader that we are in the process of interacting with an avowed Romanist who just happens to think that there is room to squeeze Evangelicals into the realm of Christendom. Neuhaus is a Roman Catholic ecumenist. But he is still Roman Catholic. As such, he is committed to the proposition that the Roman Catholic religion gave us the Bible and stands over the Bible ultimately. Yet, so stark is this affirmation to the ears of even the most liberal Evangelical ecumenist, that Neuhaus has to go on a tail chasing run to reconcile what he believes to what he knows will not fly well with Evangelicals. Listen to him on which came first, the Bible or the Church:

> "The gospel is not a theological proposition or a free-floating idea that touches down here or there, bringing into being the Church wherever it momentarily rests. The gospel is the memory, the message, and the lived experience of the determinate people through time, and that people is the Church. The gospel is God in Christ continuing to reconcile the world to himself through that part of the

[1] We recommend the very concise and quality treatment of Justification found in William Webster, *The Church Of Rome At The Bar Of History*, (Carlisle, PA: Banner of Truth, ©1995, pp. 205-207). We direct you to appendix 12 of that work, "Comments of the Fathers on the Nature of Justification." Also, we recommend the works of Martin Chemnitz, *Examination of the Council of Trent*, Part One, "The Testimonies of the Ancients Concerning Justification," (St. Louis, MO: Concordia Publishing House, ©1971, pp. 505-13). For a treatment of the overall question of Justification see author's own: *Romanism, The Relentless Roman Catholic Assault on the Gospel of Jesus Christ!* (Huntsville, AL: White Horse Publications, ©1995).

> world that is the Church, the Body of Christ. Whether that way of putting the matter is satisfactory or not is a question to be deliberated and judged by the Christian people, which is to say by the Church. In sum, it is the Church that judges the Church. The Church of the living God is 'the pillar and bulwark of the truth.' (1 Tim. 3:15 RSV). We can say, and it is important that we do say, that the Scriptures judge the Church, even though we know that there are no Scriptures apart from the Church. We can say, and it is important that we do say, that the gospel judges the Church, even though we know that there is no gospel apart from the Church."[1]

Is this so? We answer emphatically "No!" In the first place, the Gospel does precisely what Neuhaus says that it does not do:

> "Being born again, not of corruptible seed, but of incorruptible, by the word of God, which liveth and abideth for ever. For all flesh is as grass, and all the glory of man as the flower of grass. The grass withereth, and the flower thereof falleth away: But the word of the Lord endureth for ever. And this is the word which by the gospel is preached unto you" (1 Peter 1:23-25).

> "For I am not ashamed of the gospel of Christ: for it is the power of God unto salvation to every one that believeth; to the Jew first, and also to the Greek. For therein is the righteousness of God revealed from faith to faith: as it is written, The just shall live by faith" (Romans 1:16-17).

> "That we should be to the praise of his glory, who first trusted in Christ. In whom ye also trusted, after that ye heard the word of truth, the gospel of your salvation: in whom also after that ye believed, ye were sealed with that holy Spirit of promise" (Ephesians 1:12-13).

> "For this cause also thank we God without ceasing, because, when ye received the word of God which ye heard of us, ye received it not as the word of men, but as it is in truth, the word of God, which effectually worketh also in you that believe" (1 Thessalonians 2:13).

> "For the word of God is quick, and powerful, and sharper than any twoedged sword, piercing even to the dividing asunder of soul and spirit, and of the joints and marrow, and is a discerner of the thoughts and intents of the heart" (Hebrews 4:12).

---

[1] Neuhaus, in Colson & Neuhaus, pg. 208

We are not advocating that one can be saved simply by hearing the Word of God. There must be in attendance of the preaching of the Word of God the regenerating work of the Holy Spirit which works conviction, repentance and faith in the Lord Jesus Christ. But we can hardly endorse the Roman Catholic idea that the Gospel is the memory, and the message and the lived experience of a determinate people of God. If that were so, and Neuhaus would have us believe it, then there was a time when there was a church that did not yet have a Gospel! The memories and experiences had not yet accumulated to form one! *Contra* Neuhaus, the Gospel *is* a proposition based upon the knowledge of what God has done in Christ. That knowledge is found in the Word, which, furthermore, the Church did not establish. On the contrary, the Word established the Church. The Word came first and formed the ecclesia. The Word worked in the lives of sinners and created the Body of Christ. The Word attended by the supernatural persuasion of the Holy Spirit brought into existence the Church which exists to uphold the Word of God.

It is painful to watch Neuhaus chase his tail on this, but given the position of Romish authority over his head, he has little choice. Notice how contradictory he is. How can the Gospel judge the Church when there is no Gospel apart from the Church? How can the Word of God judge the Church when there is no Word without the Church? It is impossible. One has to give way to the other. Rome has made her choice and so have Christians.

The Spin Of Spins

Before leaving this section, it behooves us to look at what may be called the spin of all spins. This deals with how Neuhaus wishes to see history and theology together. When the question is put to Neuhaus as to why the Roman Catholic religion does not recant of what was said at Trent on the matter of justification, he answers with three reasons. Two are vintage Romanism. The third is religious babble:

> "First, because it is Catholic teaching that a council teaches authoritatively, and the Church is not authorized to repudiate retrospectively a conciliar decree. Second, because the Catholic Church, knowing that all theological formulations fall short of expressing the fullness of truth, trusts the continuing guidance of the Spirit in a course of doctrinal development toward the ever more adequate articulation of God's Word relative to the questions posed by the time. And third, because it is historically and theologically judged that the council fathers at Trent were right in condemning what they understood by 'justification by faith alone.'"[1]

---

[1] Neuhaus, in Colson & Neuhaus, pp. 209-210

There you have it. Rome cannot change the official teaching of an ecumenical council. But Rome reserves the right to express a more adequate articulation of God's Word should it be necessary. This is Rome's escape clause. Then, the final admission that the fathers of Trent were right all along. But now comes the spin. According to this Roman Catholic ecumenist, the real reason the Roman Catholic religion does not condemn Trent on justification is because to do so would be to condemn unnecessarily those who hold to *sola fide* but do not mean by it what the Reformers meant by it. Wonder of wonders, now we are being told that Evangelicals do not really believe what the Reformers were saying about *sola fide*, so it would be no use to condemn the formula justification by faith alone.

In a unique twist, the spin doctor has retained Romanism intact, left the Reformers in their dead past and made it look like a good thing that Trent scourged the earth of the Reformed heresy so that Evangelicals can get on with Rome as to the true meaning of *sola fide*. No doubt there are some who are duped and perhaps a little theologically illiterate. But the Christian is not buying this. The article by which Rome falls is still the justification of the ungodly by faith alone, and the authority of the Bible in the life of a believer. All attempts to destroy or to mitigate this will be resisted by God Himself. The Body of Christ will not be so easily deceived.

The Ways, The Truths And The Lives

In a parting shot at the distinctive way in which the Bible describes how one becomes a Christian and in endorsing the *Evangelicals and Catholics Together* statement, Neuhaus says, "...that the suspicions and hostilities that have attended the names Protestant and Roman Catholic will give way to a common mission among all who bear the name of Christ; that the different ways of being Christian will be embodied in ecclesial forms that the world will recognize as the continuing community of his disciples from Pentecost until the end of time."[1]

In Galatians 1, the Apostle Paul has some severe words for the Christians at Galatia who were entertaining false prophets who in turn were ruining the Gospel with their own brand of Christianity. They had a different way of becoming a Christian. The had a different ecclesial form which surrounded this different way of becoming a Christian. But Paul would have nothing of it:

> "But though we, or an angel from heaven, preach any other gospel unto you than that which we have preached unto you, let him be accursed" (Galatians 1:8).

---

[1] Neuhaus, in Colson & Neuhaus, pg. 224

In commenting on this passage of Scripture, one of the Reformers has this to say:

> "Thus they were removed from Christ, not in that they entirely rejected Christianity but because in such a corruption only a fictitious Christ was left to them. So today the Papists choose to have a half Christ and a mangled Christ and so none at all and are therefore removed from Christ. They are full of superstitions which are directly opposed to the nature of Christ. Let it be carefully observed that we are removed from Christ when we accept what is inconsistent with His mediatorial office; for light cannot be mixed with darkness."[1]

We may thank Richard John Neuhaus for proving conclusively that the words of the Reformers are as relevant today as they were in the sixteenth century. Nothing has changed. God has seen to it that His Gospel will not change. His Gospel changes men; men do not change His Gospel.

---

[1] Calvin, John, *The Epistle of Paul the Apostle to the Galatians, Ephesians, Philippians and Colossians*, (Grand Rapids, MI: Eerdmans Publishing Company, ©1965) pg. 13

Am I Therefore Become Your Enemy?

TOWARD THE END of this book we will be giving snap shots of Evangelicals who have romanced with Rome. We will also sum up the gist of this book and make some humble suggestions to remedy the loss of the Gospel of Jesus Christ in America. But before we get there, we have to expose another ecumenical work that, in our estimation, exemplifies all that has gone wrong in American Evangelicalism. This book, published by Navigator Press is entitled, *A House United? Evangelicals and Catholics Together: A Winning Alliance For The 21st Century.*

For the sake of brevity, we shall refer to this work as *A House United*. The authors are Keith A. Fournier, who at the time of publication was the executive director of the American Center for Law and Justice and the president of *Liberty, Life and Family*. The co-author is William D. Watkins, director of publications for the American Center for Law and Justice and for *Liberty, Life and Family*. Fournier is a Roman Catholic attorney. Watkins is a professing Evangelical who holds a Th.M. from Dallas Theological Seminary. What makes this book a target for our investigation is that it has all of the ingredients of apostasy stirred together into one pot.

From the cover of *A House United* we find the by now familiar assumptions found in *ECT*, Colson, Packer, Geisler & MacKenzie and Neuhaus. The essence is always the same: first, the moral sky is falling and second, Roman Catholics are *bona fide* Christians. We have seen this as *the* one-two punch of all the writers we have examined.

> "The church today is a divided house. Protestant, Catholic, and Eastern Orthodox Christians view each other with suspicion and, sometimes, open contempt. Between and within these camps, Christians frequently fight with each other over doctrine, liturgy, spiritual gifts and disciplines, social concerns, and myriad other issues. All too often Christians act like the children of a great divorce, writes author Keith Fournier: unsure of what the divorce was about but convinced they are on the right side.

"While we are occupied with these internal squabbles, a much larger battle faces us as Western civilization continues to decline. Since 1960 in America alone, violent crime has increased nearly 600 percent, illegitimate births have gone up 400 percent, divorces have quadrupled, and the teenage suicide rate has increased by more than 200 percent.

"And America's problems are reflective of the global community in which we live: Germany is experiencing a resurgence of neo-Nazi activity; political corruption is rampant in Japan; organized crime and a turbulent economy in Russia threaten newfound liberties; and the hunger, poverty political corruption, and devaluing of human life in third World countries point to a global society in desperate need of a redemptive message.

"With such real-life issues facing them, this is most certainly not a time for Christians to be quarreling among themselves. While there are legitimate issues that divide them, Christians must strive to get along with each other, cooperate on the foundation of all they hold in common, and rechannel their tremendous resources into turning back the darkness that threatens to engulf modern culture.

"*A House United?* Presents a thought-provoking case for the building of alliances among Christians of all confessions and traditions. Appealing to the Bible, church history, and the historic, ground-breaking accord 'Evangelicals and Catholics Together,' Fournier provides a challenging, hope-filled blueprint for positively impacting our culture through Christian cooperation. In addition, he provides numerous examples of individuals and groups who are already doing just that.

"Not only *can* Evangelicals and Catholics work together, for the sake of the future it is *imperative* that they do so. 'It is time for all Christians to lay down their swords and pound them into plows for the recultivation of an increasingly barren Western society,' Fournier asserts. 'The stakes are too high not to try, and with the help of our common Lord, we will succeed.'"[1]

Indeed, the stakes are high. Notice what is assumed on the cover of this book. It is taken for granted that Roman Catholicism is a *bona fide* expression of Christianity. It is taken for granted that the world is morally bankrupt and the only way to cure the problem is for all "Christians" to

---

[1] Fournier, Keith & Watkins, William D., *A House United? Evangelicals And Catholics Together: A Winning Alliance For The 21st. Century*, (Colorado Springs, CO: NavPress, ©1994) dust jacket, front and back sleeves, emphasis in original

work together. Fournier and Watkins are asking us to buy into the same thing as *ECT*, Geisler & MacKenzie, Colson, Neuhaus and Packer, among hundreds of others who are vigorously involved in romancing Rome. We are asked simply to accept Rome and, with Rome at our sides, to go out and win the world for Christ. But, which Christ? Which gospel? Giving glory to which god? The answer is painfully clear.

It appears that these ecumenicals have formed a mutual admiration society when in it comes to endorsing one another. We read the following from Fournier.

> "Finally, I wish to acknowledge the bold leadership and courage of Chuck Colson, Father Richard John Neuhaus, and the signatories of the bold accord 'Evangelicals and Catholics Together: The Christian Mission in the Third Millennium.' It is my prayer that this accord marks a new beginning for cooperation among Christians that could signal a historic turning point in our mutual efforts to proclaim the many dimensions of the gospel message and demonstrate the mission of the church to an age that so desperately needs both."[1]

Aside from the same cast of characters popping up here and there, we ask the reader to take note of the careful language used here once again. Fournier wishes for all to proclaim *"the many dimensions of the gospel message."* This is another way of saying that Rome is "in." It is the unquestioned, underlying assumption of our day and age: Rome simply has *another dimension* of the Gospel to roll out; same manufacturer, same workers just a different model. To say, "Rome is *not* in" is theologically and politically incorrect. It remains to be seen what the fall-out will be to those who dare to say No to Rome.

One professing Christian, Pat Robertson of the *Christian Broadcasting Network*, is unashamed and unabashed in his full recognition of the gospel according to Rome. Robertson views Rome as a beneficial help to the cause of God and truth:

> "When I was invited to sign the historic accord 'Evangelicals and Catholics Together: The Christian Mission in the Third Millennium' I didn't hesitate. I am convinced of the importance of such united efforts. Not 'humpty-dumpty solutions,' which Keith also mentions in this book, but true alliances rooted in our common faith in Jesus Christ and dedicated to serving Him together for the sake of our country and our world. There are many theological issues I, a Baptist, differ on with Roman Catholics. These differences are very

[1] Fournier & Watkins, pg. 6

> important. *But even more important is the common ground on which we stand and the vital mission we share at the close of this century and into the next."*[1]

Hopefully the reader is beginning to hear the siren song of the ecumenical pot stirrers. Such buzz phrases as "common ground" and "vital mission" are paraded out over and over again. Say it long enough and people will begin to believe it. Sure enough, many are believing the spin of the ecumenical spin doctors. Leaving all theological moorings behind, the ships of Evangelicalism are lining up within firing range of Rome. But the Armada has assembled not to fight, but for a much more nefarious purpose: to offload all of our cargo safely into the hull of the Vatican. The next step is to become truly united by sinking our fleet and getting on board "St. Peter's Barque," the Church of Rome. After all, our differences pale when compared with the "common ground" and "vital mission"—or so we are told. Stir, stir, stir. The brew of apostate stew is ready and being served.

So what are Pat Robertson and *NavPress* so proud of in this work of Fournier and Watkins? Let us take a look. There is much extraneous data given to us by the writers. We will not devote the time to analyze all of the thoughts tossed about in 336 pages. What we shall do is get to the heart of the matter as found in chapter 12 entitled "Sticks and Stones."

It is in chapter 12 that the authors give us a direct defense of why Rome is "in." Keith Fournier knows that for Rome to be "in" he must deal with the mighty weight of historical evidence and Christian opinion that Rome is an apostate church. He must deal with the accusations that Rome teaches a false gospel and that Catholicism is a false religion of the Antichrist. He states his position clearly and unambiguously:

> "I believe both these charges are groundless. But alas, the effects of divorce can be quite ugly, so in an attempt to set the record straight, much as the early Christian apologists did, I have chosen to address head-on what I believe are pseudo-objections based on terrible misunderstandings and misconstructions of the true Catholic doctrine."[2]

With this is mind we shall be anxious to see where we and 450 years of Reformation history have gone wrong in our biblical assessment of Rome.

Fournier begins his defense of Rome by establishing a straw man. Fournier constructs a hypothetical argument in which he has Christians believing that

---

[1] Fournier & Watkins, pg. 8, emphasis added
[2] Fournier & Watkins, pg. 208

the Catholic gospel asserts salvation by people's *own* good works. Now it may be true that some uncareful Christians run to the bottom line too quickly. They may compress Roman Catholic salvation to its essence of "salvation by what one does." But this is not the case with Christian theologians or with past Reformation theologians. We do not accuse Rome of predicating salvation on the basis of "raw works" performed solely by the individual. We address Rome where Rome needs to be addressed. Nonetheless, Fournier sets up this straw man and burns him down. We agree with Fournier that, according to Rome, "raw works" are not the basis of salvation in Rome. Rome, at Trent, did not assert this. What Fournier really needs to prove from Scripture is that "good works done with the aid of grace" are the ground of our justification. This is what Rome, at Trent, *did* assert. He also must defend the Roman dogma that salvation is contingent upon our willingness to receive the grace of God in order to perform "grace assisted good works" which merit salvation. Fournier errs at the start by assigning our rejection of Rome to non-existent arguments.

Fournier next errs in his defense of Rome by divesting the Bible from its clear teaching on the extent of man's ability to respond to God. While acknowledging that some Evangelicals believe that mankind cannot reach out in faith to God unless God first gives them the faith to exercise, Fournier rejects this:

> "Roman Catholics, however, take issue with this picture of humankind. They believe that it overemphasizes some portions of Scripture while neglecting the clear thrust of other passages. In contrast, they appeal to the full teaching of Scripture, seeking to allow it to set fuller parameters for a Christian understanding of humankind's fallen nature. Within these broader scriptural boundaries, a different picture develops.
>
> "First, the Bible presents several models of human fallenness. One model is certainly that of death: Humans are dead in sin and need new life (Ephesians 2:1-6, Colossians 2:13). But this does not mean we are unable to respond to God; rather, it means that sin has separated us from Him and that we need to be reunited to Him. The other biblical models confirm this. We are sick with sin and in need of healing (Mark 2:17). We are impoverished by sin and need God's riches (Luke 4:18, 2 Corinthians 8:9, Ephesians 2:7). We are polluted or defiled by sin and need to be cleansed (Mark 7:14-23, Ephesians 5:25-27, Titus 1:15, 1 John 1:7-9). We are lost in the darkness of sin and desperately need the light of Christ (John 8:12, 12:35). We are blinded by sin and need our sight restored (Luke 4:18, 2 Corinthians 4:3-6). We are enslaved to sin and need to be liberated from it (Luke 4:18, John 8:31-36, Romans 6:16-18). All of

these models depict our sad, desperate condition, but none of them even implies that we cannot respond to God."[1]

What shall we say the to these assertions? Well, in the first place, with the exception of Ephesians 2:1-6, the passages cited were not written to prove that man cannot respond to God. We agree. But there are two major errors here. The first is that Fournier confuses the different *effects* of depravity by calling them different *models* of depravity. To be sick with sin or blinded or polluted or defiled speaks to the *effect* or *result* of depravity. The Bible does not present to us different *models* of depravity as though so and so were sick and so and so were blind. It gives us the big picture of depravity and then describes the *effects*. The effects are often put for the whole as in the case of being polluted and defiled. But the whole does not change. The second error is the corner Fournier backs himself into by including Ephesians 2:1-6 into his "models" of human fallenness. The text clearly states that natural man is *dead* in trespasses and sins. How many kinds of *dead* are there? According to Fournier, there are the sick kind of dead, the polluted kind of dead, the impoverished kind of dead, the lost kind of dead, the blind kind of dead, the enslaved kind of dead, etc., etc. But this makes no sense. Once one is willing to grant that the Bible speaks of human fallenness as being *dead*, then it is impossible to make human fallenness something less by pointing out different modes of fallenness which are "less than dead," or "almost dead," or "partly dead." If one is dead then that is the end of it. Fournier wants us to think that dead really means sick. Why not sick really meaning dead? Is this not the better way to understand passages that discuss the effects of depravity in words that speak of it as less than dead?

We notice the bold assertion that none of the above mentioned passages, "even implies that we cannot respond to God." Yet, we are at a loss as to how to explain a dead man's ability to respond to God. Fournier already concedes the point that "dead" is at least one model of human fallenness. We have shown the error of this model analogy but let us take a closer look. If one is dead, then how can one respond to God on his own? And, Fournier, being an uncareful theologian, ruins his own religion if he says that man can respond on his own without the grace of God. We shall get to this point presently, but for now let us help out Fournier by citing passages that do imply, yea, even state emphatically, that man, being dead, cannot respond to God:

> "But the natural man receiveth not the things of the Spirit of God: for they are foolishness unto him: neither can he know them, because they are spiritually discerned" (1 Corinthians 2:14).

---

[1] Fournier & Watkins, pp. 209, 210

> "For this is the word of promise, At this time will I come, and Sara shall have a son. And not only this; but when Rebecca also had conceived by one, even by our father Isaac; (For the children being not yet born, neither having done any good or evil, that the purpose of God according to election might stand, not of works, but of him that calleth;) It was said unto her, The elder shall serve the younger. As it is written, Jacob have I loved, but Esau have I hated. What shall we say then? Is there unrighteousness with God? God forbid. For he saith to Moses, I will have mercy on whom I will have mercy, and I will have compassion on whom I will have compassion. So then it is not of him that willeth, nor of him that runneth, but of God that sheweth mercy" (Romans 9:9-16).

> "No man can come to me, except the Father which hath sent me draw him: and I will raise him up at the last day" (John 6:44).

> "But as many as received him, to them gave he power to become the sons of God, even to them that believe on his name: Which were born, not of blood, nor of the will of the flesh, nor of the will of man, but of God" (John 1:12-13).

> "That which is born of the flesh is flesh; and that which is born of the Spirit is spirit. Marvel not that I said unto thee, Ye must be born again" (John 3:6-7).

> "But though he had done so many miracles before them, yet they believed not on him: That the saying of Esaias the prophet might be fulfilled, which he spake, Lord, who hath believed our report? and to whom hath the arm of the Lord been revealed? Therefore they could not believe, because that Esaias said again, He hath blinded their eyes, and hardened their heart; that they should not see with their eyes, nor understand with their heart, and be converted, and I should heal them" (John 12:37-40).

> "At that time Jesus answered and said, I thank thee, O Father, Lord of heaven and earth, because thou hast hid these things from the wise and prudent, and hast revealed them unto babes. Even so, Father: for so it seemed good in thy sight" (Matthew 11:25-26).

Unlike many Roman Catholic writers, Fournier is at least willing to interact at a limited theological level. Because of this, we are able to catch a glimpse of the underpinnings of Catholic theology. Here we need to take a good look at where Rome goes wrong and why they have another Gospel. As we have seen, it all starts with a faulty understanding of the effect of Adam's sin on mankind. Rome has maintained that Adam's sin severely damaged his progeny but did not destroy man's ability to seek after God. Nor does

Rome believe that men are evil in themselves, as Fournier demonstrates in his citation of Roman doctrine:

> "Fourth, 'depravity' could not mean that people are evil *in themselves*. Scripture is clear: *Everything* God created is still intrinsically good, and this includes all humankind. (Mark 7:14-23; Romans 8:18-23, 14:14; 1 Timothy 4:4; Titus 1:15). In addition, human beings were created as God's image-bearers, and sin's entrance into the world did not destroy the divine image in them (Genesis 1:26-27, 9:6; James 3:9). We still reflect, however dimly, the character and presence of deity (Psalm 8:6)."[1]

It is at this point that we take serious issue with Rome. There is nothing in the Scripture that would suggest such a high view of post-Adamic man. Where do we find evidence that post-Adamic man is still intrinsically good? We marvel at the citation of Scripture adduced to prove the proposition. Listen to Mark 7:14-23, which Fournier cites to support his above assertions:

> "And when he had called all the people unto him, he said unto them, Hearken unto me every one of you, and understand: There is nothing from *without a man,* that entering into him can defile him: *but the things which come out of him*, those are they that defile the man. If any man have ears to hear, let him hear. And when he was entered into the house from the people, his disciples asked him concerning the parable. And he saith unto them, Are ye so without understanding also? Do ye not perceive, that whatsoever thing from without entereth into the man, it cannot defile him; Because it entereth not into his heart, but into the belly, and goeth out into the draught, purging all meats? And he said, *That which cometh out of the man,* that defileth the man. For from within, out of the heart of men, proceed evil thoughts, adulteries, fornications, murders, Thefts, covetousness, wickedness, deceit, lasciviousness, an evil eye, blasphemy, pride, foolishness: *All these evil things come from within*, and defile the man. (Mark 7:14-23, emphases added).

We are at a complete loss to explain how a Roman Catholic can cite this portion of the Bible as proof for the innate goodness of man. It proves just the opposite. It is that which is within (in themselves) which makes man intrinsically evil. It is what man *is* and not what is attached to man's inward parts that defiles him. Presently, we will add passages of Scripture which show conclusively that man *is* intrinsically evil. But before this, let us

---

[1] Fournier & Watkins, pg. 210, emphasis in original

examine another one of Fournier's curious proof texts for the inherent goodness of mankind. He cites Romans 14:14;

> "I know, and am persuaded by the Lord Jesus, that there is nothing unclean of itself: but to him that esteemeth any thing to be unclean, to him it is unclean" (Romans 14:14).

From this passage Fournier deducts that man cannot be intrinsically evil. But wait a minute. The context of Romans 14 is speaking about eating of meats and vegetables and the observance of one day above another. Paul argues that neither meats or vegetables nor days are to be viewed as unclean of themselves. There is nothing said about the heart of man here. Further, the text says too much to support the allegation that man has no intrinsic evil. We notice that to the one who esteems something as unclean, it is to him unclean. It is obvious that mankind is not included here. If mankind was in mind, then the one who viewed mankind as unclean of itself would make mankind unclean to him. But this is nonsense. It is not the burden of the Apostle to entertain the notion of inherent human depravity *per se*, when talking about the eating of meats and vegetables.

The next bizarre proof text of the Romanist is 1 Timothy 4:4-5;

> "For every creature of God is good, and nothing to be refused, if it be received with thanksgiving: For it is sanctified by the word of God and prayer" (1 Timothy 4:4-5).

From this the same amazing conclusion is deducted. What is completely ignored is that Paul is referring to those who were forbidding the eating of meats as though the meats were evil. Paul corrects the wrong assumption about eating meats and says that all meat is good. Paul does not mean that all meat is morally good. He does not mean that all meat is intrinsically just. Neither is he saying that the eating of humans is acceptable because humans are good. The context will not admit thoughts about the inherent nature of man in a commentary on the freedom to eat meat.

The last gasp of proof texting, in hopes of proving the innocent nature of man, is tossed out for us to examine. It is Paul's assertion in Titus 1:15;

> "Unto the pure all things are pure: but unto them that are defiled and unbelieving is nothing pure; but even their mind and conscience is defiled" (Titus 1:15).

We presume by appeal to this passage that something is to be gained by the word *pure*. But what could Paul's point—that those born from above look at life from a righteous point of view—have to do with the inherent goodness of mankind? If anything, this passage teaches the inherent evil of mankind. For, juxtaposed with the *pure* are those who are *defiled* and *unbelieving* where nothing is *pure*. So much for the "in and of themselves" goodness of mankind.

Stemming from this denial of the utter depravity of mankind is Rome's insistence that man has the final say in salvation:

> "Our minds, emotions, will, body, soul—all that we are has been affected by sin, but sin has not destroyed us or our abilities."[1]

Although the word "abilities" is left undefined here, it is clear from the context that man's ability to choose freely the grace of God in order to be saved is what Fournier has in mind. Sin has done its damage, he says, but man is not so corrupted as to lose his ability to choose God or accept the grace of God leading to salvation:

> "On the other hand, we have definitely been effaced by sin, much as rust effaces metal or as wind and water efface rock. *But humankind is not essentially evil.* Evil is a parasite. It exists in good things, but it cannot exist on its own."[2]

We take some time here to labor through this section because we have arrived at the cornerstone of Roman Catholic anthropology (i.e., what is man after the fall of Adam?). This will dictate Roman Catholic soteriology (i.e., how has God saved man?). This is, in fact, what drives their entire sacramental system.

The Romanist contention that man is not essentially evil does not hold up under the weight of Scripture. The picture of rust effacing metal is not the analogy that best depicts the Scriptural account of mankind's depravity. Depravity is more likened to a small amount of leaven in a lump of dough. Sin permeates man to such an extent that man has lost his ability to do the spiritual good. He has also lost all ability to choose God. Man's nature is corrupt to the point where he freely does not choose God and feels no remorse in his choice. Berkhof captures the point.

> "When we speak of man's corruption as total inability, we mean two things: (1) the unrenewed sinner cannot do any act, however insignificant, which fundamentally meets with God's approval and answers to the demands of God's holy law; and (2) that he cannot change his fundamental preference for sin and self to love for God,

---

[1] Fournier & Watkins, pg. 210

[2] Fournier & Watkins, pg. 210, emphasis added

> nor even make an approach to such a change. In a word, he is unable to do any spiritual good."[1]

Total depravity speaks to the extent of sinfulness within the individual. It is not just that all have sinned, but rather that sin is pervasive in all. Depravity is not measured by the number of sins. It is to be spoken of in terms of the condition in which mankind finds itself. Mankind is not as bad as he possibly can be. Total depravity is not defined by intensity of evil. God restrains the evil of mankind. Nor can total depravity be defined by the comprehensiveness of evil. No man does all of the sins all of the time. Neither does total depravity mean that mankind cannot do the relative good. Scripture is clear that man can do good to his fellow man. "And if ye do good to them which do good to you, what thank have ye? For sinners also do even the same." (Luke 6:33). But this is good in the outward sense of good. It is not fitted for Heaven. One of the mysteries of total depravity is that man does relatively good things even while depraved. But these good things become an opiate for the masses as they plunder along being content with self gratification in the things that they do. What total depravity prevents them from doing is worshiping God and bowing down before Him. "There is none that understandeth, there is none that seeketh after God" (Romans 3:11). *No, not one.*

Total depravity then is the predisposed inclination of the will to sin freely and reject God. It is the total inability to worship God and seek salvation in the righteousness of another. Sin so permeates the inwardness (heart) of mankind that the very nature of man is perverted and totally affected, infected and defected by sin so that not one aspect of man is free from sin's fatal working. Is man basically good? Is man intrinsically pure? Hardly, for "that which is born of the flesh is flesh; and that which is born of the Spirit is spirit. Marvel not that I said unto thee, Ye must be born again" (John 3:6-7).

The commentary of Moses as to the total depravity of man is straightforward:

> "And God saw that the wickedness of man was great in the earth, and that every imagination of the thoughts of his heart was only evil continually" (Genesis 6:5).

This description of mankind is not restricted to the pre-flood era as the prophet Jeremiah points out:

---

[1] Berkhof, Louis, *Systematic Theology*, (Grand Rapids, MI: Eerdmans Publishing Company, 14th printing, ©1938) pg. 247

"The heart is deceitful above all things, and desperately wicked: who can know it?" (Jeremiah 17:9).

Mankind has a depraved mind—Titus 1:15; Ephesians 4:17-19; 2 Corinthians 3:14; 1 Timothy 6:5 and 1 Corinthians 2:13,14. Mankind has depraved emotions—2 Thessalonians 2:12. Mankind has a depraved conscience—Titus 1:15; Hebrews 9:14; 10:22; 1 Timothy 4:2. Mankind has a depraved will; the heart is stubborn as a rock—Ezekiel 11:19; Jeremiah 23:29. We read in Proverbs 21:10 that the *soul* of the wicked *desires* evil, and in Ecclesiastes 9:3, that men's hearts are full of evil: "This is an evil among all things that are done under the sun, that there is one event unto all: yea, also the *heart* of the sons of men is full of evil, and madness is *in their heart* while they live, and after that they go to the dead" (Ecclesiastes 9:3).

The most revealing passages of the New Testament, which deal with the question of the state of human nature after the fall of Adam, are Romans chapter three and Ephesians chapter two. Together they are insightful as to the heart of unregenerate mankind. Together they tell us that there is none righteous, none who does good, there is no fear of God before their eyes, they are dead in trespasses and sins, they indulge in the desires of the flesh, they are by nature children of wrath and they have no hope in this world. This composite account of mankind eliminates all Romish hope of a basically good and able person emerging from the pages of Scripture. Romans 8:7 tells us that "the carnal mind is enmity against God: for it is not subject to the law of God, *neither indeed can be.*". And 1 Corinthians 2:14 tells us that the natural man is unable to comprehend the things of God:

"But the natural man receiveth not the things of the Spirit of God: for they are foolishness unto him: *neither can he know them*, because they are spiritually discerned" (1 Corinthians 2:14).

Rome builds its theology of salvation on the sand of optimism when it comes to the basic nature of man. Ultimately, a new heart must be given to mankind in a radical heart transplant that can only be done by God from start to finish (Ezekiel 11:19, 36:25-26). This is what the Scriptures define as the new birth, and it is *all* of God. Man does nothing to participate in the rebirth of his own deceitful heart. The man knows only that once he was blind and now he sees. Lydia knew only that God had opened her heart to understand the things Paul was saying (Acts 16:14). Paul understood that it was not the man who wills or the man who runs, but God who chooses (Romans 9:16), and that no one could understand and believe the Gospel unless first born of the Spirit (1 Corinthians 2:14). Jesus understood that all whom the Father would give Him would come (John 6:37). This radical event of being born from above into the kingdom of God is necessitated by the radical depravity of the human heart. Rome, on the other hand, knows that putting man in the equation of salvation is the first step in safeguarding their sacramental system of salvation. Christians know that the Bible eliminates man from the salvation equation. It judges man to be totally depraved and unable to add one thing to his salvation. In this manner, the Bible destroys all self-salvation religious systems. Christian theology preserves the true meaning of grace as it shines in all of its Scriptural brilliance: "*…and that not of yourselves*: it is the gift of God" (Ephesians 2:8). Let the reader keep this in mind, for as we have seen, Rome's solution to man's "sickness" is indeed "grace." But it is a "grace" completely foreign to the Scriptures, a "grace" that is *dependent on man and subject to man's manipulation.*

Roman Catholic apologists think they are on safe ground by asserting that metaphysical evil (man's fallenness) needs something good (man himself) to live off of in a parasitical relationship. Hence, they say, "man is basically good or else evil could not use him as a host in a parasitical relationship." Seeing human nature much like a rust-eaten car, Romanists think that God is in the business of getting the rust off so that the natural good can be preserved. However, any good auto body repair shop will tell you that once the rust has infected the metal, a replacement piece is needed. One does not get out the rust that has already deteriorated the metal. One has to replace the piece. Nowhere in Scripture are we told that we need to power wash, sand blast or grind out sin so that we can get to the good heart hidden deep within. That would be futility itself: "For though thou wash thee with nitre, and take thee much soap, yet thine iniquity is marked before me, saith the Lord God" (Jeremiah 2:22). All the work required to uncover the good heart deep inside of man would only lead one to the remarkable—and scriptural—conclusion that he does not have one. All of mankind needs a new heart—not a 'repaired heart'—as the Scriptures clearly testify:

> "A new heart also will I give you, and a new spirit will I put within you: and I will take away the stony heart out of your flesh, and I will give you an heart of flesh" (Ezekiel 36:26).
>
> "For he is not a Jew, which is one outwardly; neither is that circumcision, which is outward in the flesh: But he is a Jew, which is one inwardly; and circumcision is that of the heart, in the spirit, and not in the letter; whose praise is not of men, but of God" (Romans 2:28-29).

God's Solution, According To Rome

Having wrongly concluded that post-baptismal* Catholics are *sick* in sin rather than *dead* in it, the Roman Catholic religion has a solution to being

---

* The Romanist system claims to bring life into a dead soul through the waters of baptism. In this case, the faith of the believing parent is the condition of faith for infants while the individual faith of adults suffices for themselves.

sick in trespasses and sins. As one might expect, the person of Jesus Christ is given high accolades by Rome. Jesus is extolled and venerated as the God-man, sinless savior and the only one who can help mankind in its *sickened* state. However, the wheels of biblical exegesis and biblical exposition fall off the cart when we are told *how* Jesus is going to cure the (Romanist) problem of "sin *sickness*." So, when we examine Rome's solutions to the problems created by sin, we are talking a different language. If we cannot agree on the diagnosis, we can hardly agree on the prescription. Thus, in examining Rome's remedies, keep in mind that Rome is out to cure a sick patient. Rome is not out to bring a dead person to life, as she alleges to have already done this through infant baptism. This will become ever so obvious. Rome is wrong in the diagnosis, wrong in the treatment, and wrong in the prognosis. Listen to the way Rome remedies the problem, as we cite Fournier & Watkins:

> "According to Paul, the first and primary grace is God's free gift of Himself to humans, which is indeed 'amazing grace.' Through Christ, God has communicated Himself personally to each one of us."[1]

This may sound good but it is not *sound*! Where is this concept taught by the apostle Paul? In what sense has God communicated Himself personally to each one of us through Christ? What does this mean? This is typical religious talk. It is "filler" with hopes that no one asks any questions about these kinds of religious statements. It has a ring of truth to it but is absolutely meaningless. It leads to the following:

> "And because of His gift of free will to us, we have the potential to either accept or reject His gift. By His grace, which is free and undeserved, He makes it possible for us to respond to Him and ushers us into His life when we come by faith. In Catholic theology, faith is the assent of the mind and will to God and to the truth of what He has revealed to us. When I exercise faith in accepting God's free gift of grace in Christ, the Holy Spirit converts me and thereby brings about my justification. Moved by grace, I'm turned toward God and away from sin."[2]

Our questions for Fournier are myriad: "Where in all of Scripture are we told that God has given the gift of free will to us? And how does it follow that God personally communicating Himself to each one of us (whatever that means) leads to the gift of free will? And where are we ever told that God's grace makes it possible for us to respond to him, if only we *will*?

---

[1] Fournier & Watkins, pg. 212

[2] Fournier & Watkins, pg. 212

Where does the Bible teach us that when we come to Christ, then, after coming, we are born again? Where does the Bible teach us that we are converted by the Spirit *after* converting ourselves? Rome teaches that *when* one exercises faith, *then* the Holy Spirit converts. To Rome, one is converted *after* he exercises faith. Only then does God's work begin. But Christians know that conversion is what the Sprit *does*, not what He *responds* to. Fournier & Watkins have it backwards, making "faith" the reason that God "converts" the sinner, thereby making man's ability to convert himself the basis for God converting him. This makes faith a work, which nullifies the clear reading of Ephesians 2:8, "For by grace are ye saved through faith; and *that* (i.e., faith) not of yourselves: it is the gift of God."

Let us analyze what is being said here. First, we notice that the grace of God is God's attempt to persuade sinners to come to Him. The picture is that of God in heaven trying to give away grace accumulated through the death of His Son. It is free for the asking. One can accept or reject this grace of God. But, apparently, the grace of God makes it only *possible* to respond but not at all *probable*. This is evidenced by the majority who do not finally "convert themselves." Nevertheless, we are told by Fournier & Watkins that God does not give up so easily:

> "Catholicism teaches that God gives us the gift of causality. We have the ability to decide to accept God's love or spurn it. But God doesn't sit on His hands and wait on us. Being the Lover that He is, He pursues us, woos us, spreads His arms wide to receive us, even when we are raising our fists in defiance and shouting obscenities. In this way, grace precedes our act of faith. God paves the way for us to come to Him."[1]

We note that Fournier is so engrossed in his attempts to show forth Romanism as Christianity that he cannot see his own Romanism suffocating the Christianity he wants so desperately to show forth! Christians believe that Christ is the Way, not merely having *paved* the way. The idea that Christ's death makes salvation possible (but actually saves no onc) is the heart of Romanism. God has paved the road—now you have to decide to drive on it, says Rome. God has sacrificed His Son—now you have to decide to apply the merits of His death, says Rome. This is what Rome means when she says that God has given us "causality." God has done all He can. The onus is now on us to "cause" God to save us. We get the picture. God is in Heaven hoping that someone will pay attention to His overtures of love: "Will someone please take the grace?!" Rome has Him in heaven anxiously awaiting the outcome of a grim popularity contest for which the voter turnout has been sadly below expectations. God does all

---

[1] Fournier & Watkins, pg. 213

that He can do to get us to take His free gift, to drive on His road, but alas, few are interested. So God pursues, woos and, like a jilted lover seeking reconciliation, seeks out ways to get people to respond to His proposal. God would like more people to come and believe, but the problem is that God has given to man "causality." Man has to *cause* his own salvation by taking the grace. Thus, God waits to know who will accept the grace. If only God had retained "causality" for Himself, then He might know what will happen. As it stands, God does not know the beginning from the end. He is at a loss, waiting for us to act so he can know who will take His grace. We speak as if mad!

Where do we begin to unravel all of this? To begin with, we must question Fournier & Watkins' first premise and ask, "How is causality given? Does God, the first cause of all things, temporarily forsake causality in order to give it?" This question is self-defeating, for it has God causing man's "causality," leaving "causality" plainly in God's keeping. Causality cannot be given without having a beginning, and to have a beginning is to end causality. Thus, Fournier & Watkins' first assumption is empty of any meaning.

Next, note that all of Scripture must now bow to the Romish dogma of the freedom of the will. For Rome, it is man who decides, not God! Very well then, let us see where this dogmatic assertion shall lead in the light of Scripture. Does Scripture say that God works out all things after the counsel of His own will? (Ephesians 1:11). Yes, says Rome, but not salvation, for that is left to man. Does Scripture say that all the Father has given to Christ will come to Him? (John 6:37). This is hard for Rome to swallow, so she takes it to mean that the Father *wants* to give believers to Christ, but cannot. He knows not who will accept or take His grace. The Father, according to Rome, does not know who will come. Rome says He has left causality in man's hands. Rome has God in Heaven, not doing whatever He pleases (Psalms 115:3), but rather waiting for man to apply His Son's work by their clever choice. Does Scripture say that none can come unless given of the Father? Rome thinks this may be true in an abstract sense, but cannot bring herself to believe it. In Rome one can come or not come, based on his own free will. Therefore, he does not need to be, and indeed *cannot be*, given of the Father. All that is really given of the Father, says Rome, is the *ability* to give one's self to Christ. The rest is up to us!

Yet Luke counters all of this when he says that all those appointed to eternal life believed (Acts 13:48). Rome wants this to mean that all those who believed were appointed to eternal life. Such is her penchant for redefining words and changing meanings to suit her. The apostle Paul makes it clear that God's purpose in election was determined before time began (2 Timothy 1:9), and quite apart from the good works or good intentions of man (Romans 9:11). But since this contradicts Rome's belief that "causality" is in man's hands and that man actually *causes* God to save, she cannot bring herself to understand "grace" to mean that salvation is given "to him that worketh not" (Romans 4:5). And *worketh* he must, for causality is in his hands! Yet wherever was causality more clearly in God's hands than when Christ himself intentionally blinds the eyes and hardens the hearts of men that they *should not see with their eyes and be converted?* (John 12:40). Paul deals the death blow to man's causality when he states that *it is not man who wills or man who runs* but God who has mercy (Romans 9:16).

Christ was not mistaken when He said that his disciples had not chosen Him but that He had chosen them (John 15:16). He knew that His Father had causality the whole time. Paul was not mistaken when he told the Ephesian believers that they had been chosen by God (Ephesians 1:4). He knew that the Ephesians' holiness—yes, even their conversion itself—was because of God's election of them in Christ Jesus before the foundation of the world. Rome, on the other hand, wants their personal holiness to be the cause of their election. But the Scriptures will not yield on this point. Was not Christ delivered up by evil men according to the determinate counsel of God? (Acts 2:23). Were not Herod, Pilate and the Gentiles gathered together to do whatever the hand of God and the counsel of God determined? (Acts 4:25-28). Where is causality, except in the hands of God where it has always been? Did not God tell Moses that He would harden Pharaoh's heart long before Moses arrived in Egypt? (Exodus 4:21). Did not God determine between Esau and Jacob before they had done anything good or bad while yet in the womb? (Romans 9:11). If there was ever a place for causality to be in man's hands, it was here, for Esau sought *repentance* with the bitterness of tears, but received it not (Hebrews 12:16-17), for repentance can only be given of the Father (2 Timothy 2:25), Who, retaining causality for Himself, gave it not to Esau.

One can readily see that the god of the Roman Catholic religion is strictly a god of the imagination. How pathetic a view of God have they who would rob God of His glory and subjugate the eternal benefits of the death of Christ to the autonomous will of man. How dreadful to contemplate a god who is arriving at knowledge in his own universe as he watches patiently to see who will take the grace he offers. How pitiful to conjure up a god that is subservient to the whims of his creation. How wretched to even begin to portray God in such a manner by arbitrarily redefining the phrase "the chosen" to mean "those who choose"!

Let us be refreshed with the Word of God before we go on:

> "For I know that the LORD is great, and that our Lord is above all gods. Whatsoever the LORD pleased, that did he in heaven, and in earth, in the seas, and all deep places" (Psalms 135:5-6).

> "But he is in one mind, and who can turn him? and what his soul desireth, even that he doeth" (Job 23:13).
>
> "And all the inhabitants of the earth are reputed as nothing: and he doeth according to his will in the army of heaven, and among the inhabitants of the earth: and none can stay his hand, or say unto him, What doest thou?" (Daniel 4:35).
>
> "Remember the former things of old: for I am God, and there is none else; I am God, and there is none like me, Declaring the end from the beginning, and from ancient times the things that are not yet done, saying, My counsel shall stand, and I will do all my pleasure: Calling a ravenous bird from the east, the man that executeth my counsel from a far country: yea, I have spoken it, I will also bring it to pass; I have purposed it, I will also do it" (Isaiah 46:9-11).
>
> "But our God is in the heavens: he hath done whatsoever he hath pleased" (Psalms 115:3).

At this point the Romanist might object saying, "Precisely, and what God pleases is to leave salvation in our hands so as to not violate our free wills and keep intact our *causality*,"* to which the Scriptures say:

> "What shall we say then? Is there unrighteousness with God? God forbid. For he saith to Moses, I will have mercy on whom I will have mercy, and I will have compassion on whom I will have compassion. So then it is not of him that willeth, nor of him that runneth, but of God that sheweth mercy. For the scripture saith unto Pharaoh, Even for this same purpose have I raised thee up, that I might shew my power in thee, and that my name might be declared throughout all the earth. Therefore hath he mercy on whom he will have mercy, and whom he will he hardeneth" (Romans 9:14-18).
>
> "But what saith the answer of God unto him? *I have reserved to myself* seven thousand men, who have not bowed the knee to the image of Baal. Even so then at this present time also there is a remnant according to the election of grace" (Romans 11:4-5, emphasis added).

---

* We would highly recommend the reading of Luther's *Bondage of the Will* for any Christian who does not understand the important distinction between free *will* and free *agency*. Also, we would recommend the extended treatment on the so-called freedom of the will given to us by Jonathan Edwards, *The Works of Jonathan Edwards*, Volume One, (Carlisle, PA: Banner of Truth Trust, ©1979)

Even in light of these passages of Scripture, it is often taught in some Evangelical circles that we are converted after we believe. Everything hinges on the word "converted." Certainly there is no salvation apart from believing the Gospel. However, if we use the word "conversion" as used here by Catholicism, then the cart is before the horse. In reality, the new birth *precedes* our believing the Gospel message, for as the Scriptures say, "But the natural man receiveth not the things of the Spirit of God: for they are foolishness unto him: neither can he know them, because they are spiritually discerned" (1 Corinthians 2:14). This means that the natural man—the unbeliever—cannot comprehend or believe the Gospel until he has become spiritual, that is, until he is reborn: "That which is born of the flesh is flesh; and that which is born of the Spirit is spirit. Marvel not that I said unto thee, Ye must be born again" (John 3:6-7). One cannot believe until one has been born of God. "Whosoever believeth that Jesus is the Christ *is* born of God" (1 John 5:1). The original Greek is much clearer here than the English. It reads literally: "Everyone *believing* (present tense of the word believe) that Jesus is the Christ, *has been begotten* (perfect tense, action in the past with continuing result: *gegennetai*) of God (*ek tou Theou*)". This fits well with John 3:3,6 whereby we are told through our Lord's teaching to Nicodemus that we must be *born from above* (*gennethe anothen*). The Scriptures reserve the application of salvation to our sovereign God who does what He wills in the heavens and earth. When one is born from above, then one believes unto salvation.

A Spade Is A Spade Is A Spade!

These words are a good summary of *A House United.* Keith Fournier, despite his protestations to the contrary, is a Roman Catholic. He is not a Christian. He believes what Rome teaches about mankind, sin, salvation, justification and sacramentalism. He has believed the Roman Catholic gospel. Nowhere is this more apparent than in his miserable attempt to defend Roman Catholic infant baptism.

We would ask the reader to keep in mind that *A House United* was written with the aid of a Dallas Theological graduate and was endorsed by Chuck Colson and Pat Robertson, among others. We draw your attention to this because we want you to have it in mind as you read what Fournier has to say about baptismal regeneration. What does Rome think of baptism? Fournier, whose standard form of Roman logic warrants an extended quote, summarizes nicely:

> "To the Christian, the sign of *the invisible reality of conversion* is water baptism. Baptism is meant to be the doorway to a new way of living. It symbolically presupposes what is to come and what was left behind as it acts as *a sign of the believer's initiation into the new life in Christ…*

> "Although we often think of baptism and salvation as an adult affair, the church recognized centuries ago that they apply to children, even to infants… This practice [infant baptism] arose because Christian couples who began to have children expressed a desire to fulfill the call of Jesus so their children would be saved: 'Let the children come to me and do not hinder them. It is to just such as these that the kingdom of God belongs.'
>
> "This raises an obvious but important question: How can a baby be saved without acknowledging Jesus? …As I see it and as the Roman Catholic Church has taught, infant baptism is just one more example of grace. Even our own exercise of faith cannot earn salvation. Faith simply gives us the opportunity to receive God's gracious gift of new life and walk in it…
>
> "Now since an infant cannot exercise faith, what role could baptism possibly play in his or her salvation? The answer involves first understanding the church as the Family of families. Since its inception, a critical presupposition has underscored infant baptism, and indeed the symbolic meaning of even adult baptism: namely, *the children of Christian parents are part of a faith-filled family called the domestic church, and these children are to be raised in the midst of a faith-filled local Christian community*. The church has believed that these two experiences would ensure that children would be raised as believers…
>
> "Given the fact that baptism must be approached in faith and the church is the Family of families, I return to the original question: How can a baby be saved without acknowledging Jesus? Obviously, the infant cannot respond by faith. On the other hand, his parents, godparents, other believing relatives, and especially the church in its local expression *can respond in his behalf. The faith exercised need not be his*." [1]

If you have not been persuaded that Roman Catholic theology is a man-made religion looking for biblical credibility, then perhaps now you are convinced. We ask, "What could possibly be going on in the heads of Evangelicals endorsing this kind of anti-Christ human philosophy parading itself as biblical Christianity?" We fear that the stew of apostasy has been served and savored in places that should know better.

Rome here is awash with anti-biblical theology and open contradiction, to say the least. First, the Bible knows nothing of a "faith-filled family called a

---

[1] Fournier & Watkins, pp. 214,215, emphases added, brackets added for clarity

domestic church." There is only one Church and it is composed of those having been born from above. The *ekklesia* of God is the Household of Faith. It is composed of the saints of the living God. It is fashioned from the called out ones. It is, what Peter calls "a holy priesthood":

> "Ye also, as lively stones, are built up a spiritual house, an holy priesthood, to offer up spiritual sacrifices, acceptable to God by Jesus Christ" (1 Peter 2:5).
>
> "But ye are a chosen generation, a royal priesthood, an holy nation, a peculiar people; that ye should shew forth the praises of him who hath called you out of darkness into his marvellous light" (1 Peter 2:9).

Secondly, we marvel at how the Romanist weaves his way back and forth between "saved," "sacramentalized," "fully assented," and "raised as believers." On the one hand, the two experiences of baptism and being raised in the midst of a faith-filled local Christian community will *ensure* that the children will be raised as believers. But, does this mean "raised as though they *are* believers," or "raised as though *they should be* believers"? Rome is uncertain. At least Fournier is uncertain. This is the dilemma Rome has with her children. Are they in or out of salvation? It sounds like the children are in at baptism until we read:

> "It was assumed that the church and the family would instruct, nurture, and lead the newly baptized into a *full* assent to the faith. Full assent has necessarily included a personal decision and commitment to a lifelong relationship with Jesus Christ. Unfortunately, that commitment has sometimes been lacking in contemporary Christian experience. In other words, there are sacramentalized but unevangelized Catholics."[1]

The hopeless contradiction is vivid. The same writer who says that some Catholics are "sacramentalized but unevangelized," asks twice, "How can a baby be saved without acknowledging Jesus?" His answer, as we have quoted him directly above, is "The faith exercised need not be his." Therefore, we are to conclude that babies of Roman Catholics are saved by a faith that is not their own in baptism. But they can be saved by their own faith at a later time since there are many *sacramentalized* Roman Catholics who are not *evangelized*. Why would you evangelize a saved baby when the baby grows up? The answer, in the bizarre world of Rome, is that the infants are saved in baptism and lose their salvation later if they do not fully

---

[1] Fournier & Watkins, pg. 215, emphasis added

assent to it. All this from the same writer who, three paragraphs earlier, wants us to know that,

> "In baptism, the old man—our corrupt nature—is submerged, and the new man—our new nature in Christ—emerges clothed in Christ and His transforming power."[1]

It does not take a seminary graduate to notice everything attributed to baptism by Rome is null and void if the baptized one is in need of evangelization! So much for baptismal regeneration. So much for sacramentalism. So much for Rome.

The Merit Of "Merits"

We shall close our brief analysis of *A House United*, by moving over slightly on the theological scale to the Romish understanding of the role of merit in salvation.

Roman Catholics are a little bit squeamish about the word "merit," as it has long been a part of Roman Catholic dogma that mankind merits God's approval through works that are performed in a state of grace, or by the aid of grace. But since this sounds too much like "good works of men" meriting salvation, Romanists run for cover under the blanket of theological double-speak. The bottom line for Rome is that God instituted the merit system. He grants grace for meritorious acts, and then grants the stamp of "supernatural" on good works done by grace. Therefore there is no merit to the man—only to the works brought about by God in the man. This is to say that man cannot possibly take credit for the system of merit that God has developed. And, they say, man cannot take credit for any good works done since it was God's grace that enabled him to do them.

Ah, but there's the rub, and the heartbeat of Roman double-speak. Rome champions free will to such an extent that man is said to have to cooperate with the grace of God before that grace is effective in bringing about the meritorious act. If this be so, then who really should get the credit? Should not the credit go to the man who "allowed God" or "let God" come into his heart? Surely this is the most important aspect of any act. In essence, Rome is saying that they *allow* God to work and to will in them for His good pleasure. Moreover, Rome is saying that they can block God at any time from doing anything in them for His good pleasure. So, who is in control of salvation? In Rome, it is the man who wills and the man who runs. Not so in Christianity. Listen to Fournier & Watkins as they speak for Rome:

---

[1] Fournier & Watkins, pg. 214

"We hope in God for our complete salvation, and we're confident in what He has done for us; however, *we can never be sure that we will always be faithful to Him.*"[1]

This is Rome fully exposed. This is the gospel according to Rome. In the final analysis, it does not depend on God after all. It all depends on man and what man does. This is not Christian theology. Think about this just within the context of Romanism. Why would the same God who seeks, courts, loves, woos and ultimately desires marriage with us, leave it in our hands to *stay* with Him? Especially since, according to Rome, the only way we can stay is if God gives us the grace to *earn* the merit required for further obedience. We ask, "If we cannot do good works without His grace, then why would He withhold grace for the good works that enable us to stay with Him?" Rome answers, "God withholds nothing." However, we are obligated, they say, to go and get the grace, and of course, that is done by obedience through the sacraments. And here is where the system collapses.

In Rome, "to obtain the grace" *requires* that grace be given, (e.g., the grace instilled in man for the desire to partake of the sacraments where more grace is dispensed). So where is the *grace* that enables men to go and get the grace? If it is withheld, then no one can go and get it. And if it is left up to man, then it is preëminently meritorious, for mankind could then say that the reason God saved is because *we had the good sense to go and get the grace*. Or, in the common terms of the rank and file Roman Catholics, "God helps those who help themselves." This is fine theology for those who would boast of their obedience to accept the grace God offers. But such boasting is of no avail before the throne of God (Romans 4:2).

This is ultimately what we are left with in the Roman Catholic system of self-salvation. It is a bewildering world of condign and congruent merit. The Catholic Encyclopedia lists seven conditions for condign merit (merit which deserves a supernatural reward), four with respect to work, two with respect to the agent doing the work and one with respect to God.[2] In this, the Roman Catholic encyclopedia is clear enough on who does the work to merit the grace: man.

We shall close out our discussion on *A House United* by examining three statements made by the authors, as well as our interaction to each which shall put all of this in proper perspective.

---

[1] Fournier & Watkins, pg. 219, emphasis added

[2] We have enclosed in Appendix III a small introduction to the Romish concept of merit as we defend justification through faith apart from works of any man made system of religion.

Statement #1

> "In summary, then, Catholic Christians do not see good works as a means to justification."[1]

We question the integrity of the writers in light of the clear teaching of the Council of Trent, which says precisely the opposite:

> "Hence, to those *who work well* unto the end and trust God, eternal life is to be offered, both as a grace mercifully promised to the sons of God through Christ Jesus, and as a *just reward* promised by God himself, *to be faithfully given to their works and merits.*"
>
> "We must believe that nothing further is wanting to those justified to prevent them from being considered to have, *by those very works* which have been done in God, fully satisfied the divine law according to the state of this life and *to have truly merited eternal* life, to be obtained in its [due] time, provided they depart [this life] in grace."[2]

Statement #2

> "Christ alone merits our salvation. If this understanding is heretical, if it is truly a false gospel then all of us—Catholic, Protestant, and Orthodox—stand condemned. But this gospel is not a false gospel. It is the truth. The church has affirmed it as such since her inception. The apostles taught it because they heard it from the Lord incarnate Himself. On this Rock Catholics stand."[3]

The Roman Catholic phrase "Christ alone merits our salvation" means nothing when it comes to the articulation of the Gospel. It is an open door for all manner of cults and religions of man. It is so because it puts Christ in the position of only opening the door to heaven. It is the old heresy that "Christ has done His share, and now you must do yours," or that "God is pleased with Christ, so now here is what man must do." This means that "Christ has merited the opportunity, and now man must merit the salvation itself." Romanists think that Christ has made salvation possible and hence has merited our salvation. What they are really saying is that we could never save ourselves unless Christ had first merited the chance for us to do so.

---

[1] Fournier & Watkins, pg. 218

[2] Schroeder, *The Canons and Decrees of the Council of Trent*, pg. 41. From the sixth session, emphasis added

[3] Fournier & Watkins, pg. 221

Romanists sincerely believe that Christ enabled God to accept what sorry works we have to offer for our own salvation. Listen to Trent:

> "If anyone says that the justice received is not preserved and also not increased before God through good works, but that those works are merely the fruits and signs of justification obtained, but not the *cause* of its increase, let him be anathema."[1]

Statement #3

> "Such critics of Catholicism would do well to actually read and ponder the official documents of the Catholic Church and the theologians she honors."[2]

There is no higher source of Roman Catholic dogma than the Council of Trent. It remains the citadel of Romish thought and teaching on all matters pertaining to justification. It is not because we have *not* read Trent that we stand against Rome. It is that we *have* read Trent:

> "If anyone say that the sinner is justified by faith alone, meaning that nothing else is required to cooperate in order to obtain the grace of justification, and that it is not in any way necessary that he be prepared and disposed by the action of his own will, let him be anathema."

> "If anyone says that justifying faith is nothing else than confidence in divine mercy, *which remits sins for Christ's sake*, or that it is this confidence that justifies us, let him be anathema."[3]

We are convinced with Luther, Calvin, Knox, Whitefield, Edwards, Spurgeon, Moody and countless others that this is a different gospel. It is not the gospel revealed from faith to faith. Those who endorse such a religion poison themselves with the stew of apostasy.

As for the Roman Catholic community, we are reminded of the words of the apostle Paul in light of the sorrow he felt for his own countrymen.

> "For I bear them record that they have a zeal of God, but not according to knowledge" (Romans 10:2).

---

[1] Schroeder, *The Canons and Decrees of the Council of Trent*, pg. 45, emphasis added

[2] Fournier & Watkins, pg. 224

[3] Schroeder, *The Canons and Decrees of the Council of Trent*, pg. 43, emphasis added

Policing the Camp

IT IS BEWILDERING to us how the Evangelical world can be so easily duped by Roman Catholic sympathizers. We are astounded at how many Evangelicals are willing not only to be agreeable to Rome, but also to endorse her openly.

There are voices of dissent within Evangelicalism, to be sure. But they appear to be small pockets. And most authors find themselves swimming against the current when they try to confront American Evangelicalism with evidence of a growing trend toward apostasy.

In 1995, sensing the need to expose publicly the alarming number of ministries which were sanctioning Romanism, a pastor from the Fort Worth area of Texas published, on his own, a little booklet entitled *The Redefining of a Christian.*[1] We take interest in this booklet because the author has taken the time to document the Evangelical sell-out to the Romanist religion under the guise of moral unity:

> "In 1993 Chuck Colson, of Prison Fellowship was awarded the Templeton Prize for progress in religion. The purpose of the prize as stated by its founder, Sir John Mark Templeton, is to encourage understanding of the benefits of each of the great religions. Muslims, Hindus, Buddhists, Roman Catholics and Protestants comprised the panel which chose Chuck Colson as the one-million dollar recipient.
>
> "The announcement that Colson would receive it caused an outcry by some evangelicals who asked Colson to decline rather than endorse the ecumenical goals associated with it. We too, wrote Colson and asked him to decline and received the standard answer justifying such involvement in that it was a good opportunity to present the gospel. We wrote and asked for a copy of his speech and

---

[1] Watson, Tom, *The Redefining of a Christian*, Country Side Bible Church, 250 Ravenaux Drive, Southlake, Texas 76092. As of this writing, copies of this booklet are available upon request from the author.

> found he did not present the life-changing gospel of Jesus Christ except for one reference to John 14:6. He said nothing in reference to our Lord that would offend anyone who 'believes in God' regardless of their religion."[1]

Mr. Watson has hit the nail on the head in his probing into the affairs of Mr. Colson. As we have pointed out time and time again, there is a movement to redefine Christianity so as to include those who hold to a conservative moral stance, regardless of their theological beliefs.

Delving further into the issues, Mr. Watson shares our concern over Keith Fournier and the book *A House United? Evangelicals and Catholics Together: A Winning Alliance for the 21st Century*. Citing a highly unfavorable review of this book by Ronald Blue, President of Central American Missions International, Mr. Watson juxtaposes Blue's critique of Fournier & Watkins with the warm endorsement given the book by Charles Colson. Bewildered by the Colson endorsement of Fournier, Watson makes this penetrating observation:

> "If Fournier is as Colson claims, 'fully Evangelical in his relationship to Christ,' then we have changed the definition of a Christian or an evangelical or both. Fournier's call is a call to Romanism."[2]

Mr. Watson wrote a letter to Mr. Colson asking him, "What gives?" In letters exchanged between Mr. Watson and Mr. Colson, we can eavesdrop on Colson's response to Mr. Watson's attempts to question Colson's adoption of the religion of Rome which, as we know, does not hold to justification by faith alone. Here is Colson's response to Watson's inquiry:

> "In the end, when we speak of justification by faith, we must make an important distinction. Man is justified by faith, not by entertaining a precise and 'correct' view of the doctrine of justification. It is Christ who saves/justifies, and those who call on the name of the Lord shall be saved. Both Protestant evangelicals and official Roman Catholic teaching today confess this truth without hesitation."[3]

Where have we heard these words of apostasy before? This is the same old lie. It is the deepest heresy to throw out the biblical formula of "justification by faith alone" because belief in the formula "justification by faith alone"

---

[1] Watson, pg. 3
[2] Watson, pg. 5
[3] Watson, pg. 5

does not save anybody. It is even more reprehensible to hide the Roman Catholic religion by saying, "it too believes Christ justifies"—without explaining Rome's heretical definitions—and therefore concluding that Rome must be Christian. The entire issue of theology and orthodoxy is summed up in answering the question, "*How* does Christ justify the ungodly?" Rome, and apparently Colson with her, does not have a clue.

The remainder of Watson's booklet identifies for us some major Evangelical movements across America that have bought into Rome's sophistry and now parade boldly down main street USA flying the colors of Romanism.

Promise Keepers

Watson devotes five and a half pages to the emergence of the Promise Keepers ministry which has swept across America. While we are in full sympathy with Watson's appraisal that Promise Keepers loses the Gospel to an overriding social and moral concern, we are most intrigued by the Roman Catholic connection:

> "Charismatic Pastor Jack Hayford is a prominent writer and speaker for Promise Keepers. In July of this year, Hayford along with Paul Crouch were featured speakers at a four-day ecumenical conference of which half of the 10,000 attendees were Roman Catholic. Crouch, the head of the vast TBN television ministry has declared:
>
> > "'I have come to the conviction that Martin Luther made a mistake. He should have never left the Roman Catholic Church. …I am eradicating the word Protestant out of my vocabulary. I am not protesting anything. It is time for Catholics and non-Catholics to come together as one in the Spirit and one in the Lord.'
>
> "As we continue to hear more statements like this, should it not raise a few questions? Are these men just deceived? Do they misunderstand Romanism? Are they, for the sake of unity, willing to embrace a false gospel? Or do I dare ask, is it possible that they do not have spiritual understanding of the gospel?"[1]

---

[1] Watson, pg. 9. In response to a survey question sent to the Promise Keepers national office in Denver, Colorado we received this reply:

> "As you may know, Promise #6 from The Seven Promise of a Promise Keeper states: '*A promise keeper is committed to reach beyond any racial and denominational barriers to demonstrate the power of biblical unity.*' As this statement indicates, Promise Keepers is concerned less about a man's church label than it is about his heart and his relationship with Jesus Christ. If a man shares our faith in the biblical Jesus and is trusting in Him *alone* for salvation, he is a fellow member of the body

continued on following page

Indeed, what shall we say to these things? How shall we interpret the mounting data? It appears that the Lord has let go the virus of apostasy. If this is true, then we shall not be surprised to hear of more and more ministries becoming infected. For example, we are not in the least surprised that in 1997, bowing to Roman Catholic pressure, Promise Keepers abandoned the article of justification by faith alone from its statement of faith.[1] What next? *Christ* alone? We know from the *1994 Catechism of the Catholic Church* that Rome is not too terribly keen on that article, either.[2]

You Scratch My Back And I'll Scratch Yours!

We have maintained that an uncritical view of Romanistic theology at the higher levels of theological training will ultimately lead to chaos at the local level, be it in churches or in para-church organizations. That such is the case can be seen from this sobering observation from Tom Watson:

> "Part of the *Evangelical-Catholic Accord* was an agreement not to proselytize among the two faiths. This is only the beginning. In Colorado Springs, a non-proselytizing agreement in public schools was signed between Jews, Catholics and leaders of such ministries as Focus on the Family (James Dobson), Navigators (Terry Taylor), and Young Life (Terry McGonigal) along with area churches. A full page ad called a 'Covenant of Mutual Respect' was run in the Gazette Telegraph. The Catholic Herald reported that Bishop Richard Hanifer of the Diocese of Colorado Springs said, 'The effort to evangelize by some communities was creating an atmosphere of animosity.' Lauren Libby, Vice President of the Navigators, said the results were positive and reported the response was, 'it's good to see the body of Christ unified.' The 'body of Christ' included Jews, Protestants, and Catholics fully entrenched in

---

> of Christ, regardless of his denominational affiliation. Indeed, Promise Keepers welcomes all men, including Catholics, to participate in our conferences and other outreaches. However, this should not be perceived as a blanket endorsement of every teaching of the Catholic Church (or of any other church for that matter), but an effort to encourage inter-denominational understanding and relationship in keeping with our Savior's prayer for oneness among His fellow followers found in John 17:20,21."

We note that it is "the power of biblical unity" that is the buzz phrase used here. We also note it is not the "gospel of Jesus Christ, [which is] the *power of God* unto salvation" (Romans 1:16,17).

1 *Our Sunday Visitor*, July 20, 1997, "Making New Catholic Men?", by Michael Aquilina, pp. 10-11

2 See, for example, paragraph 1477 of the *1994 Catechism*, which informs the Roman Catholic that the righteousness "infused" into the believer is Christ's, but mixed thoroughly (and inextricably) with the righteousness of Mary and the saints.

Romanism. Pam Moore, area director for Young Life said she attended the meetings to learn from other religious leaders and that 'it is important that we respect each other's views.'"[1]

Of course, all those who sign such pacts and covenants do so under the guise of unity, love and respect hoping to capture the nation under the new gospel of Western morality, fair play, 'father knows best,' twenty-five cent hamburgers and Saturdays in the park. And this is precisely where the Gospel in America is going. This fascination with a mythical past Western morality has done much to subvert the Gospel and literally launch a campaign for Romanism. Even Christian parents are considering Catholic schools to get back to the good old days. How limited is the ecumenist at scanning the history of America in particular, and the world in general!

Watson closes his booklet with a solemn Appendix entitled "The Catholic Connection." We take the time to share with you his findings and his research.

> "The Catholic connection certainly goes far beyond the ECT and its acceptance by the Promise Keepers. In May of this year Pope John Paul II released an encyclical* making it clear that essential Roman Catholic teachings would not be compromised for unity such as the

---

[1] Watson, pg. 17. For a follow-up story on this historic pact see the "Catholic Herald," June 2, 1993.

In response to a survey we sent to a number of evangelical para-church organizations, we received this peculiar response from a staff worker of Intervarsity Fellowship. In reply to the question, "Do you believe the Roman Catholic Religion to be a legitimate, albeit diverse, Christian Community?", we received this answer:

> "Yes, Because they believe that all human beings are lost due to original sin, and that all humans need to believe in Jesus Christ for their salvation."

However, when asked later in the survey, "Do you believe Roman Catholics are lost and without God in this world and therefore it is appropriate to evangelize them?", we received this response:

> "Roman Catholics need a more biblical understanding of "justification"—the Roman Catholics who are putting their ultimate confidence for their acceptance before God in their own works, rather than in Christ (a confidence that would in turn lead to good works), do indeed need to be evangelized."

Someone has said, "If there is a mist in the pulpit then there will be a fog in the pews." Does this not serve the point that confusion reigns, and the gospel is slipping away?

* The encyclical to which Watson refers is *Ut Unum Sint*, or "That They May Be One," promulgated by John Paul II on May 25, 1995.

authority of the Pope and the Church. This encyclical was warmly received by both the National Council of Churches and the World Council of Churches.

"Twelve years ago, when Dr. J. Dwight Pentecost was teaching at Dallas Theological Seminary that the Protestant movement would once again unite with Romanism before the coming of Christ, few expected the growing list of evangelicals who have shown some openness to Rome. The following list is in no way exhaustive:

Signers of Evangelicals and Catholics Together:

Chuck Colson—Prison Fellowship
J. I. Packer—Regents College
Pat Robertson—CBN, Christian Coalition
John White—National Association of Evangelicals
Richard Mouw—Fuller Theological Seminary
Mark Noll—Wheaton College
Bill Bright—Campus Crusade for Christ

and twelve others

Covenant of Mutual Respect—a nonproselyting (sic) agreement in Colorado Springs:

James Dobson—Focus on the Family
Terry McGonigal—Director of the Institute of Young Life Ministries for Young Life
Terry Taylor—Director of U.S. Ministries—The Navigators

Other ministries and individuals who have shown openness to Rome:

Kenneth Kantzer, editor of *Christianity Today*
Jack Hayford—Church on the Way, Van Nuys, California
Luis Palau Evangelistic Association
Jack Van Impe
Hank Hanegraff—Christian Research Institute
World Vision International
Youth With A Mission
Full Gospel Businessmen's Fellowship
Inter-Varsity Christian Fellowship

Willow Creek Community Church

Although Willow Creek will not take a position on the ECT which is in keeping with the church growth philosophy of not alienating anyone, the Willow Creek Association is made up of over 50 denominations including Roman Catholic and Seventh-Day Adventist churches.

Southern Baptist Convention

Both Richard Land, Christian Life Commission and Larry Lewis, Home Mission Board signed the ECT but withdrew under pressure. They released a joint statement that 'we are not personally rejecting the intent of the document' (NIRR, April 17, 1995).

For the first time a Roman Catholic priest addressed the Southern Baptist Convention this year. Father Frank Ruff of the Diocese of Owensboro, Kentucky is the field representative for U.S. Bishop's Secretariat for Ecumenical and Interreligious Affairs. He was named an official observer of the Southern Baptist Convention (The Texas Catholic, July, 1995).

The Southern Baptist/Roman Catholic Conversation is a 17-member committee co-directed by Bishop J. Kenrick Williams of the diocese of Lexington, Kentucky and James Dixon, a Baptist from Fort Washington, M.D. representing America's two largest denominations. The committee will release jointly written material on poverty, life, racism, and healing. Meetings have been attended by Richard Land of the Christian Life Commission and James Draper, President of the Sunday School Board. The Houston Chronicle reported that Bishop Williams stated that 'we don't find any antipathy at all' and he believes that someday Catholics and Baptists might formally become one denomination (Houston Chronicle, May 21, 1994).

Navigators

Supports the ECT and published pro-Catholic books like *A House United? Evangelical and Catholics Together: A Winning Alliance for the 21st Century.*

Robert Schuller

[Stated,] 'It is time for Protestants to go to the shepherd (Pope) and say "What do we have to do to come home?" (Los Angeles Herald Examiner, September 19, 1987)"[1]

---

[1] Watson, pp. 20-22, brackets added for clarity

In the Trenches: Fighting on all Fronts

Focus On The Family

As early as 1988, we began to suspect things were not quite right in the high profile world of media-evangelicalism. We wrote a letter to *Focus on the Family* and asked James Dobson to stop endorsing Mother Teresa and other notable Roman Catholics as examples of the Christian faith. We received this telling response from Scot Marvin who was a Correspondence Assistant to Dr. Dobson at the time:

> "Please be assured that Dr. Dobson shares your concern for scriptural teaching. Consequently, both he and our program committee make thorough investigations of guests and their beliefs before considering them for our program. In so doing, Dr. Dobson has met many Catholics who share a love of Jesus, subjecting themselves to His Lordship. As in some Protestant churches, there are Catholics who are not scripturally based. However, those who are and love and serve the Lord, must certainly be embraced as our brothers and sisters."[1]

As we can see, the focus of Dr. Dobson is neither on theology nor the Roman Catholic religion. As a result, the Roman Catholic religion is not questioned by *Focus on the Family*. The dreadful oxymoron here is the assertion of "care and concern for biblical teaching" while asserting that Roman Catholics are "biblically based." In essence, Dr. Dobson is saying that there are good biblically based Roman Catholics and there are Roman Catholics who are not biblically based. The problem is that to be biblically based is to deny the entire sacramental system of the Roman Catholic religion. This is something that has apparently not even entered the minds of the people at *Focus on the Family*.

Prison Fellowship

In direct response to our letter asking Prison Fellowship Ministries to explain how Roman Catholicism can be so openly courted, we received this reply from Charles Colson as early as 1988:

> "The Bible commands me to love my brothers and sisters, to take my differences to them in truth and love, and to do everything I can to bring about healing of the Body. This is what I try to do, but I would not align anyone with Prison Fellowship who did not agree

---

[1] Letter dated August 24, 1988 from Scot Marvin on behalf of Dr. James Dobson, President of Focus on the Family.

> on the fundamentals expressed in our statement of faith, and I don't think anyone who disagreed with our statement would want to be identified with the ministry. However I must also say that I know and work with some very committed, evangelical born again Christians who happen to be Roman Catholics. Personally I have doctrinal differences with them, even as I do with some Protestants, but I cannot question their faith in God, their belief in Jesus Christ as their personal Savior, or their loving Christian spirit in reaching out to those in prison."[1]

What is so astounding, in this early response of Mr. Colson, is his insistence that one can be born from above, Evangelical, and wholly Roman Catholic all at once! This kind of statement makes all theology meaningless and absolutely obliterates the Gospel of Jesus Christ. Colson might as well have said, "I have been working with some very good square circles and some very respectable round squares."

When my sons were very small we used to talk about things that could be stated but really made no sense at all. The idea was to show my children that though some things could be said, they could not be affirmed as true. We used to talk about flying elephants and talking bears. But the little jingle that stuck in their minds was the story of two dead soldiers. I am reminded of these two dead soldiers when I read such statements as "Evangelical born again Christians who happen to be Roman Catholics." It goes like this:

One fine day in the middle of the night,
Two dead soldiers got up to fight.
Back to back, they faced each other,
Drew their swords and shot each other.

Anything is "say-able," but some things are not "affirmable" because they cancel out reality and are pure myth. Such is the case of so many of these disastrous statements coming from the pen and mouth of modern ecumenists.

Two Peculiar Responses

When the *ECT* statement was first issued it raised eyebrows among denominations and soon there were those who answered publicly. One such organization was the General Assembly of the Presbyterian Church in America. The PCA is a relatively new Presbyterian Body which broke off of the older mainline United Presbyterian Church and has had phenomenal growth since its inception. We have always applauded the break off from

---

[1] Letter dated August 22, 1988 from Charles W. Colson founder and director of Prison Fellowship Ministries.

the liberal mother organization and there is no doubt that the PCA is perhaps the strongest of the larger Presbyterian Churches in America. In general, the PCA is a staunch defender of the Westminster Confession of Faith written in London during the heat of the battle with Rome at the time of the Protestant Reformation. For this reason, we were anxious to read of the PCA response to the *ECT*. It is reproduced for you below:

> "Therefore, the Twenty-Third General Assembly of the Presbyterian Church in America adopts and directs to be sent to the signatories the following statement in response to Evangelicals and Catholics Together:
>
> "The Presbyterian Church in America remains fully committed to the Reformed doctrine of Justifications by Faith as expressed in the Westminster Confession of Faith (Chapter 11) and Catechisms (LC 70,71,77; SC 33). We reaffirm our intention to proclaim this doctrine to the world and restate our disagreement with any and all doctrinal formulations that fail to uphold the truths of the Protestant Reformation in this most important matter. We further declare that our understanding of justification is not compatible with the teaching of the official Roman Catholic Church. Therefore, we maintain that Biblical unity must be grounded in fidelity to the teaching of Holy Scripture regarding the Person and Work of our Lord Jesus Christ."[1]

We find nothing wrong with this statement although much more could have been added. But as a brief statement it serves the purpose. What is peculiar to us is the fact that the framers for some reason felt compelled to go on and add an additional dictum to this declaration. The additional comments are unnecessary and, in our opinion, open a crack in the Wittenberg Door for viewing Rome as an alternative Christian community. See if you agree. The statement continues:

> "The Presbyterian Church in America acknowledges with sadness that the failure rightly to understand and emphatically to proclaim the doctrine of Justification by Faith alone is a sin found among Protestants as well as Roman Catholics. We confess with shame, the complicity of Protestantism in the theological deterioration of Christianity."

We pause here to reflect on what is being said and the danger of this assertion. The failure to proclaim justification by faith alone is here treated as a sin of which both Rome and Protestantism are guilty. We must object

---

[1] The 23rd General Assembly of the Presbyterian Church in America Response to "Evangelicals and Catholics Together"

here. The failure to proclaim justification by faith alone is not simply a sin. It is the out and out displacement of the Gospel of Christ with another gospel. Anyone who does this is anti-Christian and is not to be considered a brother or sister in Christ. Anyone who does this boldly and as a matter of doctrinal formulation is guilty, not of sin only, but in worshiping a false god and promulgating a pagan religion. The danger is the *way* the PCA statement suggests that Protestants (presumably real Christians) have erred *just as* Roman Catholics. Also, the PCA statement fails to take into account that it is one thing to say, "Protestants have failed to accurately teach that which is part of their doctrinal confession." This is a correctable sin and should be addressed. But it is quite another thing to say, "the inadequate teaching of an already held doctrine is the *same thing* as the outright rejection of the doctrine itself." Rome is guilty of denying justification through faith alone. Some Christians are guilty of inadequately teaching justification through faith alone. There is an eternity of difference between the two errors.

The PCA document goes on to say:

> "The Presbyterian Church in America humbly acknowledges that Justification is not by faith in a doctrinal formulation but by faith alone in Christ the Redeemer and so it has often happened that people who have a living faith in Christ as their Savior have a most imperfect understanding of that faith *and of the way in which salvation comes to them* through it. With gratitude to God we gladly welcome certain developments in Roman Catholicism, especially those that have made Holy Scripture a more important part of the faith and piety of many Roman Catholics. We acknowledge that God, in his all-wise providence, has been pleased to put his loved ones in many communions whose doctrine we find unbiblical, even heretical, in important ways."

It is here, even more than what we have already commented upon, that the PCA opens the door for trouble down the line. By affirming that people can have a relationship with Christ without understanding how salvation comes to them, the PCA undermines the Gospel. The Gospel is written in a propositional form which is perfectly understandable to the pagan intellectually (although rejected) and will be understood by the elect of God who have their hearts opened to understand. All Christians inherently understand *the way* salvation comes to them. Why would the PCA want to complicate the issue here?

We must reiterate that the ploy of the Romanist and the Evangelical ecumenist is to convince us that Romanism is a safe place to be because Rome believes in Jesus. However, *what* they believe, *how* they believe it and *to what extent* their belief touches upon the Gospel of Christ is irrelevant to the likes of Colson, Fournier, Watkins, Geisler, MacKenzie, Neuhaus, etc. Here, the PCA falls prey to similar reasoning. The PCA holds out for the possibility that one can be saved without knowing what salvation really is and *how* it is given to us. Can we not see that this opens the door for an entire community of religious people who affirm many things about Jesus but lack any complete understanding of the Gospel? According to the PCA statement, this is a real possibility. But not according to the Scriptures. There is simply not a shred of evidence that those believing the Gospel do not know how salvation comes to them. They knew because God gave them eyes to see and ears to hear and therefore, through faith, they accept God's gift of salvation. To even insinuate that one can be saved without knowing *how* one is saved is falling into the hands of those who wish to deflate Christianity of all biblical air.

Secondly, we take issue to the notion that God has placed His loved ones in communities that are unbiblical and even heretical. Where does this observation stem from? There is not a hint of this in Scripture. It is wishful thinking. The Bible is quite clear that all those in Christ must flee every form of religious idolatry. There is no mistake that Christians are not to participate in any unfruitful deeds of darkness. Christians are not to eat at the table of idols. Christians are to come out from those forms of religion that deny the Word of God. What pastor, teacher, elder, deacon or leader of any Bible believing community would ever counsel anyone to stay in a heretical religion? The PCA has erred greatly in the addendum of their response to the *ECT*. We see here that rationale and justification is given to untold millions who now have been sanctioned by the PCA to stay in heretical bodies because God has placed them there. However, God has not put His loved ones in heretical communions. He has called them out:

> "And what concord hath Christ with Belial? or what part hath he that believeth with an infidel? And what agreement hath the temple of God with idols? for ye are the temple of the living God; as God hath said, I will dwell in them, and walk in them; and I will be their God, and they shall be my people. Wherefore come out from among them, and be ye separate, saith the Lord, and touch not the unclean thing; and I will receive you, And will be a Father unto you, and ye shall be my sons and daughters, saith the Lord Almighty" (2 Corinthians 6:15-18).

From The Top Down

We wish next to examine the response to the *ECT* framed by one of the most conservative and well respected seminaries in the world. We speak of Dallas Theological Seminary, long a bastion of Evangelical conservatism and bulwark for the defense of Biblical inerrancy and salvation by faith alone in the finished work of Christ alone. Although criticized as being much too dispensational and of late somewhat antinomian by outsiders, there is little doubt that Dallas Seminary has had and continues to have a broad impact on world-wide Evangelicalism. We are therefore interested in their response to the *ECT*. We are interested in particular because Charles Colson is a friend of the seminary and frequent speaker at major seminary fund raisers and devotional tributes such as the Founders Banquet and the installation of the current president, Charles Swindoll. Here is Dallas Seminary's response to *ECT*:

> "Though Dallas Seminary affirms areas of agreement in the moral and social arenas, we strongly question whether Evangelicals and Catholics can ever 'unite on the great truths of the faith.' Though both groups might use the same words and quote the same Scriptures, at least four fundamental issues separate Evangelical and Catholic doctrine.
>
> 1. Evangelicals hold to *Sola Fide* (justification by faith only in Christ alone) while official Roman Catholic doctrine teaches that justification also involves human effort.
>
> 2. Evangelicals teach that the new birth is not dependent on water baptism while Roman Catholic doctrine teaches that water baptism is a 'sacrament of regeneration.'
>
> 3. Evangelicals affirm *sola scriptura* (the Word of God alone is our final authority for doctrine and Christian life) while Roman Catholic doctrine teaches that church tradition and the authority of the pope sustain equal validity with the Bible.
>
> 4. Evangelicals hold that all believers are priests with immediate access to God through Jesus Christ while Roman Catholic doctrine teaches that the clergy, saints, and the Virgin Mary are also mediators whom individuals need to approach God.
>
> These doctrinal differences are too significant to ignore. Furthermore, these were the major issues at the heart of the Protestant Reformation and cannot be dismissed for the sake of unity. Dallas Seminary therefore cannot in good conscience endorse the *Evangelicals and Catholics Together* document."[1]

We applaud Dallas Seminary for taking such a clear stand against *ECT* but once again, we are concerned about the addendum attached to this document. We wish that they had left well enough alone. But for some

---

[1] Dallas Theological Seminary's Response to the Discussion of Evangelical/Roman Catholic Cooperation. pp. 1,2

reason there is a need to attach equivocating language to these public announcements, which language tends to undermine the strength of the position being taken in the body of the declaration.

Here then is the afterthought of the Dallas Seminary rejoinder to the *ECT*. Does it open the door a crack? We think so:

> "The document highlights the fact that a number of Roman Catholics are trusting in Jesus Christ alone for their salvation and are truly born again."[1]

We are at a loss as to why this was inserted. The *ECT* nowhere highlights that Roman Catholics are trusting in Christ alone for their salvation. As a matter of fact, the document bends over backwards to establish the point that each community, Evangelical and Roman, sees salvation in quite different ways. The theme of the document is not Rome trusting in *sola fide* but rather Rome being allowed to be Rome in her insistence upon other formulas for salvation. The entire use of the terms "born again" is foreign to the context of *ECT*. These gratuitous statements serve to undermine the gravity of the issues and the integrity of the framers of the *ECT* document, and are utterly editorial. But more importantly, they mislead the reader into thinking something is happening that actually is not, or that something is true which actually is false.

The addendum goes on to say that,

> "The document does remind Evangelicals that Roman Catholics are our allies in the fight to reclaim the basic moral and *spiritual values* under assault in our society."[2]

We come to a crossroads here with such language as "reclaim the basic moral and spiritual values under assault in our society." This uncareful language lets "the door of assertion" be swung wide open by any who wish to claim that Rome holds the same spiritual ground as Christianity. Furthermore, what are spiritual values? Do not Hindus, Muslims, Mormons and American Indians have spiritual values? We venture to say even modern movements, such as the New Age movement, have spiritual values. This jargon, used in any other context, is nothing more than a political statement that serves to tickle the ears of a diverse listening audience. But such a statement written in the context of setting straight the issue of whether Rome

---

[1] Dallas Theological Seminary's Response to the Discussion of Evangelical/Roman Catholic Cooperation. pp. 1,2

[2] Dallas Theological Seminary's Response to the Discussion of Evangelical/Roman Catholic Cooperation. pp. 1,2, emphasis added

is preaching the Gospel is totally inappropriate and damaging. Once again, the way is left open to accept Rome as an alternative Christian community sharing Christian spiritual values. This is part of the problem and not the solution. Whether intentionally or inadvertently, the framers of the Dallas Seminary Response to *ECT* have stumbled badly here and it will have a profound effect down the line if it has not already.

The Crusaders

In a letter written in the spring of 1995, William R. Bright, the president of *Campus Crusade For Christ International,* puts down his reason for signing *Evangelicals and Catholics Together*:

> "In some detail, I shared with many why I felt the Lord lead me to sign the document. Among other things, I pointed out there was absolutely no compromise on biblical truths, and that it would in no way prevent us from sharing the gospel with Catholics any more than with Presbyterians, Methodists, Episcopalians, or Baptists. There are nonbelievers in all denominations. It has, in fact, already helped us reach Catholics with the gospel in predominately Roman Catholic countries where many have staff. Now in 161 countries, Campus Crusade has a world perspective not shared by many U.S. Christian leaders, and our international leadership has affirmed how this agreement has already helped open doors and facilitated our evangelism in Catholic countries."[1]

If a supernatural blindness, for the sake of chastising this nation, has overcome the prominent leaders of professing Evangelicalism, we can find no greater illustration than this monstrous statement made by Bill Bright. We ask the reader to decide if the world has gone mad. Bill Bright says, "there was absolutely no compromise on biblical truth." Yet the *ECT* statement plainly says:

> "For Catholics, *all who are validly baptized are born again* and are truly, however imperfectly, in communion with Christ. Those converted, whether understood as having experienced the new birth for the first time or as *having experienced the reawakening of the new birth originally bestowed in the sacrament of baptism*, must be given full freedom and respect as they discern and decide the community in which they will live their new life in Christ."[2]

---

[1] Letter written by Mr. Bright in the spring of 1995 in response to meeting with key Christian leaders to discuss his signing of the *ECT*.

[2] Page 24 of *ECT*, emphasis added

We find it incredible that Bill Bright finds nothing theologically flawed with baptismal regeneration. Which gospel has Mr. Bright heard? Which gospel has Mr. Bright believed?

Furthermore, Mr. Bright says, "it (*ECT*) would in no way prevent us from sharing the gospel with Catholics..." However the *ECT* statement, which Bright signed, actually says the opposite:

> "Three observations are in order in connection with proselytizing. First, as much as we might believe one community is more fully in accord with the Gospel than another, we as Evangelicals and Catholics affirm that opportunity and means for growth in Christian discipleship are available in our several communities. Second, the decision of the committed Christian with respect to his communal allegiance and participation must be assiduously respected. Third, in view of the large number on non-Christians in the world and the enormous challenge of our common evangelistic task, *it is neither theologically legitimate nor a prudent use of resources for one Christian community to proselytize among active adherents of another Christian community."* [1]

How does this statement "help us reach Catholics with the gospel in predominately Roman Catholic countries" as Mr. Bright has so glibly stated? Which *ECT* has Mr. Bright read?

Perhaps Campus Crusade is of the opinion that it is only "unchurched" Roman Catholics who need to hear the Gospel. In this case, it is too late to do anything for Campus Crusade. They have lost it already. When Mr. Bright says that he shares the Gospel with Catholics and Baptists and Presbyterians and Methodists, etc., he is tipping his hand. By saying, "there are unbelievers in all denominations," Mr. Bright has sold the farm along with the others signing the *ECT*. The reason being that Protestant denominations who hold to confessions that clearly articulate the Gospel are worlds apart from Rome which does not. To say that there are unbelievers among theologically accurate Protestant denominations is not the same thing as saying that Rome is a Christian denomination. We wonder if Mr. Bright would be able to say, "We share the gospel with Roman Catholics, Mormons and Jehovah's Witnesses for there are unbelievers in all denominations." If this cannot be said—and indeed it must not be—then why is it so easy to slip Rome in among the Methodists and Baptists? The answer is because Rome is "in" among the Evangelical ecumenists, and the Gospel of Christ apparently no longer separates believers from unbelievers. But if it does not, then what, pray tell, does?

---

[1] Pages 22,23 of *ECT*, emphasis added

"America's Pastor"

We doubt that there is a more prominent professing Evangelical than Dr. Billy Graham. He is without question the most notable and arguably the most quoted Evangelical of our times. His work as a world wide crusade speaker, author, advisor to state and spokesman for conservative Evangelicalism has been well documented. Among his many honors, in 1996 he received the US Congressional Gold Medal for his years of effort as an evangelist. The headline for the story read, "Congress Honors 'America's Pastor.'"[1] But has Mr. Graham undone all the good of his reputation by failing to demonstrate theological accuracy and integrity when it come to appraising the Roman Catholic religion? We believe he has. As much as we admire the seemingly indefatigable work of Mr. Graham, we do not hesitate to expose the severe damage he has inflicted upon the cause of God and truth by his utter failure to recognize the apostasy of Rome. But it was not always this way with Billy Graham as explained by Mark Knoll, in *Evangelicals and Catholics Together*:

> "Billy Graham, of Southern fundamentalist extraction and nativist evangelical education, early in his evangelistic career enjoyed less than cordial relations with catholics. During the 1950s catholic officials in South America and the Philippines forbade their co-religionists to attend his meetings; in the same years local priests and bishops in the United States also often discouraged attendance at Graham crusades. During the presidential election of 1960, Graham only just succeeded in muting his enthusiasm for Richard Nixon and, again just barely, in hiding his apprehensions about a Democratic regime that would include not only a Catholic president, but also a Catholic majority Leader in the Senate (Mike Mansfield) and a Catholic Speaker of the House (John McCormack). Very soon thereafter, however, Graham began to work at improved relations with Catholics. His efforts were unusually successful. Catholics now make up a considerable portion of those who attend his meetings, record decisions for Christ, and watch the crusades on television. Tangible evidence of Graham's transcendence of interconfessional antagonisms multiplied rapidly from the late 1960s. In 1977 he was granted permission to hold a crusade in one of American Catholicism's most hallowed locations, the football stadium at the University of Notre Dame. In 1978 he became the first Protestant leader to be entertained by the abbot of the shrine of the Black Madonna in Czestochowa, Poland. In 1981 he sought and was granted an audience at the Vatican by Pope John Paul II, who short

---

[1] From Cable News Network, Inc., "Congress Honors America's Pastor," May 2, 1996, correspondent Kathleen Koch, ©1996

> years before as Cardinal Karol Wojtyla had made it possible for Graham to preach in Catholic churches during his evangelistic tour of Poland."[1]

We did a little research and came up with a July 17, 1981 article in which Mr. Graham was interviewed by *Christianity Today*. His comments in 1981 are less than encouraging and perhaps help us to understand that a shift in Mr. Graham's stance, perhaps due to a glaring weakness in his own theological education, had begun well prior to our modern ecumenical age. When asked in 1981 what he thought were the most significant changes on the American church scene in the previous 25 years, Mr. Graham answered that, among others, is "...the new understanding between Roman Catholics and Protestants. Twenty-five years ago we could hardly speak with each other openly. In crusades today, thousands of Catholics feel free to attend. I have preached in Roman Catholic schools and have even received honorary doctorates from them. This could not have happened 25 years ago."[2]

We agree with Mr. Graham's assessment of Christianity in America in 1957. However, our conclusion as to whether we were farther ahead or farther behind in 1981, given Mr. Graham's assessment of the difference between 1957 and 1981, has been answered by the climate of the 1990s. Mr. Graham may have thought we were gaining ground with the Gospel, but we were in fact losing it. We begin to take comfort in the fact that Mr. Graham was allowed to speak in Roman Catholic schools, until we read that he was given honorary doctorates. Obviously Mr. Graham said nothing that would undo the Romanist gospel and offend the Council of Trent. Therefore, we cannot rejoice at the fact that Mr. Graham spoke before Roman Catholic audiences in 1981, or, for that matter, Roman Catholic audiences in 1997.

How is it that the apostle Paul had a death sentence upon his head when he spoke the Gospel to the Jewish community, and Mr. Graham receives honorary degrees? Could it be the message? We have no doubt that it is. Somewhere early on Mr. Graham lost it, and there is not one indication today that he has retrieved the cutting edge of the Gospel.

When asked, in this same article, whether a previous meeting with Pope John Paul II was a help or hindrance to the Evangelical church in Catholic countries, Mr. Graham answered:

---

[1] *Evangelicals and Catholics Together: Toward a Common Mission,* Colson, Charles, and Neuhaus, Richard John editors, (Word Publishing, Dallas, London, Vancouver and Melbourne, ©1996) pg. 99

[2] *Christianity Today*, July 17th, 1981, "Candid Conversation with the Evangelist," pp. 18-24

> "It helped our meetings in Mexico, because Catholics felt free to attend them. They saw that I was not a bigot or intolerant."[1]

The law of the excluded middle needs to be remembered when such statements are made. To be intolerant of a false gospel is not the same as being a bigot. Mr. Graham started his spin early. We leave Mr. Graham with this rather solemn excerpt from *Christianity Today* dating back to the Fall of 1979 after the Milwaukee Crusade:

> "Some priests were skeptical about the Graham crusade because they saw Graham's conversion call as giving 'one moment of excitement and not lasting commitment,' said Sister Maureen Hopkins of the archdiocesan ecumenical office. 'My argument to them was that its not up to Graham, but to the local church, to make a lasting commitment.' Some of the priests became less critical, she said, when they learned that the Graham team emphasizes local church involvement for new converts and would not challenge their own ministries. A Graham team member conducted a seminar last November for area priests and lay leaders, in which he explained the Graham operation.
>
> "The Archdiocese of Milwaukee arranged a special eucharistic celebration for Roman Catholic inquirers. The celebration, held a week after the crusade, would indicate that the sacraments are 'still an important part of the church,' said sister Hopkins, and *that Roman Catholic doctrine and Graham's message need not be contradictory."*[2]

How remarkably prophetic—and deadly to the Gospel of Jesus Christ—this Roman nun's words have proven to be.

"The Walking Bible"

As a seminary student I was more than impressed with an answer given by one of my professors to the question, "Professor, how many times have you gone through the Bible?" The professor paused a moment and answered, "It is not how many times the man goes through the Bible but rather, how many times *the Bible goes through the man* that really counts." He meant by this that one needs to be inundated with the wondrous theological constructs and meanings of things in the Bible. The Bible is to penetrate deep into us both for good living (sanctification) and right thinking

---

[1] *Christianity Today*, July 17, 1981, pg. 21

[2] *Christianity Today*, September 7, 1979, "Reconfirmation for Milwaukee: Surprise Affirmation for Graham," emphasis added

(doctrinal foundations). As Paul wrote, "Let the word of Christ dwell in you richly in all wisdom; teaching and admonishing one another in psalms and hymns and spiritual songs, singing with grace in your hearts to the Lord" (Colossians 3:16).

Perhaps this is the telling tale of so many Evangelicals who are well known for their ability to quote verses and cite historical backgrounds to biblical events. But it is apparent that many have not taken the time to be good theologians. Good theology comes from weaving solid exegesis in and out with solid systematic theology. It is integrating the part with the whole and the whole with the part that makes a good theologian. Bible verses are all too often memorized and thrown around in a willy-nilly fashion to "prove" this point or that. Seldom is there any solid exegesis of the text and rarely is there any systematic approach to the theological question.

With neglectful exegesis and impoverished theological investigation, it is no wonder that the modern "Bible Man," be he on radio or television, is often the recipient of too great a respect for simply memorizing the text. He is equally far too often given excessive credit and not enough scrutiny when it comes to good doctrine and sound theology.

We have received personal letters from home and abroad asking us to investigate the writings or sayings of several who have publicly announced an affinity for Romanism. We need not fill the remainder of this book with name after name of those who have a decided lean toward Rome. We have highlighted the problem well enough with those we have mentioned. However, we think it fitting to close this section by allowing the reader to ponder a recent critique of a ministry that has been brought to our attention time and again. We speak of Mr. Jack Van Impe, who in some circles is known as "the Walking Bible."

This review of his ministry matches our assessment after having watched Mr. Van Impe on video tape extolling the virtues of the Roman Catholic religion:

> "Wherever I go, in this country and abroad, I'm repeatedly asked this same question. Jack Van Impe claims to be seen by millions in 25,000 cities and many other countries. Tragically, Jack is without excuse for the misinformation he is presenting to those millions. He claims to have studied Catholicism in detail and to be as well informed on this subject as anyone can be. Yet if he were a paid agent of the Pope, Jack could not do a better job of propagandizing his viewers into Catholicism.
>
> "Rexella begins this particular program by enthusiastically saying that Jack is going to give some 'shocking and surprising informa-

tion. ...You've spent a lot of time in preparation for it,' she says to Jack. He replies, 'I've been collecting articles for over a year. I study between 6 and 8 hours a day. I love to do research work. I finished the new Catholic *Catechism*... there are 2,850 points and I love much of what I've read in there... I just finished 602 pages in the *Catholic Encyclopedia*, so *we know what we're talking about...'* (He never even hints that anything might be wrong.) Jack then says that Paul commands believers to 'keep the unity of the Spirit... for there is one Lord, one faith.' The implication is that Catholics and Evangelicals preach the same gospel and are united in the true faith. Not so! In *A Woman Rides the Beast*, book and video, and in past newsletters we have fully documented Catholicism's false gospel.

"Rexella then says she wants to share with viewers 'some of the wonderful sermons Pope John Paul II has been preaching.' The *contents* of the sermons are not given, but only the *titles* of some sermons: 'Jesus Christ, the way to conversion,' 'Only Christ satisfies the human thirst,' 'We must preach Christ wherever we live,' 'Proclaim Christ, light of all people,' and 'Faith is the greatest gift.' Rexella then reports that the Pope 'stood in Rome and said, "I'm praying that we will have a conversion of this city to Christ."' (The implication is that the Pope means the same conversion to Christ that evangelicals preach, which any ex-Catholic knows is not true.)

"Jack then further commends the Pope: 'He's fulfilling what Jesus asked us to do... for Jesus said, in John 12:32, "If I be lifted up I'll draw all men unto me."' (Jack doesn't tell his viewers that the 'Christ' the Pope 'lifts up' is the wafer he holds over his head and worships at Mass and that Catholicism's 'Christ' is continuously being sacrificed for sin in contradiction to the biblical teaching that His sacrifice was completed 1,900 years ago at Calvary: "[We] are sanctified through the offering of the body of Jesus Christ *once for all...* [and] *after* he had offered *one sacrifice for sins for ever,* [He] sat down on the right hand of God;... there is *no more offering for sin*" - Heb. 10:10,12,18). Jack then quotes many salvation verses from the Bible, giving the false impression that this is the message of the Pope and Roman Catholicism.

"Jack Van Impe goes on to say that at the turn of the century fundamentalism was represented by five basic tenets: 1) inerrancy of the Bible; 2) Christ's deity from all eternity; 3) Christ's virgin birth; 4) salvation through Christ's shed blood; and 5) the resurrection of Christ. He then says, 'I'm glad that the Pope is preaching these and it's all in the *Catechism*... but we've not been willing to recognize our Catholic brethren and sisters because of prejudice.' No, it is not *prejudice* that causes us to oppose Catholicism's false gospel of works and ritual, but concern for lost souls.

"We lack space to analyze the rest of the tape, but it's in the same vein. As for all five points being in the *Catechism*, that is not true (Feb. 97 TBC). But it appears to be the case to those who don't understand the real meaning of the words Catholicism uses. Yes, one can find sound biblical statements in the Catholic *Catechism* and in what the Pope says; but the same is true of Mormons, Jehovah's Witnesses, Christian Scientists and other cults. Consider this ad which the Mormon Church places in newspapers around the country at Easter:

"During the Easter season we again rejoice with all of Christendom, and gratefully commemorate the resurrection of our Lord and Savior, Jesus Christ... At this sacred season we solemnly testify that Jesus Christ is the Son of God, the Savior and Redeemer of the world. We know that He lives! We know that because He lives, we too shall live again!

"It all sounds so biblical! From this quote, using Jack Van Impe's method for accepting Catholicism, we could show that Mormons are also our brothers and sisters in Christ. The truth, however, is that the biblical terminology used has a different and unbiblical meaning for Mormons, who deliberately camouflage their counterfeit gospel beneath evangelical language. The same is true of Roman Catholicism.

"For example, in the new *Catechism* which Jack commends, one finds that 'God's saving plan was accomplished 'once for all' by the redemptive death of his Son Jesus Christ' (par 1067). That sounds good, but other sections in the *Catechism* declare that the benefits of that 'redemptive death' are kept in 'the treasury of the Church' (Vatican II) and are dispensed in installments in exchange for good works, sacraments, rosaries, intercession of saints, purgatory and indulgences. There are endless steps one must take for salvation. The same *Catechism* clearly states, 'Outside the Church there is no salvation' (par 846); But Van Impe doesn't inform his viewers of such Roman Catholic 'damnable heresies' (2 Pt. 2:1)."[1]

Upon contemplation of what has been revealed in this section, one can only wonder and ask, "How many?" How many Evangelical churches, Bible

[1] *The Berean Call*, April 1997. For a complete critique of Mr. Van Impe write to P. O. Box 7019 Bend, Oregon 97708. Mr. Hunt has had a consistent testimony in an ongoing effort to warn Christians of the false gospel of Rome. For this we are grateful.

Colleges, Seminaries, High Schools, Church Schools and Evangelical Ministries are involved in what Peter Kreeft calls an "Ecumenical Jihad"? How many have RSVP'd the invitation to the Roman Ball in order to romance with Rome? How many are waiting gleefully on the other side of the ballroom, hoping Rome will ask them to dance? We cannot venture a guess. But our fear is as real as Elijah's who lamented:

> "And he said, I have been very jealous for the LORD God of hosts: for the children of Israel have forsaken thy covenant, thrown down thine altars, and slain thy prophets with the sword; and I, even I only, am left; and they seek my life, to take it away" (1 Kings 19:10).

Some would call this comparison of the prophet Elijah and the "Ecumenical Jihad" of his day to the acceptance of Rome by Evangelicals in our day absurd, or paranoid at best. We allow the reader to decide. As for us, we have set out to verify the Gospel's worst nightmare. We think we have done so and we pray that the warning is not too late. The battle may be just beginning. We have one hundred percent confidence that the elect of God will stand firm. We also know that they will pay the price. Let us rejoice,

> "...to be put in trust with the gospel, even so we speak; not as pleasing men, but God, which trieth our hearts" (1 Thessalonians 2:4).

Where Do We Go From Here?

IT APPEARS TO US that erosion of sound doctrine comes quickly, almost suddenly. Corresponding to that, it seems to take a long time to put things right again. This is perhaps due to the reality of opposing forces that wage war in the trenches of theology and power. As a generation of true believers leaves this earthly sojourn, it is critical that the next generation of true believers move into positions of authority and credibility. This is where we seem to have lost the battle. It appears as though most of the mainstream media ministries, mega-churches, Bible Colleges and Seminaries have failed us in the quest to maintain sound doctrine in any meaningful way. There are perhaps many reasons for this, but none greater than the influence of money in American professing Evangelicalism. Our best guess is that materialism has eroded away the Gospel from one end and fear is nibbling away from the other. Toss in a little liberalism, humanism, anti-supernaturalism, sacramentalism, easy-believism, and Pelagianism, and we get a glimpse of forces grinding away at the Gospel of Christ.

But let us focus on what we believe to be just two of the main culprits. The first is materialism. By this we mean the ego-motivated preoccupation with church size in America today. Stemming from a rather deficient and deformed view of the Body of Christ, and an increasingly pastor-dominated Evangelical church, we see an erosion of doctrinally sound churches replaced by user-friendly, program-oriented fellowships. The steady defection from sound theology toward a "need-meeting" fellowship fits nicely into the ego-centric psyche of pastors who, in many cases, derive a sense of success from the size and prosperity of "their" church. "How many people are in your church?" is the most frequently asked question at pastors' conferences. One never asks, "Are you biblically grounded in the Protestant Reformation?" Or, "Are you teaching the doctrines of the Scriptures against the heresies of this day, and taking a strong stand against anti-Christian cults and movements?" If "personal peace and affluence" mark the sin of this generation of unbelievers, then "respectable churches with growing budgets and nifty programs" may be the sin of the Christian equivalent.

Certainly the emphasis has grown away from the offense of the Gospel to a sociological medicinal approach to society. The Evangelical world seems detached from the biblical mandate to be on the cutting edge and to preach the Word in season and out of season (2 Timothy 4:2). It seems that this mandate has been replaced with "extend a friendly hand and sponsor a retreat somewhere." This is no small criticism, for it leads to bigger things. When the Body of Christ is more concerned with size and programs oriented toward growth in order to satisfy the pastoral staff and placate the ego of those in leadership, we have lost the Gospel to materialism. It is no wonder that accommodation is rampant among "socially acceptable churches." They have yielded to the temptation to fit into the world in order to minister to it. This material bent has proven to weaken the Gospel and compromise the witness of Christ, a witness which, at the core, is in confrontation with culture, not an accommodation to it.

We have observed a very disturbing correlation between the Evangelical appetite for growth and the Evangelical distaste for sound doctrine and careful biblical exegesis. One need not peruse the American ministerial scene long before finding an insatiable appetite for money, growth and a corresponding disinterest in theological training. Unless this trend is preëmpted by the prophetic Word of God it shall continue until Christianity is nothing more than a social ritual measured and informed by conservative ideological considerations rather than the Bible. Such a state of affairs appears to be emerging as the ecumenical spin doctors spell out Christianity in terms of "men keeping promises," "the moral majority," "contract with America," "Couples for Christ," "World Wide Marriage Encounter," "Focus on the Family," "The Family Research Council," "Prison Fellowship Ministries," "Operation Rescue," "Operation Blessing," and a vast network of in-house and para-church organizations designed to meet felt needs. But these have no clear sound when it comes to the Gospel of Jesus Christ. We say "no clear sound" because the emphasis is upon cooperation and integration rather than on clarification.

In our estimation, the way back to God is going to be painful for professing Evangelicalism. It must begin with a renewed commitment to the Word of God and a resolve to follow the definitions and parameters set forth in Scripture. This will take a sober evaluation. For instance, the Body of Christ is composed of those who have entered by the blood of the lamb and confessed faith in Christ, according to the testimony of the Gospel of Christ. These then are baptized in light of their salvation. These are the saints of God. They compose the Body of Christ and make up the constituency of the Body of Christ. No one else is to be mistaken as a member of the Body. The Church is defined, according to Scripture, as those who have been given the same faith as the early disciples of Christ. The Body of Christ is the Church of the living God. It is not an institutional entity entered into by ritual or marriage or without individually confessing faith in the Savior on the terms of His Gospel. Within the formation of this Body of Christ, the Lord has established a rule of order and oversight to be adhered to within the Fellowship of the saints. Elders/Bishops (presbyters/episcopos) are the leaders of the New Testament Body of Christ. Yet, how often is leadership thrust upon one man called "the pastor"? How often does faithfulness to the meeting of the Church end at Sunday morning? How often is the collection plate or the number of programs used as the measure for the success of a Church? Even the words "success" and "church" are somewhat of an oxymoron in light of the New Testament. How many Evangelical churches even care to have a membership with accountability to the leaders over the flock? How many Evangelical churches are measured by their size and not by their faithfulness to the Word of God, which clearly says they shall be judged by their faithfulness to it ? (John 12:48, Titus 1:7-9, Revelation 3:8-10). How many Evangelical leaders are put in positions of authority because they are successful businessmen? How many Evangelical churches model their assembling together after the world and not in accordance with the Word? How many Evangelical churches have forsaken strict and careful doctrinal statements and fail to hold their leaders accountable to the Word of God in theology and doctrine? How many Evangelical churches align themselves with organizations or missions without a care for the doctrine or theology of that mission?

In light of the absence of biblical "Christianity" within what is being called "the Body of Christ" today, what is one to conclude? We suggest that the Body of Christ is much smaller than anyone has imagined, and it thrives only before the Lord. It is simply too great a stretch to continue to call "Christian" all the aberrations out there, when there is no biblical warrant to do so. Like a giant rubber band that has been stretched to its limit and comes back with stinging force, clearing a path in its wake, so God will snap off all the bogus organizations which parade themselves as "Christian" but have no affinity for the Bible. How long can we continue to describe as "Christian" things which, by definition and substance, defy the revelation of God? Michael Horton offers this sobering indictment which captures our sentiments nicely:

> "We live in a fascinating time. Over the mere span of a few months in 1995, *Newsweek* magazine asked churches why sin and forgiveness have been thrown overboard for more psychological and 'seeker-sensitive' themes; *Time* reminded us of the Resurrection and asked us why it is no longer central (or, for that matter, believed by all who call themselves Christians). Although the Reformation is perceived by many evangelicals as an irrelevant event somewhere in the foggy past, it was recently celebrated and sympathetically mined for its resources by the *Wall Street Journal*. And one cover story of

> *U.S. News and World Report* was on the commercialization of evangelical Christianity.
>
> "During this same span of time, I watched the ABC television special with Peter Jennings 'In the Name of God,' as the church growth movement and the signs and wonders movement (especially the so-called 'laughing revival') were described by their own supporters. One entrepreneurial evangelical pastor announced that he did not 'bore' people by telling them to turn to particular places in Scripture. Another parroted David Letterman's 'Top Ten List' on Sunday morning, with the images of Letterman and other icons of pop culture facing the congregation (rather, audience) from the stage. Still another leading church growth pastor told Jennings that the reason he did not have a cross anywhere was because, as important as the cross is to the church, Christianity cannot be reduced to one message or symbol. On the signs and wonders side of things, it was utter bedlam, with men and women exhibiting the most astonishing hysteria. One leader, himself struggling with a terminal illness, said that he had to see miracles regularly and reminisced about his pre-signs and wonders days, during which he frequently asked himself, 'I gave up drugs for this?' In his wrap-up, Jennings asked the viewing audience whether these bold enterprises are actually making Christianity relevant by abandoning the gospel.
>
> "My point in this litany is to observe that there seems to be more common sense in popular culture—even among some of those who may not be Christian believers themselves—than one often discerns in the evangelical movement. The unregenerate may not understand the things of the Spirit of God (1 Cor. 2:14), but many certainly understand the things of the world, and they can tell when the church and the world are no longer distinguishable. As the lines continue to blur, a crisis looms on the near horizon. The church must be reminded that, when the text of Scripture is no longer regulating her doctrine, life, and worship, her authority and power, which is grounded in the Gospel of Christ revealed in Scripture, will soon be lost."[1]

Can we not detect one of the undermining causes for this malaise as the sin of materialism in this sobering portrayal of professing American Evangelicalism? Can we not see that the Gospel of Christ is not "of the essence" among those holding to what amounts to their own religion? With this in mind, is it any wonder why American Evangelicalism has nothing to say to the Roman Catholic religion? With the infrastructure of basic

---

[1] *The Coming Evangelical Crisis,* John A. Armstrong, General Editor, (Moody Press, Chicago, ©1996) pp. 245,246

ecclesiology falling apart at the seams and the advent of a "people-nourishing," "growth-minded" pastorate fearful of rocking the boat, what definition of Christianity should we expect?

Furthermore, we sense that fear has invaded and taken a stronghold within Evangelicalism. Materialism and fear go hand in hand. There are two kinds of fear operating against the Gospel. The first is a fear of rejection. Everyone wants to be someone and everyone wants to be accepted. It is sad but true. We find that the majority of pastors who refuse to get involved in the Roman Catholic controversy do so out of fear of recrimination from within their own church and from within the community as well. There is a fear of being too strong or being too dogmatic or being too doctrinaire. There is also the fear of losing one's job. Outspoken and vocal pastors and teachers are at the mercy of the boards who hire them. It is not easy to risk it all with kids in school and a mortgage to pay. We believe an unhealthy fear has dominated those already weak in theology causing them to side step any meaningful protection of the Gospel. Also, there is a fear found even in the more solid defenders of the Gospel that they may be offensive and perhaps lose some popularity or political clout. We have had firsthand experience with one such TV personality who is very sound in doctrine but inconsistent in his 'after hours' when it comes to applying the Gospel to at least one board that he sits on.[1] We have good reason to believe that consistent application of the Gospel will cost well known and well heeled Evangelicals some choice positions on socially active political and religious organizations.

The second fear is less subtle but no less insidious. This is the fear of which we have already written early on. It is the fear of making a disintegrating culture worse by taking a strong stand for the Gospel. It is often alleged that such a stand will alienate too many people and thus prevent the church from ministering effectively. No greater lie has been proposed by the forces of

---

[1] We marveled at the testimony of D. James Kennedy and his articulation of the gospel in contrast to the false hope of Romanism as exhibited in the tape series put out by John Ankerberg. We applauded and still highly recommend this tape series that featured Dr. Kennedy, Dr. Sproul and Dr. John MacArthur. What we cannot understand is Dr. Kennedy's involvement on the Board of Care-Net. Care-Net is a national umbrella organization that serves the Crisis Pregnancy Centers (CPC's) nationally. Care-Net endorses Roman Catholicism as an alternate worshiping community and has no qualms with staffing evangelically funded CPC's with Roman Catholic workers. After telling the nation that Rome was apostate, we asked Dr. Kennedy why Care-Net was endorsing Rome. After sending Dr. Kennedy a thirteen page letter, over a year ago, we are still awaiting his response. This is what we mean by a lack of consistency. We feel Dr. Kennedy should either work to effect a change at Care-Net or leave the board. The gospel is too important. We wonder, "What gospel will a Roman Catholic give to an unwed pregnant teenager?"

darkness than this. And yet, it appears to have handcuffed and paralyzed even those who should know better. We are appalled at the ease with which men can take matters into their own hands and fashion remedies that have nothing to do with the Gospel of Christ, and then have the gall to call themselves Christian. Such is the case of those driven by fear.

It is time to come to grips with this fear and flood it out with the Word of God. God has not set His Word on this world for the propagation of an Americanized Western culture. He has not set His Word on this world to establish a nation of any kind. Rather, He has set His Word in the hearts of men and women to preach the Kingdom of God and to proclaim salvation in the name of Jesus Christ. This salvation crosses all political and ideological boundaries and is enslaved to none of them. For in the final analysis, Christianity is the sharing of faith to faith the story of One who came to seek and to save the lost from their sins. He did not come to establish America or Western Europe. He came to set His people free from sin and death. He came to die that all those given to Him by His Father would live eternally with Him. Christianity is about liberation from the bondage of death and eternal hell suffered by those outside of Christ. It is *not* about protecting our borders from the secularists. Christianity is about worship and living lives out before the face of God. Christianity is about the Body of Christ and living in a world within the world. It is about the household of faith. It is *not* about world relief programs and conservative think tanks. Christianity is given to us by God in propositions that cannot be changed. The chief proposition is the Gospel of justification apart from works of any law (Romans 3:28). This essence of the "essence" of Christianity must never fall to the worries of any troubling age. Without it there is no Gospel. Without the Gospel, there is no cure for sinful man. Those who wish to heal the culture by inoculating it to the only known cure are agents of death and darkness. Truly those who follow them will find themselves teetering on the edge of apostasy. Should they fall in, they would be without God, having no hope in this world.

It is high time that Christians reclaim lost ground. The biggest area of loss is created by the guilt manipulators who, in their preaching, substitute the effects of the Gospel in the world and in the heart, for the Gospel itself. Good things done by real Christians must not be put in place of what makes one a Christian. Neither can we go on and say that good things done must make men Christian. We do not disparage the doing of the good, but when the doing of the good is put up for Christianity, then the doing of the good becomes a replacement for Christianity. This is blasphemy and idolatry. It is a false gospel; it is no gospel at all.

If there is to be a change in our culture, it will come about through the clear teaching and preaching of the Gospel of Jesus Christ. It will come about from fearless men and women who are not afraid to call a false gospel a false gospel. It will come about from men and women who are uncompromising with the Word of truth. It will come about from those who are unwilling to compromise and unwilling to yield to those who have poisoned themselves with the stew of apostasy and flattered themselves with their false courage by forming alliances that lead others to the edge of apostasy. May we have in mind and heart these words penned by men who have gone before us for the cause of God and truth. And then having done everything, may we stand firm in this dimly lit hour of our travail:

> "It is the bounden duty of every Christian to pray against Anti-Christ, and as to what Anti-Christ is no sane man ought to raise a question. If it be not the Popery in the Church of Rome there is nothing in the world that can be called by that name …because it wounds Christ, because it robs Christ of His glory, because it puts sacramental efficacy in the place of His atonement, and lifts a piece of bread in the place of the Saviour, and a few drops of water in place of the Holy Ghost, and puts a fallible man like ourselves up as Vicar of Christ on earth; if we pray against it, because it is against Him, we shall love their souls though we loathe and detest their dogmas, and so the breath of our prayers will be sweetened, because we turn our faces towards Christ when we pray."[1]

> "I remind you that the Protestant Reformers were not just bigoted zealots or fools. Their eyes were opened by the Holy Spirit; Luther, Calvin, Knox, all of them. They saw this horrible monstrosity depicted in the Bible and the warning against it. At the risk of even losing their lives they stood up and protested. They confronted Rome, ...The Roman Catholic Church is a counterfeit, a sham, it represents prostitution of the worst and most diabolical kind. It is indeed a form of the antichrist; it is to be rejected and denounced, but above all, it is to be countered. And there is only one thing that can counter it and that is a Biblical, doctrinal Christianity. A Christianity that merely preaches 'Come to Christ' or 'Come to Jesus' cannot stand before Rome. Probably what that will do ultimately, will be to add to the numbers belonging to Rome. People who hold evangelistic campaigns and say, 'Are you Roman Catholics? Go back to your church,' are denying New Testament teaching. We must warn them."[2]

And warn them we shall. Indeed, we have endeavored to do so.

---

[1] Charles Spurgeon, as quoted in de Semlyen, Michael, *All Roads Lead to Rome?* (Dorchester House Publications, England, ©1993) pp. 174-175

[2] Excerpt of a sermon given by Dr. Martin Lloyd-Jones taken from *the Bible League Quarterly,* October/December 1981 as found in de Semlyen, pg. 173

Appendix I: ECT II, the Disappointing Sequel

DUE TO THE NEGATIVE fall-out which ensued upon the March 1994 release of the *Evangelicals and Catholics Together Statement*, there has been a reformulation of sorts among its signers. This reformulation appears in the document entitled, *The Gift of Salvation* (*GS*), released on November 12, 1997 by many of the original signatories of the *ECT*.* Having already analyzed the original *ECT*,† it behooves us now to examine this new document.

We first notice that the fundamental theme of *ECT* appears as well in the opening statement of *GS*. This theme is that Roman Catholics and Evangelicals are (falsely) assumed outright to be brothers and sisters in Christ:

> "We give thanks to God that in recent years many Evangelicals and Catholics, ourselves among them, have been able to express a common faith in Christ and so to acknowledge one another as brothers and sisters in Christ." (*GS*)

The grounds given to us by *GS* for avowing that Catholics and Evangelicals are one in Christ are as follows:

> "We confess together one God, the Father, the Son and the Holy Spirit; we confess Jesus Christ the Incarnate Son of God; we affirm the binding authority of Holy Scripture, God's inspired Word; and we acknowledge the Apostles' and Nicene creeds as faithful witnesses to that Word." (*GS*)

---

* Though not all. The list of signatories of *GS*, a little smaller than that of *ECT*, is contained in Appendix II.

† See Appendix I: "Disturbing Alliances" in Robert M. Zins', *Romanism: the Relentless Roman Catholic Assault on the Gospel of Jesus Christ!*, (Huntsville, AL: White Horse Publications, ©1995)

What is missing from this confession should warn all who hope to find consolation in this new statement. The missing element is the *Gospel* of Jesus Christ. We also note that the language used in this confession is *safe* language. But being *safe* is not the same thing as being accurate. Even at the outset we notice that *Sola Scriptura* (the Bible *alone*) is negotiated away by only "affirming the binding authority of Holy Scripture." The word "alone" is conspicuous by its absence.

We also invite the attention of the reader to the subtle but important issue that "Holy Scripture" and "God's inspired Word" are not the same thing Roman Catholicism. This distinction is necessary because Rome cannot confess that the Bible *alone* is the Word of God. In Rome, God is said to speak through Tradition, the Magisterium and the Popes. Thus, the Romanists who constructed this document cleverly avoid the issue of *Sola Scriptura* by affirming a) the Holy Scripture, and b) God's inspired Word. In Rome, a is only a subset of b! We wonder if the professing Evangelical authors understand this subtle deception. Whether they do or not, we see that yet another document designed to show forth commonalities between Roman Catholics and Evangelicals, begins by glossing over irreconcilable differences.

To continue, confessing belief in the Trinity, Jesus Christ as the incarnate Son of God, the binding authority of Scripture and the Nicene/Apostles' creeds does not give evidence that Christianity is present. In order to have Christianity, we must have the Gospel. But, according to this document, the glue which holds Evangelicals and Catholics together is something different than the Gospel, something called "the gift of salvation in Jesus Christ." Hence the title of the document.

Once again, we caution that the terminology "gift of salvation in Christ" is carefully chosen. This catch phrase can mean different things to different people. We know Romanism views everything as a *gift* stemming from the "gift of salvation in Christ." The entire Sacramental System, as well as temporal suffering and Purgatory, is considered a *gift* from God (see pages 88 to 104 of *On the Edge of Apostasy*).

So to speak in terms of the "gift of salvation in Christ" is futile unless it is spoken of in biblical nomenclature. Also, all terminology must be fleshed out to see if it withstands all non-biblical models of the Gospel. The jargon employed by the framers of *GS* in their introductory paragraphs is not sufficiently defined in such a manner as to indicate that Christianity is present. Later, *GS* will go on to say, "The restoration of communion with God is absolutely dependent upon Jesus Christ." But as we shall see, this means one thing to the Roman Catholic religion, and quite another to the Christian.

As we maneuver through the document, there are some statements which tip us off as to the direction the signers are going. We begin by experiencing an unsettling discomfort with this telling admission:

> "...we have found that, notwithstanding some persistent and serious differences, we can together bear witness to the gift of salvation in Jesus Christ." (*GS*)

From this we gather that *how* one understands the "gift of salvation in Jesus Christ" is not an issue with the signers of *GS*. We are told that there are persistent and serious *differences*, but they do not inhibit or prohibit the proclamation of the "gift of salvation in Jesus Christ." It is alleged that either community can proclaim the *same "gift"* in the *same terms* meaning the *same thing* from the *same Bible*. We shall see, however, that the persistent differences make it impossible to assert that the "gift of salvation in Christ" in Roman Catholicism is the same as in Christianity.

We take a moment to point out another observation found early on in this document. The point may appear small at first, but it is not. The document states this concerning the creation and fall of man:

> "God created us to manifest his glory and to give us eternal life in fellowship with himself, *but our disobedience intervened* and brought us under condemnation." (*GS*, emphasis added)

We point out that, according to Romans 5:12-21, it was not the sin of *us* that did us in. *It was the sin of Adam.* We only make this point because *GS's* mediate view of our condemnation in Adam opens the door for a mediate view of our justification in Christ. The Roman Catholic religion is well known for an infusionary, mediate view of justification stemming from an infusionary, mediate view of condemnation. This makes a big difference when redemption, "the gift of Salvation," is concerned. The Bible teaches that *Adam's* disobedience was immediately imputed to all of his offspring. In accordance with this, Christ says the world is "condemned already" (John 3:18), because in Adam, *all sinned* (Romans 5:12). Thus, the Christian Gospel teaches that our only hope is for the righteousness of Christ to be immediately imputed to us through faith: "For if by one man's offence death reigned by one; much more they which receive abundance of grace and of the gift of righteousness shall reign in life by one, Jesus Christ." (Romans 5:17). Rome, however, teaches that it is Adam's sin, residing in us (concupiscence in the case of those who have received Romish baptism), which causes us to sin, bringing about our condemnation. Thus, our sins (*and ours only*) become the ground of our condemnation. Rome's solution, as we have documented in *On the Edge of Apostasy*, follows this error. Rome surmises that our righteousness (*and ours only*), stimulated and energized by the infusion of grace, becomes the ground of our justification. This is the root and foundation of Rome's whole sacramental system which is believed (by Rome) to give us the grace to be righteous enough through our good works to be finally justified. But this is not the Christian view; the Christian view holds to an immediate imputation of Christ's righteousness, which righteousness is the *sole* ground of our justification, through faith. As can be seen, the difference between "our disobedience, occasioned by Adam's sin," as the ground of our condemnation, and "Adam's sole disobedience" as the ground of our condemnation, is the difference between two radically divergent religions leading to two opposite gospels! The authors of *GS* have been very careful and clever *not* to correct the Romish error right from the start.

We now move into the heart of the document. The framers of *ECT* were called into question for their failure to affirm the biblical doctrine of Justification through Faith Alone. The *ECT* failed miserably to protect the Gospel from Romish errors pertaining to justification. In hopes of improving things, the authors of *GS* have found more convincing language. But is it an improvement over *ECT*, or simply smoke and mirrors? Once again, we find "safe" terminology which both the Romanist and the Christian can affirm, but with different interpretations:

> "We agree that justification is not earned by any good works or merits *of our own*; it is entirely God's gift conferred through the Father's sheer graciousness, out of the love that he bears us in his Son." (*GS*, emphasis added)

Christians can affirm the above statement because we know what we are saying when we say "no works or merits of our own." It means that nothing we do or *can* do, regardless of the source of our motivation, can assist in God's verdict of justification. Romanists, however, could affirm the above statement, but with a totally different bottom line understanding. To the Romanist, "no works or merits of our own" only means *passivity* in the Sacrament of infant baptism as the process of justification *begins*. It also means "God inspired, God induced good works stimulated by graces received in the Sacraments" are absolutely necessary to *complete* justification. Christians and Roman Catholics have absolutely antithetical and contradictory understandings of what it means to be justified by the grace of God, *completely apart from* any of our own works and merits (Romans 3:28). So, merely to state this formula, as the framers of *GS* have done, means nothing. Christianity is not guaranteed to be present unless the *meaning* of the assertion is fleshed out and words are defined. Unfortunately, this was not done in *GS*, and if it had been, the document itself would have withered on the vine.

Another "safe" declaration attempted by the authors of *GS* serves to open another door for scrutiny which will eventually sound the death knell for this ill-fated attempt to mix the unmixable:

> "The New Testament makes it clear that the gift of justification is received through faith, 'By grace you have been saved through faith; and this is not your own doing, it is the gift of God' (Ephesians 2:8). By faith, which is also the gift of God, we repent of our sins and freely adhere to the gospel, the good news of God's saving work for us in Christ. By our response of faith to Christ, we enter into the blessings promised by the gospel. Faith is not merely intellectual assent but an act of the whole person, involving the mind, the will, and the affections, issuing in a changed life. *We understand that what we here affirm is in agreement with what the Reformation traditions have meant by justification by faith alone (sola fide).*" (*GS*, emphasis added)

We need to unpack this carefully drafted paragraph a little at a time. *First*, the formula "through faith" [dia pisteos], given to us by the apostle in Ephesians 2, needs to be understood. Faith is the *alone instrument*, but not the *ground* of justification. Justification comes "through" or "by" faith, but never "because of" or "on account of" faith.

Second, the authors' focus here is on "faith itself" and not the *ground* of justification. While the Reformed Tradition would champion faith over and against works, it would be equally careful to include a discussion on and a definition of the *ground of justification,* i.e., the imputed righteousness of Christ. But *GS* is careful to avoid this, and thus nullifies any meaningful connection with the Gospel of Christ. Here again, the Roman Catholic and the Christian can both affirm the above assertion but from radically different definitions. In Rome, "saved by grace through faith" means "saved on account of grace given through the sacramental system when partaking in faith."

Third, the "by our response of faith to Christ" in Roman Catholicism means faithful participation in the Mass, Adoration of the transubstantiated wafer, adulation of Mary and a firm faith in the existence of Purgatory, among other things. This is not the "by faith" of the Christian.

Fourth, the framers of *GS* proclaim that what they have affirmed here from Ephesians 2:8 (despite two radically opposite grids of interpretation) is in agreement with what the Reformation traditions have *meant* by "justification by faith alone." Notice the document does not affirm "justification by faith alone" (*Sola Fide*). It only affirms that what has been said here is what the Reformers *meant* by "justification by faith alone." We take sharp exception.

The Reformation produced specific and clear language that often juxtaposed the Christian doctrine of *Sola Fide* with the Romish doctrine. Therefore, *GS* can only be in agreement with what the Reformation *meant* by "justification by faith" if what *GS* says is understood through the grid of the Reformers. But without out additional data as to what "justification by faith alone" really *meant* to the Reformers, it is an empty boast. Furthermore, any Roman Catholic could filter what little has been said here through his own sacramental grid and conclude that the Reformers were in essential agreement with Rome, which is absurdity epitomized!

But worse, it is patently untrue that what has been said in this *GS* agreement *is* what the Reformers *meant* by "justification by faith alone." If *GS* means to say that *only* what is said here is what the Reformers *meant* by *Sola Fide*, then *GS* is a lie. The document leaves this impression. The fact is that any correspondence between what has been said in *GS* about *Sola Fide* and what the Reformers *meant* by *Sola Fide* is analogous to the tip of an iceberg and the iceberg itself. The Reformers were never so careless as to limit a definition of "justification by faith alone" to "the gift of justification is received through faith." This is *not* what is *meant* by *Sola Fide*. The Reformers knew that all Romish theologians could affirm language like that which is employed by *GS*, and still miss the Gospel. Here is a small taste what the Reformers *really meant* by *Sola Fide*. Note how their definitions rule out Rome's view of justification altogether:

> "Those whom God effectually calleth he also freely justifieth; not by infusing righteousness into them, but by pardoning their sins, and by accounting and accepting their persons as righteous; not for any thing wrought in them, or done by them, but for Christ's sake alone; nor by imputing faith itself, the act of believing, or any other evangelical obedience to them, as their righteousness; but by imputing the obedience and satisfaction of Christ unto them, they receiving and resting on him and his righteousness by faith; which faith they have not of themselves, it is the gift of God." (*Westminster Confession of Faith*, Chapter XI)

> "Hence also it is proved, that it is entirely by the intervention of Christ's righteousness that we obtain justification before God. This is equivalent to saying that man is not just in himself, but that the righteousness of Christ is communicated to him by imputation, while he is strictly deserving of punishment. Thus vanishes the absurd dogma, that man is justified by faith, inasmuch as it brings him under the influence of the Spirit of God by whom he is rendered righteous. This is so repugnant to the above doctrine (of justification) that it can never be reconciled with it." (John Calvin, *Institutes of the Christian Religion*, Book III, Chapter XI)

The *GS* document not only fails to tell us exactly what the Reformers *meant* by *Sola Fide*, it is silent on what *Rome* means as well. Here is what Rome *really* means by justification by faith:

> "If anyone says that justifying faith is nothing else than confidence in divine mercy, which remits sins for Christ's sake, or that it is this confidence alone that justifies us, let him be anathema." (Council of Trent, 6th Session, Canon 12)

The *Gift of Salvation* statement fails to capture the meaning of the Reformers, and fails to report the meaning of the Romish religion pertaining to justification. Instead, it tries to accommodate both by deliberately using language that can be affirmed by both religions. Such attempts are to be rejected and the authors should be held accountable for their sleight-of-hand and sleight-of-theology.

We move next to the issue of Christian baptism. Something has to give before the Romish sacrament of infant baptismal regeneration can be squared with Christian baptism of confessing believers. We listen carefully to *GS*:

> "By baptism we are visibly incorporated into the community of faith and committed to a life of discipleship. By their faith and baptism, Christians are bound to live according to law of love in obedience to Jesus Christ the Lord." (*GS*)

In yet another attempt to use *safe* language, the authors have managed to say something which can be taken any way we want to take it. If I am a Romanist, I highlight the word *incorporated* and read that infant baptism for admission into the Body of Christ begins my life of grace and obedience. If I am a Christian, I highlight the word *visibly* and read that I am showing publicly my faith in the risen Savior and allegiance to His Body by my public baptism.

However, a careful theologian would never be comfortable with the wording of the document. Baptism does not *incorporate* anyone into the Body of Christ. Only the Lord can do this and it is in virtue of regeneration, i.e., being born from above. This has nothing to do with baptism. And baptism does not grant supernatural faith for the ongoing Christian life. To say that it does is implied by the wording, "By their faith and baptism, Christians are bound to live..." etc. This, of course, is news to the Christian but not to Rome. The authors must have greatly feared the ire of Rome here in order to formulate such a patently Roman Catholic assertion on baptism.

As we come toward a summation of this document, we are left with uneasiness over the language employed by the authors to summarize important theological constructs and doctrine. We are left uneasy over the use of terms which can be taken any number of ways. The terms appear to be deliberately vague in their context to allow for ingestion by either the Romanist or the Christian reader. Here are some examples:

On Sanctification

> "Sanctification is not fully accomplished at the beginning of our life in Christ, but is progressively furthered as we struggle, with God's grace and help, against adversity and temptation. In this struggle we are assured that Christ's grace will be sufficient for us, enabling us to persevere to the end." (*GS*)

There is no definition of grace offered to us in *GS* with which to digest what the rest of this means. The grace of Christ in Rome refers to a "treasury of merit" that Christ has allegedly purchased. From this treasury of merit Christ is said to dispense grace through the Sacramental system. Yet, to Christians, grace is the unmerited kindness of God toward His own in Christ. It is not something they earn or obtain by their obedience to the sacraments.

On Forgiveness

> "When we fail, we can still turn to God in humble repentance and confidently ask for, and receive, his forgiveness." (*GS*)

We have no idea if the forgiveness of God here mentioned is through the Romish or Christian understanding of forgiveness. In Rome, the penitent confesses to a priest and does penance for forgiveness of sins. He ultimately hopes to go to Purgatory to finish paying off the penalty of sins committed. In Rome, sins are forgiven but still have to be paid for through penance or time in Purgatory. This is not Christian forgiveness. The language here is "safe," but also empty of any meaning.

The Basis Of Hope

> "As we have shared in his sufferings, we will share in his final glory." (*GS*)

That Christians suffer for being in Christ is no secret. But to say, "as we have shared in his sufferings," admits to an alien understanding of Christ's atonement. In Rome, sharing in Christ's suffering means just that. In Rome, one merits grace through suffering with Christ. Hence, the advent of the monastery and the cloistered monks. There is also a "hope" based upon such sufferings which is part of the Romish religion. But this is not Christian.

On The Gospel

> "As believers we are sent into the world and commissioned to be bearers of the good news, to serve one another in love, to do good to all, and to evangelize everyone everywhere. It is our responsibility and firm resolve to bring to the whole world the tidings of God's love and of the salvation accomplished in our crucified, risen, and returning Lord." (*GS*)

There is not a word of definition as to what this *gospel* might be. What exactly is the good news that is to be shared in the world? The authors do not say. The closest we come to a definition is their firm resolve to bring "the tidings of God's love and the salvation accomplished in our crucified, risen and returning Lord." But exactly how does one participate in God's love? Exactly how does one become a recipient of the salvation accomplished by the Lord? What was accomplished by the Lord? When Rome can say, and it has, "Christ's death is complete, but not closed,"[1] they can hardly agree with us that Christ *accomplished* anything. Christians believe that He did. Rome cannot. All of these questions require an answer. As we have seen, the gospel according to Rome is contrary to the Gospel of Christianity. In Rome, salvation possibly awaits all those who by faith attend the Romish system. In Christianity salvation is given to all those who through faith take for themselves the righteousness of Christ.

In light of this it is startling to find the authors' insistence that "Evangelicals must speak the gospel to Catholics and Catholics to Evangelicals." What could possibly be meant by this? Surely, the mandate of the document is not that Evangelicals should convert Rome and Rome should convert Evangelicals. This would be absurd.

More to the real point is the authors' willingness to do an end run on the Gospel and reframe the question in terms of "fulfillment" and "completion" language. Once you have brought Rome "in" by testifying that Rome has the Gospel, what do you do with real Christianity? The answer is this: we are essentially asked simply to accept Rome as Christian and "fulfill" Rome with what Evangelicals have to offer. Also, we are asked to take a less than full "evangelicalism," and "complete" it with what Rome has to offer. In this way one community can "speak the gospel" to the other without endangering either's right to be called Christian. The document does not say, "Evangelicals must evangelize Catholics or vice versa." It only says, "We [Evangelicals and Catholics] must evangelize everyone." Hence, the document allows for the *speaking of the Gospel* to Rome and from Rome,

---

[1] John Paul II, Apostolic Letter *Salvifici Doloris* (On the Christian Meaning of Human Suffering), February 11, 1984, paragraph 24

but does not allow for evangelization from one religion to another. This is very clever. However, it is neither pleasing nor clever to God.

Thankfully, if our assessment of this document does not derail the Evangelical and Roman Catholic *Ecumenical Express*, perhaps the document itself will. We read at the end of *The Gift of Salvation* all that makes it an exercise in futility. The authors mention some *differences* that need to be hammered out:

> "...we recognize that there are necessarily interrelated questions that require further and urgent exploration. Among such questions are these: the meaning of baptismal regeneration, the Eucharist, and sacramental grace; the historic uses of the language of justification as it relates to imputed and transformative righteousness; the normative status of justification in relation to all Christian doctrine; the assertion that while justification is by faith alone, the faith that receives salvation is never alone; diverse understandings of merit, reward, purgatory, and indulgences; Marian devotion and the assistance of the saints in the life of salvation; and the possibility of salvation for those who have not been evangelized." (*GS*)

We are truly at a loss here. If the Evangelical signers of *GS* really wish to "urgently" explore the Roman Catholic meaning of such things as baptismal regeneration, the Eucharist, merit, purgatory and indulgences, they need only read up on Rome's assertions of these doctrines in the Council of Trent and the *1994 Catechism*. They both address them all! And if the Roman Catholic signers also wish to explore such things "urgently," they can explore the same documents and find that their religion condemns to hell people who assert what some of the Evangelical signers have here and elsewhere asserted. What is there left to explore? It is troubling to us that despite all that has been observed *and readily admitted* by the authors, they would insist that those holding such nefarious doctrines as purgatory, indulgences and Eucharist adoration, among others, are Christian:

> "All who truly believe in Jesus Christ are brothers and sisters in the Lord and must not allow their differences, however important, to undermine *this great truth*, or to deflect them from bearing witness together to God's gift of salvation in Christ." (*GS*, emphasis added)

We ask, "All who truly believe *what* in Jesus Christ?" We ask, "What exactly *is* God's gift of salvation in Christ?" How can two absolutely and diametrically opposite views of the Gospel of Jesus Christ be right? The authors may as well have said, "All Mormons and Jehovah's Witnesses who truly believe in Christ are our brothers and sisters and we must not allow their differences to undermine *this great truth*." We submit that the "great truth" of the Gospel of Christ is completely missed by the authors.

The "great truth" is that "All those who believe in the true Jesus and His true Gospel are brothers and sisters in the Lord." The issue is not "those who truly believe;" it is rather, "those who believe the truth."

We close our analysis with some reflections on the ending of the *GS* document. The writers are completely disingenuous when they boldly say:

> "As Evangelicals who thank God for the heritage of the Reformation and affirm with conviction its classic confessions, as Catholics who are conscientiously faithful to the teaching of the Catholic Church, and as disciples together of the Lord Jesus Christ who recognize our debt to our Christian forebears and our obligations to our contemporaries and those who will come after us, *we affirm our unity in the gospel that we have here professed*." (*GS*, emphasis added)

The authors do not in fact affirm with conviction the classic confessions of the Reformation as they touch upon *Sola Fide* and *Sola Scriptura*. They seem to have deliberately ignored the entire reason for the Protestant Reformation. Incredibly, they wish us to believe that they can affirm the confessions of the Reformation while affirming Romanism as Christian. This, of course, is precisely what the classic confessions of the Reformation were quite unwilling to do.[1]

The Roman Catholics who signed this document cannot possibly think that they can affirm *Sola Fide* as *meant* by the Reformers and all Christians since. To do so would fly in the face of the teaching of the Roman Church.

It is sheer lunacy when professing Evangelicals can commit themselves to the classic Reformation Creeds while affirming Romanism as Christianity.

---

[1] We urge any careful student of history and Theology to revisit the classic creeds of the Evangelical Reformed Churches as well as the early Baptist and Presbyterian Creeds. One will come away with a hearty denial of the Romish Sacraments, Purgatory and the Roman Catholic definition of justification, among other distinctives of the Roman Catholic religion. The writers of *GS* would have done well to have borrowed from the Belgic Confession of 1561: "As for the false Church, she ascribes more power and authority to herself and her ordinances than to the Word of God, and will not submit herself to the yoke of Christ. Neither does she administer the Sacraments, as appointed by Christ in his Word, but adds to and takes away from them as she thinks proper; she relieth more upon men than upon Christ; persecuting those who live holily according to the Word of God, and rebuke her for her errors, covetousness, and idolatry. These two Churches are easily known and distinguished from each other" (*Belgic Confession*, Article 19, AD 1561). At least they were "easily known and distinguished" to the collected minds of the classic Creeds of the Reformation. The authors of *GS* here try unsuccessfully to have the Creeds and Romanism. Instead, they end up with 436 years of egg on their collective face.

It is beyond lunacy to affirm a conscientious faithfulness to the Roman Catholic religion while affirming the Gospel of the Reformation Creeds.

The above foolishness of unscrupulous wordsmithing is only outdone by their outrageous conclusion which mercifully marks the end of this tawdry folio:

> "We affirm our unity in the gospel that we have here professed." (*GS*)

We have no doubt that the signers are in unity of affirmation regarding the gospel which *they* have professed. But it is neither the Gospel of Christ nor the gospel of Rome. It is the gospel of ecumenism. And as such, it is both ludicrous and dangerous. Ludicrous because it lacks both truth and mooring to anything Christian. Dangerous because it is believed and advanced by those who have gained the confidence of some in the genuine Christian community, which confidence, we hope has been thoroughly decimated by this discussion.*

* We refer the reader to Appendix II, a list of those who signed this follow-on to the *ECT* accord.

Appendix II: Signers of "The Gift of Salvation"

Evangelicals

Dr. Gerald L. Bray (Beeson Divinity School)
Dr. Bill Bright (Campus Crusade for Christ)
Dr. Harold O. J. Brown (Trinity Evangelical Divinity School)
Dr. Charles Colson (Prison Fellowship Ministries)
Bishop Williams C. Frey (Episcopal Church)
Dr. Timothy George (Beeson Divinity School)
Dr. Os Guinness (The Trinity Forum)
Dr. Kent R. Hill (Eastern Nazarene College)
Dr. Richard Land* (Christian Life Commission)
Rev. Max Lucado (Oak Hills Church of Christ, San Antonio, TX)
Dr. T. M. Moore (Chesapeake Theological Seminary)
Dr. Richard Mouw (Fuller Theological Seminary)
Dr. Mark A. Noll (Wheaton College)
Mr. Brian O'Connell (Interdev)
Dr. Thomas Oden (Drew University)
Dr. James J. I. Packer (Regent College, British Columbia)
Dr. Timothy R. Phillips (Wheaton College)
Dr. John Rodgers (Trinity Episcopal School for Ministry)
Dr. John Woodbridge (Trinity Evangelical Divinity School)

Roman Catholics

Father James J. Buckley (Loyola College in Maryland)
Father J. A. Di Noia, O.P. (Dominican House of Studies)
Father Avery Dulles, S.J. (Fordham University)
Father Thomas Guarino (Seton Hall University)

---

* Dr. Land, under further consideration of the implications of *The Gift of Salvation*, removed his name from the document the day after it was released. (Baptist Press Release — 11/13/97)

Dr. Peter Kreeft (Boston College)
Father Matthew L. Lamb (Boston College)
Father Eugene La Verdiere, S.S.S. (Emmanuel)
Father Francis Martin (John Paul II Institute for Studies on Marriage and Family)
Mr. Ralph Martin (Renewal Ministries)
Father Richard John Neuhaus (Religion and Public Life)
Mr. Michael Novak (American Enterprise Institute)
Father Edward Oakes, S.J. (Regis University)
Father Thomas P. Rausch, S.J. (Loyola Marymount University)
Mr. George Weigel (Ethics and Public Policy Center)
Dr. Robert Louis Wilken (University of Virginia)

Appendix III: the Marketing of Merit in Rome

IN THE OCTOBER 1995 issue of *This Rock* magazine, the feature article was devoted to a Catholic exposition on the meaning of "merit" in the Roman Catholic religion. The author, a free lance writer named Mark P. Shea, is a former "evangelical" converted to the Roman Catholic religion in 1987. The title of Mr. Shea's article is: "The Meaning of Merit." This article is meaningful to us because it shows to what depth a Roman apologist will go to make palatable his religion in the hopes of marketing it as Christianity.

The essence of Mr. Shea's article is to explain the meaning of Canon 32 of the Council of Trent. Canon 32 is one of 33 Canons following 16 Chapters on the subject of Justification in the 6th Session of Trent (January, 1547). We produce the entirety of Canon 32 for the reader:

> "If anyone says that the good works of the one justified are in such manner the gifts of God that they are not also the good merits of him justified; or that the one justified by the good works that he performs by the grace of God and the merit of Jesus Christ, whose living member he is, does not truly merit an increase of grace, eternal life, and in case he dies in grace, the attainment of eternal life itself and also an increase of glory, let him be anathema."[1]

Mr. Shea has felt the sting of rebuke from the evangelical community which has cited this Canon as proof that Rome teaches a meritorious salvation. Mr. Shea, however, believes that evangelicals not only misunderstand Trent, but basically teach the same thing using different words. So sure is Mr. Shea that he is willing to say:

> "It appears to many Christians that this teaching of Trent says, 'We get our salvation the old fashioned way: We earn it.' If it does, then,

[1] Schroeder, *The Canons and Decrees of the Council of Trent*, pg. 46

> as a Christian, I quite agree with them that Trent falls under the curse spoken by Paul against 'anyone, even an angel' who preaches a gospel other than the one the Apostles preached."[1]

If Mr. Shea has any integrity, we suggest that he call his local Bible church and ask them to get the Baptismal font ready for a repentant sinner who is now ready to come to Christ on the basis of a full confession of error.

Trent And Merit

Let us examine the language of Trent and proceed to analyze Mr. Shea's attempts to redefine vocabulary in his hopes of vindicating Romanism.

Trent grants that the good works of the one justified are, in fact, the gifts of God. It is worded in this way to protect Rome from the Pelagian heresy that man can merit his salvation unaided by the grace of God. Trent teaches that all good works of man are from God since God first gives grace for their accomplishment. However, Trent goes on to say that these good works are "the good *merits* of him justified" and that "the good works truly *merit* an increase of grace, eternal life,..." etc.

Christian theology has long balked at this terminology because it compresses together the words "merit" and "grace." R.C. Sproul explains:

> "Rome's view of merit and grace contains an unresolved paradox. On the one hand Rome insists on speaking of merit, while on the other she insists that this merit is rooted in grace. The Germans expressed this paradox by coining the *Gnadenlohn,* 'gracious merit.'"[2]

So committed is Rome to the notion that merit is real and is man's share in his own salvation, that they have devised a two-tiered level of merit. On the one level is *congruous* merit. This kind of merit evokes God's reward to natural man alone, apart from prevenient grace. Congruous merit is said to be 'fitting merit' for those who, apart from the grace of God, do good works to the best of their ability. Congruous merit is a reward given by God as is fitting to the man who works according to his own power. On the second tier is *condign* merit. The word condign means 'worthy' or 'deserved.' Condign merit is not merely suitable, but actually a reward deserved. The *Catholic Encyclopedia* explains for us the difference between condign merit and congruous merit:

---

[1] *This Rock* pg. 25

[2] Sproul, pg. 148

> "From an ethical point of view the difference practically amounts to this, that, if the reward due to condign merit be withheld, there is a violation of right and justice and the consequent obligation in conscience to make restitution, while, in the case of congruous merit, to withhold the reward involves no violation of right and no obligation to restore, it being merely an offense against what is fitting or a matter of personal discrimination (*acceptio personarum*)."[1]

R.C. Sproul gives us confirmation of the Roman Catholic understanding of condign (deserved) and congruous (fitting) merit by citing for us Thomas Aquinas:

> "A man's *meritorious work* may be considered in two ways; in so far as it proceeds from his own free will, and in so far as it proceeds from the grace of the Holy Spirit. There cannot be condignity [deserved merit] if a meritorious work is considered as it is in its own substance, and as the outcome of a man's own free will, since there is then extreme inequality. There is, however, congruity [fitting merit], since there is a certain relative equality. For it seems congruous that *if a man works according to his own power, God should reward him according to the excellence of his power*. But if we are speaking of a *meritorious work* as proceeding from the grace of the Holy Spirit, *it merits eternal life.*"[2]

Clearly the Roman Catholic religion teaches a two-tiered level of meritorious actions performed by man. One is worthy of eternal life since it proceeds from the grace of the Holy Spirit. The other is fitting of honor but not demanding of honor. To withhold a reward for condign merit would be unjust. To withhold a reward for congruous merit would be only an offense against what is fitting.

Roman Catholic theology is unabashed in its insistence that God has obligated Himself to reward condign merit with eternal life. Trent is adamant about this:

> "Hence, to those who work well unto the end and trust in God, eternal life is to be offered, both as a grace mercifully promised to the sons of God through Christ Jesus, *and as a reward promised by God himself, to be faithfully given to their good works and merits*."[3]

---

[1] *The Catholic Encyclopedia*, Volume 10 pg. 203

[2] Sproul, pg. 150

[3] Schroeder, *The Canons and Decrees of the Council of Trent*, pg. 41, emphasis added

We notice the language here, as well as in the 32nd Canon of the 6th session of the Council of Trent, is explicit:

> "The *good works* of the one justified," "*the good merits* of the one justified," "or that the one justified by *the good works* that he performs by the grace of God," "*truly merit* an increase of grace, eternal life."

No one can deny with integrity the fact that Rome teaches that those who work well receive a reward of eternal life to be given faithfully to their good works and merits. Also, according to Rome, good works truly merit an increase of grace.

How then does Mr. Shea avoid all of this in hopes of convincing us that Rome means what it says but still is Christian? Mr. Shea has two methods of affirming the teaching of his newly found religion. He first erects some straw men and burns them down—he tells us what the term merit does not mean coming from the Council of Trent.

> "On the lips of the Council of Trent, merit does not mean 'earned grace' or 'do-it-yourself salvation,' nor does it mean 'good deeds to supplement Jesus' inadequate saving work.'"[1]

The problem here is that no one is accusing Trent of these odd definitions of merit.[2] Merit at Trent and everywhere else in Roman Catholic theology means something deserved by virtue of fulfilling a condition, or by virtue of performing an act. The *Roman Catholic Almanac* is sufficiently clear on this point:

> "*Merit:* In religion, the right to a supernatural reward for good works freely done for a supernatural motive by a person in the state of and with the assistance of grace. The right to such reward is from God, who binds himself to give it. Accordingly, good works, as described above, are meritorious for salvation."[3]

Mr. Shea seeks to divert attention away from the fact that merit means 'the right to a supernatural reward for good works freely done in a state of grace and with the assistance of grace.'[4] In order to soften the value of merit, he

---

1 *This Rock*, pp. 25

2 While the term "merit" does not mean "to earn grace," it is merit, in fact, which is rewarded with grace in the Romish system

3 *1994 Catholic Almanac*, pp. 317

4 It remains for another day to explore how one does something "freely" while in need of being in a "state of grace" as well as in "need of grace" before it can be done! How much *continued on following page*

falls back on the old Romanist position that eternal life is all of grace, since man is rewarded for his works that could not have come about apart from grace. We keep in mind that Rome sees real merit to good works but calls the works 'of grace' because God starts the works with grace. The apostle Paul did not have such a high view of works, and neither did he wish to polish up works by saying they must be 'of grace' since God starts everything by His grace! Paul did not rely on abstract philosophical contortions to try to prove that, after all, everything is really of grace. He was blunt and to the point:

> "*And if by grace, then is it no more of works*: otherwise grace is no more grace. But if it be of works, then is it no more grace: otherwise work is no more work." (Romans 11:6)

Since Mr. Shea is fully aware that the Roman Catholic religion teaches that all good works of merit (condign merit) have their starting point with the grace of God, he is free to be clever in the mixing and matching of his terms. This is his second method of convincing us to swallow Rome's teaching on merit salvation. Mr. Shea wishes to bring the word merit up to 20th century meaning. He wants to change the word merit to the word "fruitfulness," and then thinks he can find common ground with the Gospel by triumphantly announcing that meritorious works are nothing more than God-produced fruit. This fruit is then what matters to God in the final analysis of salvation:

> "Essentially Trent is saying that grace, incarnate in us, has tangible and eternal effects on us and our relationship with God according to our cooperation with it. If we freely respond to grace and do good, this changes us and makes us able to respond to more grace, which God seeks to give. We indeed bear fruit for eternal life. We indeed are rewarded for what we do. Yet it is all the works of grace."[1]

The fly in the ointment of all of this is the fact that the Gospel of Jesus Christ and the testimony of Scripture does not make justification dependent upon our good works or our merit. It is the common Roman Catholic position (dressed up here by Mr. Shea) that good works done in faith, as prompted by the grace of God, are the ground of our justification. But the Reformers knew full well that the only ground of justification was the righteousness of Christ imputed to the poor sinner (Romans 5). They also knew that this imputation of Christ's righteousness was given through faith alone (Romans 4). They saw that circumcision was a gift of God to His

---

of condign merit is reserved to the cooperation of man? The Catholic Encyclopedia gives us 7 conditions for condign merit, 4 with respect to the work, 2 with respect to the agent doing the work, and 1 with respect to God.

[1] *This Rock*, pg. 28

people but even so, they could not rename this 'work' as grace and demand it for justification (Acts 15). They saw the Law of Moses as a gift of God to His people but they could not redress it and market it as grace to those who wished for salvation in Christ alone (Galatians 5). The Reformers viewed correctly the Pharisaic mindset that clung to 'good works' done in faith as a guarantee that God would accept them (Luke 18). They could not fit the new wine of the Gospel into the dead wineskin of the self-righteous. The Reformers, in the light of Titus 3, correctly exposed the arrogance of Rome which boasted that meritorious (or, for Mark Shea, fruitful) works done under grace "truly merit an increase of grace, eternal life... and the attainment of eternal life itself." Seeing that Rome had seized upon the ethical teaching of Jesus to construct a system of personal merit through surrender to a man-made system of grace, the Reformers preached the righteousness of Christ alone for justification. They dismantled the Romish system of sacramental grace dispensing and indulgences, and replaced it with the righteousness of Christ. Mr. Shea has attempted to avert our eyes away from Christ alone for justification. He instead wishes to hold forth the 'fruit' of grace as the ground of our justification. He does so to the ancient drum beat of a dead religion. It is the 'same old same old,' albeit dressed in 20th century terminology. But whether it be the articulate and careful garb of the Council of Trent, or the witty, whimsical attire of 20th century pop theologians, the finery of Rome is as filthy rags compared to the garment of holiness in Christ alone.

Mr. Shea closes his article with this dreadful conclusion:

> "Under the guidance of the Spirit it is really possible for Catholics and Evangelicals to say, concerning faith and merit, 'How good and pleasant it is when brothers dwell together in unity.'"[1]

We respond by encouraging the reader to take careful note that Mr. Shea is in fact teaching the same old heresies when it comes to salvation. The Romanist religion has always wished to make the 'fruit' of justification *the cause* of justification. The Roman Catholic religion has always accused the Reformers of *"merely satisfying"* the Law of God in the verdict of justification. (In reality, the Reformers knew that satisfaction of God's law was at the heart of justification, and no amount of good works done in faith could satisfy the holiness of God and His unrelenting law.) The Romanist religion has, likewise, accused Christians of paying scant attention to the value of good works. They say we should elevate them where they belong as the ground of our salvation. They say it is our cooperation with the grace of God in producing these good works that merits our justification. We answer "No, not now and not ever!" The Bible is clear that justification is a

---

[1] *This Rock*, pg. 28

free gift of God and not dependent upon good works done in righteousness (Titus 3:5). The Bible is equally clear that regenerative grace, given freely by God to His own, will not fail to produce that fruit of sanctification without which no man shall see God. But to put the *fruit* produced by the graciousness of God as the *cause* of that graciousness, robs God of His glory, reduces salvation to the 'cooperation' of man, and diminishes Christ's mighty atonement by sharing it with the goodness of man. Or worse yet, Rome wishes to make God's salvation contingent on the willingness of man to let God make him good, or 'fruitful.' This pollution can only be purified by the strong rivers of the Word of God.

> "Now to him that worketh is the reward not reckoned of grace, but debt. But to him that worketh not, but believeth on him that justifieth the ungodly, his faith is counted for righteousness." (Romans 4:4,5)

It is said, "a rose by any other name will smell as sweet." So it is with Rome. Its odious fragrance will be the same when called by any other name. Christians cannot bear the illicit religion of Rome. In the final analysis, "And what concord hath Christ with Belial? or what part hath he that believeth with an infidel? And what agreement hath the temple of God with idols?" (2 Corinthians 6:15-16a).

In the insightful words of John Murray, former chair of theology at Westminster Seminary, we conclude:

> "If we once allow the notion of human satisfaction to intrude itself in our construction of justification or sanctification then we have polluted the river, the streams whereof make glad the city of God."[1]

Mr. Shea, using popular language in hopes of beguiling the uncareful, has done just this. Rome and her apologists continue to pollute with human merit the streams whereof make glad the city of God.

---

[1] Murray, John, *Redemption Accomplished and Applied*, (Grand Rapids, MI: Eerdmans Publishing Company, ©1955) pg. 51

Bibliography

Armstrong, John (gen. ed.), *Roman Catholicism: Evangelicals Analyze What Divides and Unites Us*, (Chicago: Moody Press, ©1994)

Berkhof, Louis, *Systematic Theology*, (Grand Rapids, MI: Eerdmans, 14th printing, ©1938)

Calvin, John, *The Epistle of Paul the Apostle to the Galatians, Ephesians, Philippians and Colossians*, (Grand Rapids, MI: Eerdmans Press, ©1965)

Calvin, John, *The Necessity of Reforming the Church*, (Dallas, TX: Protestant Heritage Press, ©1995)

Canons and Decrees of the Council of Trent, trans. Rev. H. J. Schroeder, O. P. (Rockford, IL: Tan Books, ©1978)

Catechism of the Catholic Church, the (1994), (Washington, DC: US Catholic Conference, ©1994)

Catholic Almanac, (1994) (Huntington, IN: Our Sunday Visitor Publishing, ©1993)

Chemnitz, Martin, *Examination of the Council of Trent,* translated by: Fred Kramer, (St. Louis, MO: Concordia Publishing House, ©1971)

Christian Faith, The, Neuner, J. & Dupuis, J., (New York: Alba House, ©1981)

Christianity Today, July 17th, 1981, "Candid Conversation with the Evangelist"

Clark, Gordon H., *Today's Evangelism: Counterfeit or Genuine?*, (Jefferson, MD: The Trinity Foundation, ©1990)

Cranfield, C. E., *The International Critical Commentary: Epistle to Romans, Volume I,* (ICC series, Edinburgh, Scotland: T & T Clark, ©1975)

de Semlyen, Michael, *All Roads Lead to Rome?* (Bucks, England: Dorchester House Publications, ©1993)

Edwards, Jonathan, *The Works of Jonathan Edwards*, Volume One, (Carlisle, PA: Banner of Truth Trust, ©1979)

Evangelicals and Catholics Together: The Christian Mission in the Third Millennium, March 29, 1994

Evangelicals and Catholics Together: Toward a Common Mission, Colson, Charles, and Neuhaus, Richard John, editors, (Dallas, TX: Word Publishing, ©1996)

"Evangelicals and Catholics Together in Cult Ministry Panel Discussion," Evangelical Ministries to New Religions annual conference, Atlanta, GA, USA, October, 1995. Tape 1 Side 1. (©1995, Evangelical Ministries to New Religions, PO Box 20352, Philadelphia, PA, 19137)

Fournier, Keith & Watkins, William D., *A House United? Evangelicals And Catholics Together: A Winning Alliance For The 21st. Century*, (Colorado Springs, CO: NavPress, ©1994)

Geisler, Norman L. & MacKenzie, Ralph E., *Roman Catholics and Evangelicals: Agreements and Differences,* (Grand Rapids: Baker Books, ©1995)

John Paul II, *Crossing the Threshold of Hope*, (New York: Alfred A. Knopf, Inc., ©1994)

Keating, *Catholicism and Fundamentalism*, (San Francisco: Ignatius Press, ©1988)

Murray, John, *Redemption Accomplished and Applied*, (Grand Rapids, MI: Eerdmans Publishing Company, ©1955)

New International Dictionary of the Christian Church, The, J. D. Douglas editor, (Grand Rapids, MI: Zondervan, ©1978)

Our Sunday Visitor, July 20, 1997, "Making New Catholic Men? Promise Keepers' 'gospel for guys': Is it just the thing Catholic men need? or is it bound to loosen male bonds to the Church?", by Michael Aquilina, pp. 10-11

Peter Kreeft, *Ecumenical Jihad*, (San Francisco: Ignatius Press, ©1996)

Reed, Kevin, *Making Shipwreck Of The Faith: Evangelicals and Roman Catholics Together*, (Dallas, TX: Protestant Heritage Press, ©1995)

Schaff, Philip, *The Creeds of Christendom*, Vol. I, (Grand Rapids: Baker Books, ©1993)

Schroeder, H. J., *The Canons and Decrees of the Council of Trent*, (Rockford, IL: TAN Books and Publishers Inc., ©1978)

Sources of Catholic Dogma, The, Translated by Roy J. Deferrari from 13th. Edition of Henry Denzinger's *Enchiridion Symbolorum*, (St. Louis, MO: Herder Book Co., ©1957)

Sproul, R. C., *Faith Alone: The Evangelical Doctrine of Justification,* (Grand Rapids, MI: Baker Books, ©1995)

Spurgeon, Charles Haddon, *The Sword and the Trowel,* January 1873

The Berean Call, PO Box 7019, Bend, Oregon 97708.

The Coming Evangelical Crisis, John A. Armstrong, General Editor, (Moody Press, Chicago, ©1996)

Watson, Tom, *The Redefining of a Christian*, (Southlake, TX: Country Side Bible Church, 250 Ravenaux Drive, Southlake, Texas 76092, ©1995)

Webster, William, *The Church Of Rome At The Bar Of History*, (Carlisle, PA: Banner of Truth, ©1995)

Zins, R. M., *Romanism: The Relentless Roman Catholic Assault on the Gospel of Jesus Christ*, (Huntsville, AL: White Horse Publications, ©1995)

Subject Index

Scripture Index